LANCELOT-GRAIL

THE OLD FRENCH ARTHURIAN VULGATE AND POST-VULGATE IN TRANSLATION

LANCELOT-GRAIL

LANCELOT-GRAIL

THE OLD FRENCH ARTHURIAN VULGATE AND POST-VULGATE IN TRANSLATION

NORRIS J. LACY, GENERAL EDITOR

VOLUME X

CHAPTER SUMMARIES
by Norris J. Lacy
with Carol J. Chase, Martha Asher,
Cynthia K. Hood, Anne P. Longley & David S. King

INDEX OF PROPER NAMES
by Samuel N. Rosenberg
with Daniel Golembeski

D. S. BREWER

Published by arrangement with Routledge, Inc., part of Taylor & Francis Group LLC

First published 1993-1996
Garland Publishing Inc., New York

New edition 2010
D. S. Brewer, Cambridge

ISBN 978 1 84384 252 1

Set ISBN 978 0 85991 770 4

D. S. Brewer is an imprint of Boydell & Brewer Ltd
PO Box 9, Woodbridge, Suffolk IP12 3DF, UK
and of Boydell & Brewer Inc.
668 Mt. Hope Avenue, Rochester NY 14620, USA
website: www.boydellandbrewer.com

A catalogue record for this book is available
from the British Library

This publication is printed on acid-free paper

Printed in Great Britain by
CPI Antony Rowe, Chippenham and Eastbourne

CONTENTS

VOLUME II

THE STORY OF MERLIN

VOLUME III

LANCELOT, PART I

LANCELOT, PART II

VOLUME IV

LANCELOT, PART III

LANCELOT, PART IV

VOLUME V

LANCELOT, PART V

LANCELOT, PART VI

VOLUME VI

THE QUEST FOR THE HOLY GRAIL

VOLUME VII

THE DEATH OF ARTHUR

Volume VIII

The Post-Vulgate, part I. The Merlin Continuation

VOLUME IX

THE POST-VULGATE, PART II. THE QUEST FOR THE HOLY GRAIL

THE POST-VULGATE, PART III. THE DEATH OF ARTHUR

Chapter Summaries for the Vulgate and Post-Vulgate Cycles

by Norris J. Lacy

with

Carol J. Chase

Martha Asher

Cynthia K. Hood

Anne P. Longley

David S. King

CHAPTER SUMMARIES FOR THE VULGATE AND POST-VULGATE CYCLES[*]

VOLUME I

THE HISTORY OF THE HOLY GRAIL

1.   Prologue.

The scriptor begins by praising the Trinity and by explaining why he chooses not to reveal his name. He then recounts events that occurred seven hundred seventeen years after the Passion, when he received orders to set in writing the history of the Grail. A voice announced that it was bringing news of the Trinity and that this was the voice of the Great Master. The Master gave him a book in which His great secrets were contained. Amid marvels, the scriptor began to read the book. Later, he was commanded to leave, and his travels took him to a chapel, where the power of the book was used to cast out a devil. The voice commanded him to copy the book, and he undertook the work, beginning with the account of the Crucifixion.

2.   Joseph of Arimathea Lays Christ's Body in a Sepulcher and Is Imprisoned.

At the time of the Crucifixion, Joseph of Arimathea, one of the few to believe in Christ, seeks something belonging to Him. In the house where the Last Supper was

---

[*]   Norris J. Lacy prepared the summaries of the Vulgate *Quest for the Holy Grail, The Death of Arthur,* and a portion of the Post-Vulgate. He also provided the remaining summaries, but they are based on drafts made by others, as follows: Carol J. Chase for *The History of the Holy Grail;* Cynthia K. Hood for *The Story of Merlin;* Anne P. Longley for the Vulgate *Lancelot;* Martha Asher for most of the Post-Vulgate chapters and David S. King for others.

held, he finds the bowl Christ used. He asks Pilate for Christ's body and lays it in the sepulcher he had prepared for himself. Angry at this, the Jews seize Joseph and imprison him.

3. Vespasian Is Healed; Joseph of Arimathea Is Liberated.

Titus seeks a cure for his son Vespasian, who suffers from leprosy. A knight from Capernaum, who tells him he could be healed by something belonging to Christ, is sent to find something; he returns with an image of Christ, and Vespasian is cured. Vespasian then sets out to avenge Christ's death. He liberates Joseph of Arimathea.

4. Joseph and His Followers Depart; Joseph Preaches Before Evalach in Sarras.

Joseph sends for his friends and relatives; seventy-five are converted and depart with him. They spend the first night in a wood, where the Lord sends them all the food they desire. In a city called Sarras, Joseph preaches before King Evalach, who has just been routed on the battlefield by the Egyptians.

5. Evalach's Vision.

As King Evalach lies in bed, worried about defending his land and thinking about what Joseph told him, he has a vision: he sees a tree that appears to be three and yet one. Then he sees a beautiful child enter and depart through a secret door without opening it. A voice explains the meaning of that vision: it illustrates how Christ entered and left the womb of the Virgin while leaving her virginity intact.

6. Joseph Prays for Evalach's Conversion.

Eager to convert Evalach, Joseph arises and prays, asking God to demonstrate His power. A voice tells Joseph that during the night Evalach saw a sign; it then says that Joseph's son Josephus will be ordained as a priest.

7. Josephus's Investiture.

Joseph and his people gather to worship at the ark. The Lord calls Josephus forward; inside the ark, he and then his father see a red man, surrounded by angels holding the objects associated with the Crucifixion. The Lord invests Josephus as a bishop, explains the symbolic value of the vestments, and establishes the sacrament of Communion.

8. Josephus Preaches Before Evalach; Evalach Battles Tholomer.

Joseph and his son Josephus go before King Evalach; one of Evalach's priests, who attacks the idea of the Trinity, loses his sight and speech. Josephus tells Evalach that because he did not believe the signs sent to him, God will punish him by putting him under his enemy's hand for three days and three nights. At the temple Josephus exorcises the devil, and the gods are all broken. A message comes that Tholomer has besieged the castle of Evalachin. Before Evalach's departure for battle, Josephus prepares a shield with a red cross, which Evalach must look at only when he fears for his life. Evalach departs, gathers his forces, and goes to Evalachin. In the ensuing battle, Evalach is forced to flee to La Choine.

9. Evalach and Tholomer Join in Battle Again.

Evalach receives a message from the queen, warning him that Tholomer intends to besiege La Choine; she learned the details of the battle from Josephus. Evalach and his men head for Sarras; on the way, they meet Evalach's brother-in-law Seraphe, who has come to help him. They decide to go to Orcaus to gather forces; Tholomer's army arrives, and a fierce battle ensues.

10. The White Knight.

In the continuing conflict, Seraphe performs marvelous feats of arms. Evalach is captured by Tholomer; fearing for his life, he tears off the cloth covering the cross on his shield. A white knight arrives, rescues him, and helps defeat the Egyptians.

11. The Story of Sarrasinte's Conversion.

Evalach's wife, Sarrasinte, sends for Josephus, who tells her that Evalach cannot avoid being under Tholomer's power. She promises to believe in Jesus Christ and convert her husband if he returns in honor from this war. When Josephus begins to instruct her, she sends everyone away and lays out the articles of the faith as well as any clerk. She then tells Josephus the story of how she and her mother became Christians.

12. Evalach's and Seraphe's Conversion.

King Evalach seeks the White Knight in vain. He and Seraphe depart for Sarras, where Josephus tells him that his victory is due to the Lord's intervention. A man whose hand has been cut off in a melee is healed when he touches the shield with the red cross. Seraphe and Evalach convert and are baptized, receiving new names: Nascien and Mordrain. Josephus baptizes people throughout the land; at Orcaus he exorcises a devil in the temple. At the king's order, those who do not wish to convert depart and are struck with various ills. Hearing this, Josephus rushes to the city gates and is punished by an angel, who strikes him in the thigh with a lance. He removes the lance, but the tip stays in the wound, and he is unable to stanch the bleeding.

13. Josephus Is Healed; the Grail Quest Is Announced.

Once Sarras is converted, King Mordrain asks Josephus to show him the ark. When Nascien sees the Grail, he gives it that name, because he finds it pleasing or agreeable [Old French *agreer, Greal* or *Graal*]. He looks inside the vessel and is punished for this offense by losing his eyesight. An angel removes the lance head from Josephus's thigh. With blood that drips from it, the angel heals Josephus's wound and Nascien's eyes. Josephus interprets the king's vision, explaining the meaning of the three trees (the Trinity) and of the child (representing the Holy

Spirit) who entered the king's room. Then he has the king destroy the idol he keeps in an underground room. Josephus and his followers depart.

14.   King Mordrain's Vision.

King Mordrain has a vision in which he sees his nephew, Nascien's son, carried off by a bird to a strange land. A lake and nine rivers spring forth from his stomach; a man comes down from the heavens and washes himself in the waters. The priests Josephus left behind are unable to interpret the dream. Lightning and thunder strike Mordrain's palace, and he is carried away by the Spirit of Our Lord.

15.   Nascien's Imprisonment.

After King Mordrain's disappearance, Nascien is found weeping and in despair. At the instigation of a traitorous man named Galafre, Nascien is accused of treachery and is imprisoned. Despite his treatment, he never loses his faith in God.

16.   The Rock of the Perilous Port.

King Mordrain is left on a rock in the middle of the ocean. A pirate named Foucaire once built a house there, from which he attacked passing ships. He was defeated by Pompey, but this deed was kept secret.

17.   The Silver Ship and the Black Ship.

King Mordrain is visited alternately by a man in a silver ship, who brings him great comfort, and by a lady in a black ship, who invites him to depart with her. Each time she disappears, she is followed by a storm. In one of the storms, the rock is cleft in two. The next morning the king finds bread, which is knocked out of his hand by a marvelous bird. At the end of the week, the king leaves on the silver ship.

18.   Nascien's and Celidoine's Liberation.

Nascien and his son Celidoine are held in prison by the traitorous Galafre. After seventeen days, a hand carries Nascien away in a cloud. When Galafre follows, he is marked by the being in the cloud. Galafre has Celidoine thrown from the battlements, but he is caught and carried away by nine hands. Fire descends from heaven and destroys the tower, killing Galafre. The nobles ask Queen Sarrasinte for mercy and urge her to send messengers to seek Nascien.

19.   Flegetine Sets out to Seek Nascien.

Flegetine takes refuge with one of her vavasors. One night she has a vision: Nascien appears and tells her to follow him to the West. She sets out in this direction with the vavasor and his oldest son.

20.   Description of the Turning Isle.

Nascien is carried to an island in the Western Sea that turns with the firmament. The reason for this characteristic is explained: it derives from the original separation of the four elements. After Nascien awakes, he sees a ship approaching; once it has landed, he boards, despite a warning in Chaldean. Inside he finds a bed on which are a crown and a sword. Nascien examines the sword and its scabbard, both of which bear inscriptions.

21.   The Tree of Life.

At the end of the bed is a portico constructed from three spindles of different colors. The origin of the spindles is explained: they are from trees derived from a branch plucked by Eve from the Tree of Knowledge. The ship in which the bed is found was constructed by Solomon, who, having been told by a divine voice that his lineage would be ended by a chosen knight who will surpass all others in goodness and chivalry, sought a way to let that knight know that his coming was known in advance. In the ship he placed the bed and the sword of his father, King David; only the chosen knight could draw it without disastrous results.

22.   Nascien's Lack of Faith.

Because Nascien doubts the natural color of the spindles, the boat opens up, and he finds himself in the water. Once he has swum to shore, he prays and finally sleeps. The next day, a man who arrives in a ship explains the meaning of the ship, the bed, and the three spindles. Nascien finds his words so sweet that he falls asleep. He dreams that a serpent attacks him; he defends himself in vain, but the serpent flees when a little worm comes to Nascien's defense.

23.   Celidoine Converts King Label.

Celidoine is carried to an island. A storm comes up. and two ships land. Celidoine approaches and is brought before King Label. When Celidoine interprets the king's dreams and says that they predict the latter's death, King Label converts to Christianity and is baptized by a hermit, who interprets another vision. Label stays with the hermit and soon dies. His men, having refused to convert, seize Celidoine.

24.   Celidoine's Adventures at Sea.

King Label's men avenge their lord's death by putting Celidoine in a boat with a lion. Celidoine arrives before the wonderful boat with the bed inside and boards it. The next day, he finds his father, Nascien, on an island. They board the boat again and travel to another island, where Nascien fights a giant. When he tries to use the sword from the bed, it breaks. He then puts himself under the Lord's protection and finds a sword with which he wounds the giant. He and Celidoine set out again; they find King Mordrain, who boards their ship and joins the two pieces of the sword. A voice tells them to leave the ship. Nascien, who is slow to do so, is wounded by a flaming sword.

25.   Messengers Set out to Seek Nascien.

The messengers seeking Nascien travel for a long time without hearing any news. The youngest has a vision: Joseph of Arimathea shows him where to find Nascien, in a ship near Greece. The next day the messengers set out toward the sea; one of them dies because of the excessive heat. They reach a boat, where everyone except a young woman, King Label's daughter, is dead. She explains what happened. After burying the dead, they go to sleep on the ship. During the night, the wind takes them out to sea. They arrive at an island where the ship breaks up on the rocks, and two of the remaining messengers die. There they find a beautiful house that has fallen into ruin.

26.   The Story of Hippocrates: His Powers, His Trouble with Women, and His Downfall.

Hippocrates becomes renowned in Rome for his knowledge in healing, but he is tricked by a woman and dishonored. When he hears about Jesus Christ's power, he leaves Rome to seek Him. He heals the son of the king of Persia, who retains him. They travel to visit the king's daughter, who is married to the king of Sur. There he falls in love with their daughter and obtains her hand in marriage. He builds a castle and a fabulous home on an island. His wife, who hates him, deceives him, and he dies. The house is later destroyed by the king of Babylon.

27.   The Messengers Are Tested and Reunited with Nascien.

Several visitors come to the messengers and King Label's daughter on the island. Finally, a man arrives in a small boat and has them take his place. The boat takes them to the ship, where they join Nascien, King Mordrain, and Celidoine. They arrive before a castle belonging to King Mordrain's son. Before they land, Nascien is healed by a white-robed man who comes across the water on foot and who tells them that Joseph of Arimathea will cross the water in the same way that night. He tells Celidoine to leave in a small boat. The others then land; Nascien sends messengers to find his wife, who returns.

28.   Nascien Departs for Britain; His Adventures on Land and Sea.

Nascien and his wife seek news about Joseph of Arimathea and Celidoine. Nascien has a vision in which he is told to go to the sea, where he will find a ship. He departs, and his men search for him. Nabor finds him fighting a giant and saves his life, but is killed when he tries to force Nascien to return. Some of Nascien's other men arrive; the lord of Karrabel is also punished by God for his acts and dies. Nascien, leaving instructions to bury all three, departs for the sea. He embarks in a ship and has several dreams about his lineage, with particular reference to the eighth and ninth male descendants (that is, Lancelot and Galahad). Coming upon another ship, he boards it. An old man chastises him for wanting to know too much and interprets his dreams for him, explaining that the descendant in the eighth generation will live in mortal sin and that that man's son, of the ninth generation, will be born in sin but will soon be full of great prowess and goodness.

29.   Flegetine Has the Towers of Judgment Built.

Flegetine is frightened for her husband and her child, for she does not know what
has become of them. Finally, the men of Karrabel arrive to give her news of Nascien
and to tell her what he wants done. Following his instructions, Flegetine has the
Towers of Judgment built, and she has three splendid tombs placed there, each
bearing an account of the way its occupant died.

30.   Josephus and Some of His Followers Cross the Sea Without a Ship and Arrive
in England.

Joseph and his companions travel for a long time. Galahad I is conceived. One
hundred fifty of them cross the sea on Josephus's undertunic, but four hundred
sixty are left behind because of their lack of faith; they will cross later in ships and
galleys.

31.   Nascien Arrives in Great Britain with the Rest of Josephus's Followers.

Nascien's boat stops to pick up the sinners left behind when Joseph crossed the sea.
They cross and find Joseph. During their ensuing travels, God performs a miracle,
multiplying twelve loaves of bread. They reach the castle of Galafort, where they
find Celidoine, who is to debate with the clerks of the Saracen law.

32.   Duke Ganor's Conversion; The First Christian Victory over the Saracens in
England.

Duke Ganor has a dream, which Josephus interprets. He then tells the duke about a
childhood experience and explains its symbolic import. The duke and his ministers
immediately convert; those who refuse Christianity depart and perish in a storm.
Galahad I is born. The King of Northumberland besieges the duke but is vanquished
through the help of Our Lord.

33.   King Crudel Imprisons the Christians; Mordrain Defeats Crudel and Liberates
Them.

Joseph and Josephus, who leave with some of their followers to preach, are
imprisoned by King Crudel. King Mordrain has a vision: the Lord calls upon him
to avenge Him against King Crudel. Mordrain sets out for Great Britain. During
the voyage, the devil claims one of his men. Upon reaching Britain, Mordrain is
met by Nascien and Celidoine. He defeats King Crudel and liberates Josephus.
During the Mass that follows, King Mordrain goes too near the Grail and loses his
eyesight and strength. The Lord grants his request not to die until Galahad comes
to visit him. The entire party returns to Galafort, where Celidoine and King Label's
daughter are married. Mordrain then retires to an abbey.

34.   King Agrestes Becomes a False Christian; Moses Sits at the Grail Table; Bron's Son Alan Is Named Future Guardian of the Grail.

Josephus and his relatives set out again. At Camelot they convert a large number of Saracens. King Agrestes pretends to convert, but after Josephus's departure he makes his people return to the Saracen law, martyrs the twelve companions Josephus left behind, and goes mad. The people send for Josephus, who buries the martyrs and has a church built. After his departure, Moses sits in the empty chair symbolizing Christ's place and is carried away in flames. Josephus grants the wish of Bron's youngest son to be the guardian of the Holy Vessel after his own death. Some time later, the Grail serves everyone but the sinners; Bron's son catches a fish that miraculously multiplies to feed them.

35.   Joseph Converts Matagran; The Christians Cross a Deep River, Then Visit Moses; Canaan and Simeon Sin.

Joseph sets out alone; at a Saracen castle he is wounded in the thigh, and half the sword is left in the wound. He resuscitates a dead Saracen and heals the dead man's brother, thus converting them. He removes the broken sword from his thigh; it will drip blood until the two halves are rejoined by Galahad.

Joseph departs and rejoins Josephus and the other Christians on the shore of a river too deep to cross. They pray; a white stag accompanied by four lions crosses the river. Josephus and his people follow in safety. However, one person, Canaan, is left behind; he crosses in a ship, which capsizes immediately afterward. Josephus explains the meaning of the stag and the lions: the stag, which rejuvenates itself, represents the Master. He and his followers continue their travels. In a castle they find Moses burning in a fire, and his burden is lightened by Josephus's prayer. As the group proceeds, everyone except Simeon and Canaan is served by the Grail. Envious, Canaan kills his twelve brothers, and Simeon wounds Peter. The Christians decide that the two are to be buried alive. As the pits are being dug, Simeon is carried away in flames.

36.   Canaan's Burial and Peter's Illness.

As the Christians bury Canaan, he repents. His request that his brothers be buried around him is fulfilled. The brothers' swords are placed on the tombs. The next day, the swords stand upright on each tomb; Canaan's tomb is burning and will do so until Lancelot comes to extinguish the fire, whereas Simeon and Moses will be delivered by his son. Parent remains behind to pray for Canaan; Peter, whose wound is poisoned, stays with him. As the wound worsens, he asks Parent to take him to the sea; there they find a boat, in which Peter departs, leaving Parent behind.

37.   Peter's Healing and King Orcant's Conversion.

Peter arrives at an island, where King Orcant's daughter takes pity on him. She brings a Christian imprisoned there to heal him. At a feast at King Orcant's castle, the son of the King of Ireland is poisoned. Orcant is accused of treachery and must defend himself before King Luce. To find a defender, the king challenges all the knights in his kingdom to fight a foreign knight (who is in fact the king himself in disguise) . No one can defeat him until finally Peter does so. He then defends the king successfully, obtains his conversion, and marries the king's daughter. King Luce also converts. Peter's heirs are listed; Gawain descends directly from Joseph of Arimathea (through Peter).

38. Josephus's Brother Galahad Is Made King of Hoselice; He Lightens Simeon's Torment.

Josephus continues his travels, converting people. Finally, after an absence of fifteen years, he returns to Galafort. He makes his brother Galahad king of Hoselice. Yvain is descended in a direct line from him. One day Galahad comes across Simeon, who is burning in a fire. Galahad founds an abbey there; later he is buried there.

39. Josephus Makes a Cross on the Shield Mordrain Used in Battle Against Tholomer and Then Dies.

Josephus travels to the abbey where King Mordrain dwells. When the king learns that Josephus will die the next day, he asks for something to comfort him. Josephus has him send for the shield he gave him for the battle against Tholomer and makes a cross on it with his own blood. No knight will hang it around his neck until Galahad comes. The next day Josephus dies; later Scotsmen come and take the body away.

40. The Holy Vessel Is Passed on to Alan.

Shortly before death, Josephus confides the Holy Vessel to Alan, who sets out with his brothers and relatives. They arrive at the Land Beyond, where the king converts and is healed. The king asks Alan to leave the Holy Vessel there. He gives his daughter in marriage to Alan's brother Joshua and builds a stronghold for the Holy Vessel. After the wedding, the king sleeps in the palace where the Holy Vessel is kept; an angel strikes him in both thighs with a lance. The king and Alan die on the same day; Joshua and his descendants are the Grail guardians. One of his descendants, King Lambor, wars against King Varlan; fleeing, the latter boards the splendid ship, takes the sword, and strikes King Lambor, causing great devastation in the land. King Lambor's descendants are listed.

41. Nascien's Death; Celidoine's Lineage.

Nascien, his wife, and Mordrain's wife all die. Nascien is buried in an abbey. King Mordrain has the shield with the cross brought to this abbey, where it will stay until Galahad hangs it around his neck. Celidoine's knowledge of the stars and astronomy saves his land from two catastrophes: a famine and an invasion by the Saxons. After Celidoine's death, his descendants are listed. The story of Lancelot I's death is recounted.

THE STORY OF MERLIN

1.   Merlin's Conception and Childhood Deeds.

Angry that Our Lord has freed the sinners from hell, devils resolve to retaliate by creating a human with devilish powers. They have an incubus impregnate a virgin. When her pregnancy becomes noticeable, judges arrest her and lock her in a tower until the birth of the child, who is Merlin. Because of the mother's piety, the Lord allows the child to retain knowledge of things past and also gives him knowledge of things to come. The infant Merlin, soon able to talk, reveals that his mother's judge was fathered by a priest, rather than by his mother's husband. Merlin's mother is spared, and Merlin proves his powers of prediction by correctly forecasting the priest's suicide. Merlin has these events recounted to Blaise, who is to make a book of everything Merlin tells him.

2.   Merlin Explains Why Vortigern's Tower Will Not Stand.

Vortigern orders that a tower be built. As it is built, it collapses repeatedly. Vortigern consults his clerks, who are unable to find an explanation, but each has a vision of a fatherless boy who will be responsible for the clerks' deaths. To save themselves, they concoct an explanation that the tower needs the blood of this boy in its mortar in order to stand. Vortigern sends messengers to find this fatherless boy. They find Merlin, who reveals that he knows why they have come and promises that, if the messengers will ensure his safety until he has spoken to Vortigern, he will explain why the tower will not stand.

    Merlin explains to Vortigern that the tower collapses because beneath it is a great pool in which there are two dragons who turn over when they feel the weight of the tower's construction. Vortigern orders the pool drained, and the dragons are found. Merlin predicts correctly that the dragons will fight to the death. He then explains that one dragon signifies Vortigern, and the other, the sons of Constant. He then informs Vortigern that Uther and Pendragon are on their way to fight him, having assembled a great army. Vortigern sends an army to the port to meet them, and Merlin returns to Blaise.

3.   Uther Pendragon and the Round Table; the Perilous Seat.

Vortigern dies in a fire, as predicted by Merlin. Pendragon becomes king, and the Saxons recruited by Vortigern continue to wage war against the Christians. Pendragon is assured that Merlin can help them take Vortigern's castle, but Merlin says that will not happen until Hengist is dead. Eventually, Merlin informs Pendragon that Uther has killed Hengist.

On Merlin's advice, messengers conclude a truce with the Saxons. Merlin later warns the brothers that Hengist's kinsmen wish to avenge his death. He tells them that one of the two will die, but he will not say which. When Pendragon sees a red dragon moving through the air, he begins the battle. All the Saxons die, as do Pendragon and many of his men. Uther is now king.

To help Uther prepare his brother's burial, Merlin magically has huge stones brought from Ireland and arranges them upright. He then tells Uther the story of the Table of the Last Supper and of the Grail Table and orders Uther to set up a third table at Carduel in the name of the Trinity. The table is built, and Merlin chooses fifty knights to join the king at the table, leaving an empty seat for the one who will fulfill the adventures of the Grail. One person tries to assume the empty seat and is immediately destroyed.

4.   Uther's Love for Ygraine; Arthur's Conception and Birth.

Uther has his barons bring their wives and vassals to court. He loves Ygraine, the wife of the duke of Tintagel, upon seeing her. She tells her husband of the king's advances, and the two of them leave Carduel. For safety, the duke puts his wife in the castle of Tintagel.

Uther besieges the castle but cannot take it. Merlin promises to help the king lie with Ygraine if he will give Merlin what he wants. Uther agrees, and Merlin transforms him into the likeness of the duke. Thus disguised, Uther sleeps with Ygraine, and Arthur is conceived. Merlin tells Uther that, in return for his help, he wants the male child who was conceived. Merlin advises Uther to marry Ygraine; he later takes the infant and has Antor and his wife raise the child as their own.

Eventually, rebels strike throughout the land, and the king suffers great losses. Merlin tells him how to win the war. Then Merlin says that Uther will die soon, leaving the land without an heir. (Ygraine is by now dead.) Everything takes place as Merlin said, and, just before the king dies, Merlin informs him that Arthur will be the next king. After Uther's death, Merlin assures the barons that God will pick their leader at Christmas. Meanwhile, Antor has raised Arthur, now sixteen, and loves him as much as his own son, Kay. All three go to Logres at Christmas.

5.   The Youth of King Arthur; The Sword in the Stone.

All the clergy and barons are gathered at Logres to pray for a new leader. Leaving the church, they find a huge stone on which there is an anvil with a sword in it, with the message that the one who pulls the sword from the stone will be king. All those present try in vain to draw it. Later, Kay sends Arthur to get his sword. Unable to find it, Arthur pulls the sword from the stone and delivers it to Kay, telling him where he found it. Kay claims that he himself drew the sword but is then forced to tell the truth. Arthur returns the sword to the stone, and Antor asks him to make Kay his seneschal should he become king. Arthur again pulls the sword from the stone for all to see. The barons, protesting that he is of low birth, have Arthur's coronation postponed many times while they test his wisdom and generosity; finally he is crowned king, and a long period of peace follows.

Some jealous barons threaten Arthur with death if he does not leave the country. He withdraws from Carlion and awaits the arrival of Merlin, who then tells the barons the truth of Arthur's origins. The common people and the clergy take Arthur's side, but the barons refuse to accept a bastard as their king and prepare to attack Arthur. Merlin tells Arthur that the knights of the Round Table left this land for the bordering kingdom of King Leodagan of Carmelide; Arthur should go there and take Leodagan's daughter as his wife. With the help of Merlin and Excalibur, Arthur routs the traitors.

Merlin advises Arthur to meet the brothers King Ban of Benoic and King Bors of Gaunes and take them with him to Carmelide, for they will help him defeat his enemies. When summoned, King Ban and King Bors, though at war with Claudas, return to Britain.

6.　The Brother Kings, Ban and Bors, Pay Homage to Arthur.

Arthur honors Ban and Bors. Later, the king sends for Merlin, who tells the brothers that Arthur is their lord, and the following day Ban and Bors swear fealty to Arthur.

Merlin explains that Arthur is still opposed by the six traitor kings of his land, and efforts must be made to defeat them. Then they should all go to Carmelide, for if giants take this neighboring land, Arthur will never have peace. In addition, Arthur will receive King Leodagan's daughter, Guenevere, as his wife. Merlin goes to Blaise, then to Gaunes to summon Ban's and Bors's men to help Arthur. Meanwhile, Arthur secretly moves his men into position for battle.

7.　The Six Kings' Renewed Forces; the Brother Kings and Arthur's Victory over the Saxons.

The six kings swear revenge on Arthur and Merlin for previously routing them. They gather a huge army. Merlin tells Arthur to be generous; then, telling Arthur and the brother kings that this land holds the greatest treasure there ever was, he places a marker where it is located. Arthur assembles his battalions, and they ride out. Meanwhile, the Saxons lay waste the land of the traitor kings and besiege the castle of Vandalior in Cornwell. King Arthur's forces arrive before the traitors can fully arm themselves, and a great battle ensues. Arthur's side thoroughly defeats the traitors, and Merlin tells Arthur to return to his land with his friends, while Merlin goes to Blaise.

8.   Merlin as a Bird Catcher.

Arthur and his men make their way back to Logres. Pharien and Leonces of Payerne return to their country to protect it from Claudas. The next day, a poor bird catcher gives Arthur his birds and upbraids him for not sharing his buried treasure. Arthur is amazed that the bird catcher knows of it, and when Ban and Bors press him, he reveals that Merlin told him of it. Ulfin realizes that the bird catcher is Merlin and teases Arthur for not recognizing him. Arthur is further convinced of Merlin's love for him. Arthur befriends a maiden, Lisanor, and together they conceive Loholt. The king takes leave of Lisanor to ride into Carmelide with forty knights.

9.   Rebels' Defenses Against the Saxons.

The defeated barons stop in King Urien's city of Sorhaut. Messengers arrive with news that the Saxons have invaded their lands, and King Tradelmant advises them to fortify the lands bordering Saxon country and gather their kinsmen to break the siege. They close the borders so well that hardly any supplies get through to the Saxons, and thus they win most of the battles.

   Blasine, the wife of King Neutres of Garlot, is Ygraine's half-sister, and their son Galescalain is distressed that his father fought against Arthur, his uncle. He proclaims his ill will toward anyone who opposes Arthur, and he seeks his cousin Gawainet's help in becoming Arthur's knight.

10.   King Lot's Young Sons; Mordred's Parentage.

King Lot and an army of three thousand go to Orkney, where they are all welcomed joyfully, and successfully defend the city against the Saxons. Lot is married to Arthur's half-sister, and their sons are Gawainet (Gawain), Agravain, Guerrehet, and Gaheriet. Lot's wife is also the mother of Mordred, Arthur's son, for one night, when Arthur was still a squire, he joined her after her husband had secretly left to go to court. She thought Arthur was her husband, and they conceived Mordred. The next day Arthur told her what had happened; she was ashamed and knew she was pregnant, but they did not reveal the incident.

   Lot's wife tells Gawainet that Arthur is his uncle, and Gawainet swears to become Arthur's knight and never again to set foot in his father's house until his father befriends Arthur. His brothers agree, and they prepare to go join Arthur.

11.   Young Sagremor; Dispersal of the Routed Rebel Leaders.

The three kings leave Sorhaut to fortify strongholds One of the kings, Brandegorre, has a wife who is the daughter of the emperor of Constantinople. She has a son, Sagremor, from a previous marriage. Sagremor hears about King Arthur and yearns to be his knight. His grandfather wants him to be a knight, for he will inherit the throne, and sends him off to Britain. Meanwhile, the Saxons overrun Arthur's land, and the traitor barons are angry that Arthur does not defend his land himself.

12.   Young Galescalain and King Lot's Sons; Battle with the Saxons.

Gawainet and his brothers go to their cousin, Galescalain, in response to his message. Gawainet tells his cousin that he intends to be knighted by Arthur. With all the knights and squires they can muster, the youths leave for Logres, and on the third day they meet a group of Saxons destroying the land. A peasant tells the youths that Arthur is in Carmelide, and they decide to fight the Saxons for Arthur. Gawainet fights especially fiercely, and the youths destroy a train of three thousand Saxons. Gaheriet slices off the arm of Guinebal, who he believes has killed his brother Guerrehet, and the Saxons surround him. Gawainet and the others rush to defend Gaheriet. The Saxons retreat.

13.   Gawainet and His Brothers Defeat the Saxons.

The people learn of the youths' pledge to fight for Arthur. Five thousand men are sent to help them in their struggle against the Saxons, who are led by King Medelant and King Guinemant. Gaheriet kills Guinemant, and the Saxons strike back. The youths are having the worst of it when the reinforcements from Logres arrive, and a bloody battle ensues. Doon of Carduel pins King Medelant, and Gawainet, fighting better than anyone, deals the king the death blow. The Saxons, aghast, flee toward Vambieres, the site of the great siege. The youths pursue them and rout them, returning to Logres with all the goods stolen by the Saxons. The people of Logres hold Gawainet in high esteem, and he stays on there.

14.   Arthur's Support of King Leodagan Against the Saxons.

King Arthur and his companions ride to Carmelide, where they find a frightened King Leodagan, whose lands have been invaded by King Rion and fifteen other kings. The companions (including Merlin) appear before Leodagan and tell him that they are there to help, but they will not yet reveal their identities. Leodagan summons all his people capable of bearing arms. Saxons lay waste the countryside around Carhaix, and the two hundred fifty knights of the Round Table arm themselves, as well as the knights of Carmelide and the companions. Merlin carries the standard for the latter group, magically opens the city gates, and leads them into battle, bringing on a dust storm to disorient the enemy. The other groups join them, and the companions and the knights of the Round Table do wonders, though they are greatly outnumbered. The Saxons defeat Leodagan and take him prisoner. Leodagan faints from distress, and his daughter, Guenevere, nearly kills herself.

15.   Guenevere Witness to the Battle Below Carhaix; the Two Gueneveres.

Merlin, leading Arthur and his companions to where Leodagan had been taken, orders them to charge. They rescue the king, arm him, then follow Merlin back to help the knights of the Round Table. Guenevere rejoices. She watches Arthur and wonders who he is. As the Saxons flee, many knights chase them, but the companions and Leodagan rush to help the knights of Carmelide, led by the seneschal, Cleodalis. The story says that Leodagan once raped Cleodalis's wife and fathered a daughter on her. Earlier that same night, he had fathered a daughter with his wife. Both girls were baptized Guenevere and locked exactly alike, except for a crown-shaped mark on the queen's daughter's back. The king locked up Cleodalis's wife for more than five years; yet the seneschal never stopped serving him.

16.   Rout of the Saxons at Carhaix.

The Saxon kings Sornegrieu and Sapharin rally their men about them, and a great battle ensues. Merlin advises the companions and the knights of the Round Table to rid themselves of ten giants who are a threat. Eventually, the companions rout Sornegrieu and his army, and the survivors ride to help Sapharin. The knights of the Round Table and the companions follow Merlin to where Cleodalis and his men are struggling. Arthur fights fiercely, and Guenevere and all the maidens pray for him. Sapharin and his men injure many knights and almost kill Leodagan. Merlin calls Arthur a coward, shaming him so that he attacks Sapharin. The Saxons suffer such great losses that the survivors flee to King Rion. Rion swears that he will avenge his losses by taking Leodagan prisoner. He sends for more troops and supplies.

17.   The Victorious Arthur Falls in Love with Guenevere.

Leodagan gratefully rewards those who helped him rout the Saxons, but the three kings give away their winnings. The companions are never without the company of the knights of the Round Table. The king's daughter and Arthur gaze at each other, while Leodagan wonders who Arthur is and imagines his daughter marrying the unknown knight. Meanwhile, Leodagan's daughter serves wine to Arthur, who is preoccupied with her beauty. The maiden tells the unknown knight not to be shy and declares her gratitude for his actions during the battle. Leodagan says that he would gladly give his daughter and will his land to a man who would fight for him. Merlin knows that Leodagan is speaking of Arthur. Arthur daydreams about marrying Guenevere. She is the wisest, fairest, and best-loved woman in Britain, except for Elaine the Peerless, the Fisher King's niece and keeper of the Holy Grail until Galahad's conception.

18.   News of the Young Heroes; the Battle Before Arundel.

Merlin tells Arthur of the battle waged by his nephews against the Saxons and of the imminent arrival of Sagremor. Meanwhile, in his fortified city in North Wales, King Tradelmant learns that Saxons have invaded his land; he and his men ride out to meet the invaders. Many Saxons are slain, with some escaping to the Castle of the Rock, where they arm themselves and counterattack. Tradelmant is almost routed when the King of the Hundred Knights arrives with help, causing the Saxons to flee to Saxon Rock. The King of the Hundred Knights explains that God has brought them these troubles in order to raise up His true religion, and he proposes summoning all of their people to fight the Saxons in God's name. Tradelmant agrees.

19.   King Urien's Sons and Nephew; King Neutres Against the Saxons.

Hearing of the great slaughter committed by the Saxons, King Aguisant and his men take up arms against the Saxons. They suffer many losses and are saved only by the arrival of Urien and his nephew Bademagu. Urien's sons Wonet (Yvain the Great) and Yvain the Bastard, with Bademagu's son Meleagant, stay behind to guard the city. Nightfall puts an end to the fighting, and on his way back to Sorhaut, Urien slaughters a group of unarmed Saxons and restocks Sorhaut with the booty. On hearing the news of King Lot's sons and Galescalain, Wonet joins his cousins in Logres to fight for his uncle, along with Wonet the Bastard. King Neutres is upset that he has lost his son, Galescalain, and hearing about King Aguisant's trials, he decides to patrol the borderland near the Welsh causeway. A huge army of Saxons invades the land, and a fierce battle ensues. Neutres and his army lose more than they win. When night falls, they go to Wissant to rest.

20.   Dodinel the Wildman.

The Saxons invade the land of Tadelmont's brother, Belinant, who has a fourteen-year-old son, Dodinel the Wildman, so named because all he does is hunt wild animals in the forest. (Belinant's wife is Eglantine, King Neutre's sister; thus, Dodinel is Galescalain's cousin.) The Saxons also invade King Brandegorre's land, which borders Belinant's land. Brandegorre's men fight the Saxons on a bridge over the river Severn, which flows past Estangort, held by King Carados. Seeing shields and lances floating down the river, Carados realizes that Brandegorre is fighting the Saxons and summons his own men to help. Reinforcements arrive from Belinant's land as well, and the Christians slaughter the Saxons. As night falls, the battle breaks up, and the surviving Saxons retreat to Saxon Rock. The next morning, seeing that the Saxons have left, the Christians part company. As word spreads about Lot's, Urien's, and Neutre's sons, Dodinel decides to join them, and he sets off with Kay of Estral and Kay's nephew Kehedin.

21.   The Plight of the Saxons; King Clarion Opposes the Saxons.

King Clarion leaves Sorhaut and garrisons Northumberland. Meanwhile, King Bramangue of the Saxons mourns his losses at the Castle of the Rock and laments the dearth of food. Oriel leads a group to plunder Northumberland; his cousin Soriondes does the same in Cornwall, while their cousin Arrant pillages Loonois and Orkney. The Saxon kings decide to take the cities of Vambieres and Clarence by starving out the people. Clarion sends for Duke Escant of Cambenic to help him battle the Saxons, and there is fierce fighting for three days.

22.   King Clarion of Northumberland and Duke Escant; Sagremor's Arrival in Britain.

At Leodagan's castle, where the victory celebration continues, Merlin tells the three kings that he must return to Logres to help those who are fighting the Saxons. First he goes to Blaise to relate to him the adventures of Carmelide and Logres, while Oriel and his army begin to invade Northumberland. Meanwhile, Sagremor arrives in Britain and comes across the Saxons led by Oriel. People fleeing the Saxons explain the situation to Sagremor and give him directions to Camelot. Sagremor prepares to fight the Saxons and calls his men to arms.

23. Merlin and the Young Heroes Against the Saxons.

Merlin appears in Camelot and bewails the fate of the youths and of Sagremor; he accuses Gawainet of cowardice and thus lures him and the other youths into fighting with Sagremor against Oriel and his army. The youths fight well, and Oriel attacks Agravain. Gawainet strikes down Oriel, thinking he has killed his brother. Merlin, disguised as a knight, advises the youths to return to Camelot; Gawain and Sagremor leave. Meanwhile, Oriel is determined to avenge himself. The Saxons overtake the Christians and engage Gawainet, Sagremor, and Galescalain in battle, while the others ride on. Oriel recognizes Gawainet and charges him, but Gawainet strikes him down again.

As the three youths ride on to Camelot, Oriel regains consciousness and threatens Gawainet.

Meanwhile, Guerrehet, Agravain, and Gaheriet ride out to seek the three who had stayed behind. They encounter Merlin, who upbraids them for their cowardly behavior in leaving the other three behind to fight Oriel. The three shamed youths meet the other three, and they ride back together to Camelot. There they rejoice over Sagremor, who explains why he has come.

24. The Victory of King Clarion and Duke Escant; Bylas Attacks Urien's Sons.

Oriel returns to fight against Clarion and Escant. Unable to drive the Christians from the crossing at the narrows, the Saxons post guards there to hem in the Christians, then plunder the countryside. Clarion, Escant, the lord of Palerne, and a group of men ride out at night and slaughter a group of Saxons. A great battle with the Saxons ensues, and there is a great slaughter on both sides. The Christians are nearly massacred, but nightfall and the woods save them, and they return to Corbenic Castle. The Saxons seek them out the following morning but are routed by the Christians. Thus, Oriel and his men ride on to the city of Clarence, where Hargodabran is waging war against the Christians.

The two Yvonets leave Sorhaut and withdraw to Arundel. Gawainet summons men from throughout the kingdom to ride to Bredigan. The two Yvonets leave the castle of Arundel and are caught unawares by Bylan. The Christians fight hard and successfully defend themselves.

25. Merlin as Messenger Boy; King Yder and the Exploits of Arthur's Nephews.

Merlin, disguised as a messenger boy, runs to Bredigan to deliver a letter to Gawainet, claiming that Yvonet sent it. The letter describes the predicament of the two Wonets and requests Gawainet's assistance. Gawainet and his companions rush to help.

Meanwhile, King Yder routs a group of Saxons, but his men suffer great losses at the hands of Margalant. Soriondes goes on to help in the fight against the Wonets at the bridge, just as Gawainet and his companions come to help the other side. The

Wonets wonder who the men are who have helped them. Aces of Beaumont tells the brothers to fight so well that the others will want to know their identities; the brothers fight very boldly. At length, the Saxons begin to gain the upper hand.

26.   Ascendancy of the Young Heroes; Growth of the Heroic Circle.

The youths are greatly outnumbered and are about to be overrun when Gawainet arrives with a large army; the Saxons are driven back. Night falls, and the Christians celebrate and rest in Bredigan, while the Saxons set out to meet the main army at Vambieres.

    The youths go to rescue the young men in the garrison at Arundel. They, with other Christian knights, do battle with the Saxons. The Saxons surround the Christians as Gawainet arrives with the other youths. Merlin appears disguised as an unarmed old man and advises Gawainet to turn back, because the Saxons greatly outnumber the Christians. Gawainet follows this advice. King Lot watches the Saxons surround the stronghold. Lot and his wife, their son Mordred, and 5000 men escape to Glocedon. On the way, they meet a group of Saxons who rout them from their encampment and kidnap Lot's wife.

27.   Help from a Mysterious Knight.

A mysterious knight calls Gawainet a coward. Gawainet and all the others follow the knight and encounter a squire carrying Lot's youngest in a cradle. This squire explains what happened to Lot and the others, and Gawainet tells him to lead him to the Saxons. Gawainet notices a beautiful woman (his mother) in a meadow, being dragged by her hair and beaten by two Saxons on horseback. Gawainet and his brothers rescue the woman, then slaughter the Saxons. Gawainet's mother explains that she has lost Lot and Mordred. Gawainet tells her they have found Mordred.

    Later, they leave for Logres, taking Lot's wife and Mordred with them and swearing that Lot will not get his wife back until he has made peace with Arthur. They conclude that the knight who led them to rescue Lot's wife was Merlin.

28.   Merlin Warns Leonce of Payerne, Then Meets Viviane and Teaches Her His Magic.

Merlin goes to see Blaise, but must soon leave for the kingdom of Benoic, which is in danger of being taken over by Claudas and the Romans. He says that the wolf has come into that land to bind the lion so that he cannot move, that a wondrous leopard will come from the kingdom of Benoic, and that a great lion will come out of Britain; but he will not explain the meaning of these words. He reassures Blaise that the Saxons will soon be driven out of Britain, and that he, Merlin, must help to fulfill the adventures of the Holy Grail. In Benoic, Merlin goes to Leonce of Payerne to warn him of the imminent invasion by Claudas.

    Merlin promises to teach Viviane his tricks if she will swear her love to him, which she does. She is eager to learn Merlin's magic, and he teaches her a few tricks. Then he leaves for Carmelide.

29. Arthur Weds Guenevere; Battle Against Rion.

Merlin is back in Carmelide, and the three kings ask him how to break King Rion's siege. Merlin tells them what to do, tells Arthur of the adventures of the kingdom of Logres, and informs Ban and Bors that Claudas intends to strip their land. He then describes the fate of Britain, again using the animal metaphors, and the kings are perplexed. The three kings and Merlin meet with Leodagan, who seeks and receives advice concerning King Rion. Merlin asks Leodagan to give his daughter in marriage to Arthur; Leodagan enthusiastically agrees. Merlin finally reveals the forty-one companions' identities for all to hear.

   Leodagan sends knights to the places indicated by Merlin. They take forty of Rion's spies as prisoners and then, with Merlin in the lead, surprise the enemy. Merlin blows his horn, and the Christians attack. A great slaughter ensues, with Nascien fighting better than anyone else.

30. Victory of Leodagan and Arthur over Rion.

The fierce battle continues. Finally, Rion and his men flee as the Christians pursue them. Arthur chases Rion into a valley, where they reveal their identities to each other, then attack. Rion flees in fright, and Arthur pursues him. Kahanin tells Arthur he will fight him for Rion, and Arthur strikes him down. When the five other kings see what has happened to Kahanin, they attack Arthur, prompting the three companions to come to his rescue, and the Saxon kings run away after Rion. Meanwhile, Ban and Bors are slaughtering other Saxon kings when Rion happens upon them, with Arthur close behind. Arthur and Rion fight fiercely, and the latter again flees, nearly going mad and swearing revenge on all of Britain. Night falls, and the Christians let him go. Arthur tells Ban he has won the richest prize there is: Rion's sword.

31. Arthur Fights the Saxons.

Leodagan, Arthur's companions, and the knights of the Round Table chase the giants, and a number of battles ensue. The Christians who did not pursue any giants fear that Arthur and the others are dead.

   Meanwhile, Merlin makes use of his magic, creating a giant river and a great fog to rout Galahad, lord of the Land of the Grazing-Grounds, and his company of ten thousand men. King Amant, who once fought Uther, learns that Arthur is in Leodagan's land and decides to take revenge. He encounters Galahad and his men; Galahad thinks Amant belongs to Leodagan, and fierce fighting ensues.

   Merlin urges Arthur and the others to hurry on to help Leodagan and Cleodalis. They arrive in time to help them, but the fighting is so intense that the Christians require Merlin's assistance to rout the rest of the Saxons. Arthur and his companion ride back to the meadow near Aneblayse. The king distributes the booty and then leaves with his men, promising Leodagan to come to his aid should he ever need him again in the future. Bors rides with them for a while, then turns toward the castle of Charroie.

32.   Bors Kills Amant; Gawain and his Brothers Knighted.

Amant and Galahad fight, but a group of Saxons rescues Galahad. Amant is routed.
Leodagan asks Arthur to marry Guenevere. Merlin says that Arthur must first go to
Benoic to accomplish a difficult task.

Arthur and his men head for Bredigan, and Ban sends Bors a message to meet
them there. Bors, along with Guinebal, comes to the Perilous Forest. He arrives in
a meadow where maidens, ladies, and knights dance, watched by a maiden and an
old knight. Guinebal, smitten with the maiden, promises that, if she will grant him
her love, he will keep the dance going until the knight faithful to Love arrives to
break the spell.

Bors and Amant fight, and Bors is victorious. Arthur sends workers to dig up a
treasure that Merlin told him about. They send it to Logres, where Arthur's nephews
are waiting. When Arthur arrives, he agrees to knight them all, and he girds the
sword from the stone on Gawainet.

Meanwhile, Merlin and Morgan become friends, and he teaches her about
astronomy and necromancy. Then Merlin tells Arthur and his men that Benoic is in
danger. Merlin orders Gawainet to ride to the port of Dover to gather a large fleet.
Gawainet obeys, and once all is arranged, Arthur and the brother kings set out.
Merlin goes to Blaise to tell him about all that has happened and about the lady he
loves. Blaise fears that she will betray Merlin.

33.   Arthur's Forces Battle Claudas's at Trebes.

Arthur and his men sail to La Rochelle, and Merlin arrives the next day. Leonce
of Payerne and Pharien of Trebe, warned by Merlin of the threat from Claudas,
Pontius Anthony, and Frollo of Germany, send word throughout Benoic and
Gaunes, gathering men and securing valuables. Claudas finds little to destroy or
take. The three enemies and Randol the Saxon besiege the castle of Trebe. Inside
are Queen Elaine, her sister, Gratian, and his son Banin. Learning that the castle is
under siege, Leonce sends word to Anselm the Seneschal and to Pharien to wait for
their men in the forest of Briosque.

Meanwhile, Merlin orders the Christian forces to leave for the forest. Then he
goes to Leonce and his men and tells them that Arthur and his men are coming
to help. Blioberis leads Arthur's men close to the siege, and the Christian forces
inflict great damage on the besiegers. The youths, and especially Gawainet, all
fight well against Frollo, while Ban's echelon combats Claudas, Bors's fights
Pontius Anthony, and Arthur's battles the men of Randol. Eventually, seeing
how well Gawainet is fighting, Ban asks him to help take revenge on his deadly
enemy, Claudas. The two pursue Claudas, but then Gawainet notices Agravain,
Guerrehet, and Galescalain all fallen or in grave danger and abandons the chase
in order to rescue them. Once safe, Gawainet's brothers continue to fight. Finally,
the Christians drive the four enemy echelons together, and the fighting grows even
heavier and more wondrous.

34.   Victory of Arthur's Forces; Elaine's Dream.

Arthur is gladdened at the sight of Pharien, Leonce, Gratian, and Anselm, riding out of the forest of Briosque. Meanwhile, the fighting is heavy; when Pharien arrives with five thousand men, Claudas charges him Pharien attempts to withdraw toward the forest and is chased by Claudas. Leonce and his men arrive. Merlin scolds Gawainet, Ban, Bors, and Arthur for hiding in the woods when they are needed. The Christians are nearly routed until the men inside the castle ride out to help them. Arthur and the others rejoin the battle, fighting so fiercely that the enemies begin to retreat. At the castle of Trebe at nightfall, the Christians celebrate their victory, and the sister queens rejoice at the safe return of their husbands. That night, Ban and Elaine conceive a child, then Elaine has a strange dream that symbolizes with animals the fate of the child she just conceived. Ban prays to be allowed to die when he wants, and a voice in a dream tells him his wish will be granted, but first he will commit adultery. Arthur stays on in Benoic for a month to plunder and lay waste Claudas's land.

35.   Merlin and the Emperor of Rome.

Ban seeks out Merlin to explain the meaning of his and his wife's disturbing dreams; Merlin interprets Elaine's dream. Then he goes to his lady and teaches her many things, after which he goes to Rome, where Julius Caesar is emperor. Caesar's wife is a nymphomaniac who keeps twelve young men disguised as her maidens. The daughter of a Duke in Germany, whose birthright was stolen from him by Frollo, comes to Caesar's court disguised as a squire and calling herself Grisandoles. One night Caesar has a frightening dream and broods about it the next day. Merlin changes himself into a stag and comes into the hall where the emperor is dining. The stag tells the emperor that he will not know the meaning of the dream until the Wildman vouches for it. The stag then leaves.

   The emperor offers a reward to anyone who can bring back the stag or the Wildman. One day the stag approaches Grisandoles and tells how to take the Wildman. She then catches Merlin in the form of the Wildman and leads him to the emperor. Merlin interprets the emperor's dream, revealing that the empress's maidens are really men with whom she sleeps when the emperor is away. Caesar has the maidens stripped to verify the Wildman's words. Then he has the twelve men and the empress burned to death. The Wildman tells the emperor that Grisandoles is really a beautiful woman named Lovely, and that there is a treasure buried near the abbey and the church. He explains the evil effect of money and also expounds on the vile nature of woman. Merlin tells Caesar to wed Lovely and give her father back his birthright. He then leaves, writing above the door that the Wildman and the stag were both Merlin of Northumberland.

36.   The Saxons Defeat the Rebellious Princes.

The emperor makes peace with Frollo and gives Lovely's family back their lands; then he marries Lovely and gives his daughter to Patrick. A messenger arrives, telling about a dispute between the barons of Greece and the emperor Hadrian. Merlin returns to Blaise to tell him of all that has happened.

Ten kings and a duke gather at Cambenic to fight the Saxons. They ride to Clarence, where they ambush the Saxons at night. The surprised Saxons jump on their horses and begin to fight. The Christians are driven back, but the King of the Hundred Knights inspires them with his words. They fight well but are forced to give ground. Night falls, and the Christians again attack the unsuspecting Saxons. At daybreak, the Saxons fight hard to avenge their losses, and since they outnumber their enemies, they ultimately rout the Christians. Feeling less secure, the Saxons now have forty thousand men guarding their army. The Christians all go back to their own countries.

37.   The Tournament at Carhaix; the False Guenevere.

King Arthur and the high barons are joyfully welcomed back in Logres. Three days later, Arthur, Gawainet, Ban, and Bors, accompanied by three thousand men, ride to Carmelide and are greeted by Leodagan. The next morning, Leodagan asks Arthur when he will wed his daughter, and Arthur says he must wait a week, for Merlin's arrival.

The twelve princes who were routed return home and pray for peace with Arthur. Lot, however, plots to take Arthur's wife from him. Merlin, who knows Lot's thoughts, goes to Carmelide to be with Arthur. Wealthy men who hate Leodagan plot to kidnap Guenevere, then put the false Guenevere in Arthur's bed on the wedding night. Merlin knows their plans and tells them to Ulfin and Bretel, who prepare to rescue Guenevere. The next morning, the wedding takes place, followed by a tourney.

That night, as everyone prepares for bed, the traitors seize Guenevere and replace her by the false Guenevere. Ulfin and Bretel rescue the queen, throwing the traitors down the cliff. Merlin tells Leodagan what happened, and three ladies prepare his daughter for bed. Arthur returns and goes to bed with his wife.

That night, Bertelay the Red, one of Leodagan's worthy knights, kills another knight, who killed one of Bertelay's cousins in order to have his wife.

38.   Bertelay Condemned; Arthur to Hold Court.

The kinsmen of the knight slain by Bertelay bring their suit to the king. The king sends for Bertelay, and at a trial, it is decided that Bertelay should be stripped of his land and sent into exile. There he finds the false Guenevere and broods about revenge.

Nine days after his wedding, Arthur leaves for Logres, where he plans to hold court in mid-August. Lot waits for Arthur in the Forest of Sapinoie, as his spies have informed him that the king is on his way to Logres. Merlin goes to see Blaise.

39.   Lot Surrenders to Arthur, and Gawain Becomes the Queen's Knight; News of the Grail.

Arthur, warned of a trap, puts the queen in the care of forty knights, then rides to meet Lot; Gawainet and his companions arrive to join the battle. Gawainet fights Lot and takes him prisoner. Lot and Gawainet then reveal their identities, and Gawainet forces his father to make peace with Arthur.

They all ride on to Logres, and Arthur and Guenevere hold court. Gawainet asks Guenevere to retain all the companions as her knights. She agrees, and they are henceforth known as the knights of Queen Guenevere. A tourney begins between the knights of the Round Table and Queen Guenevere's knights; the latter rout the knights of the Round Table.

News of the Holy Grail arrives in Logres. The companions of the Round Table begin a quest to learn the identity of the best knight, the one who will bring about an end to the adventures.

40.   Arthur to Propose a Truce with the Remaining Rebellious Princes.

Ban suggests that, in tournaments, Arthur's knights no longer fight against one another, but rather with the noble men in Arthur's borderlands. Lot then proposes a truce with the barons who still hate Arthur, so that they can join forces to drive out the Saxons. It is agreed that Lot should deliver the message to the barons and that his four sons should go with him. Arthur is afraid for Gawainet, but Guenevere persuades him to accept the arrangement. Gawainet beseeches Guenevere not to let a tournament take place again between his companions and Arthur's. The knights all go to rest, except for Guiomar, who goes to see Arthur's sister, Morgan, and makes love with her all night long.

41.   Gawain and His Brothers Battle the Saxons.

Lot and his sons ride to the Plains of Roestoc, where they encounter thousands of Saxons. Lot and his sons courageously defend themselves but are forced to flee. After a second battle, in which Gaheriet is injured, the Christians flee again. Eventually, the Saxons return to the siege that Lot and his sons had interrupted.

42.   The Children of Pelles; Galahad Predicted.

King Pelles's son says he will not become a knight until the best knight in the world gives him arms. This knight will fulfill the adventures of this country that will soon begin and will thereby heal his uncle's wound through the thighs. King Pelles reminds his son that this knight must come to them on his own and ask about the Holy Grail, which his daughter has, and he must father a child on her. His son wants to go to Arthur's court and serve Gawainet. He leaves the next morning and rides until he comes to the Plains of Roestoc, where there are five hundred Saxons. The Saxons surround Pelles's son, but he defends himself and manages to get away. The Saxons continue to pursue him.

43.   Agravain and Gaheriet Discuss Love; the Saxons Routed.

As Lot and his sons ride through the forest, Agravain, Gaheriet, and Guerrehet discuss what they would do if one of the daughters of the forester with whom they stayed were with them now. Agravain would take her by force, Guerrehet would take her only if it pleased her, and Gaheriet would simply protect her. Gawainet and Lot judge Gaheriet to have spoken the best, Agravain the worst. Agravain tries to justify uncourtly behavior toward women, and Lot correctly predicts that evil will befall his wicked son. They then see Lidonas, the Fisher King's son's squire, bemoaning the fate of his master. He tells them how his master is being attacked by Saxons, so Agravain and Gaheriet hurry to his defense, with Lot and the others following. Pelles's son fights alongside Gawainet, and together the six men slaughter many Saxons, including two kings, and rout the rest.

44.   Agravain Quarrels with his Brothers; Gawain and Eliezer Rescue a Lady.

Agravain and his brothers continue to quarrel about maidens and cowardliness. The Fisher King's son, Eliezer, explains who he is and why he has come. They stop at a hermitage to sleep, but Gawainet and Eliezer hear a knight moaning and a woman screaming; both are being beaten. While Gawainet rescues the woman, Eliezer goes to help the knight. They both succeed, though with difficulty. On their way back to the hermitage, they learn that the woman is the sister of the lady of Roestoc, and the knight is her cousin.

   The next day, they ride to Roestoc, where they ask the castellan to send a message to the King of the Hundred Knights about the truce with King Arthur. The next morning Lot and his men leave. The King of the Hundred Knights joyfully receives the message.

45.   The Saxons Again Routed; The Rebellious Princes Agree to a Truce.

Lot heads for Cambenic, where the Saxons have routed Duke Escant. Lot promises to help him fight the Saxons. The Christians fight boldly, and at noon, Gawainet does wonders. The Saxons take the duke prisoner, but Gawainet and Gahariet rescue him. The Christians then slaughter so many Saxons that the remaining ones flee.

   The duke promises to attend the peace talks. Lot and his sons leave the duke and go to Arestel in Scotland to wait for the other princes. After they arrive, Gawainet speaks to them about the truce, guaranteeing safe conduct for all until Christmas in order to drive the Saxons out of the land. Lot tells them about the adventures that led him to swear fealty to Arthur. The barons agree to the truce and agree to fight on the Plain of Salisbury, but they add that once the Saxons are beaten, Arthur should again beware.

46.   Merlin Visits Blaise; the Queen's Knights Battle Knights of the Round Table.

Lot sends word to Arthur that the truce has been granted. Agravadain, Minoras the Wicked, and Moneval leave Arthur's court in disguise, intending to fight the queen's knights without being recognized. Merlin goes to Little Brittany and tells the Lord of Payerne and Pharian to gather as many men as possible and go to the Plain of Salisbury. After visiting Viviane, Merlin goes on to Lambal, where he tells Gosengos to take men to the Plain of Salisbury; then he takes the same message to the barons of Carmelide and King Bademagu. Finally, Merlin arrives in Logres and tells Arthur to assemble his men.

   Then Merlin tells Arthur that the three men he saw ride into the forest are mad knights of the Round Table who will fight the queen's knights. Kay, Yvain, and Girflet are sent out to break up the battle. They do so, and then all the knights return to Logres, where Merlin explains that jealousy has provoked the strife between the two groups of knights. Arthur sends messengers to gather all his men at the Plain of Salisbury, then goes to see the three wounded knights and rebukes them for their foolishness. Arthur and his men ride to Salisbury. The Saxons hear of the gathering and lift their sieges in order to gather at Clarence.

47. Eliezer Knighted by Gawain; Further Battles Against the Saxons.

All the princes hurry to Salisbury. Arthur arrives last, and Merlin advises the others to make peace with the king. This counsel upsets the barons, who came only to drive out the Saxons. Merlin next advises that they all ride to Clarence, where the Saxons are. Eliezer asks Gawainet to knight him, and he does so.

The next morning, the knights leave for Clarence. Meanwhile, some Saxons have returned to Garlot and have besieged the city. The queen and her seneschal try to leave the city at night, but the Saxon spies catch them and kill the seneschal. Learning what happened, the Christians go to rescue the queen, and they fight boldly with the Saxons. Merlin tells Gawainet, Eliezer, Ban, and Bors that forty Saxons are taking the queen to Clarence. These four knights agree to go after them.

48. A Great Victory over the Saxons.

Gawainet and his companions ride until they see the queen and her captors. They slaughter all the Saxons except one. After rescuing the queen, they head back to the battle, which the Christians win. The next day, the Christians head for Clarence. King Hargadabran sends fifty thousand of his men to Garlot. They meet Merlin and the other Christians; the armies charge each other, and the Saxons are routed. The Christians chase the Saxons to the sea, where they board galleys and escape. Arthur and his men return to their tents in the meadowland.

The next day, they go to Clarence, where Merlin assures them victory if they are willing to do as he says. They swear it, and he orders everyone to make peace with Arthur. Spurred on by Merlin, the Christians fight fiercely, and those within the city ride out to help. They slaughter most of the Saxons, with the others escaping to sea.

49. The Castle of the Fens.

All the Christians return to their lands, while Arthur and his companions go to Camelot. Merlin accompanies Ban and Bors, who come upon a castle where the daughter of the castle's lord is so lovely that Merlin wants to lie with her. Remembering Viviane, he casts a spell so that Ban and the maiden fall in love. Ban is distressed by his feelings for the maiden, because of his love for his wife. Merlin knows, however, that the union of Ban and the maiden will produce a child who will become a man of great prowess. Thus, at bedtime, Merlin casts a spell, causing all to sleep except Ban and the maiden; then he leads her to Ban's bed, where they make love all night. Merlin undoes the spell, and everyone awakens. As the kings prepare to leave, Ban tells the maiden she is pregnant with a son. Finally, the kings are back in Benoic; Merlin leaves them for Viviane, then leaves her to visit Blaise.

50.   Arthur's Mid-August Court; King Rion's Challenge.

Arthur announces that he will hold court, and the barons and princes arrive with their ladies. At dinner, a blind man enters and plays the harp. Meanwhile, King Rion, downcast by his defeat at the hands of Leodagan's forces, gathers his men to avenge their shame. They lay siege to Carmelide but cannot take it. Rion, receiving word that Arthur is celebrating his rout of the Saxons, vows to have Arthur as well as Leodagan in his power. He sends messengers to inform Arthur of his intentions, then resumes the attack on Carmelide, which the castle's inhabitants successfully fend off time after time. Rion's messenger delivers his letter to Arthur, requesting Arthur's fealty and asking for the king's beard, which he wishes to add to his cloak's fringe. Arthur refuses.

51.   The Battle Before Carhaix.

Everyone marvels at the harper's playing and wonders who he is. He asks to bear Arthur's ensign in his next battle. Ban realizes that the harper must be Merlin, but Arthur refuses to grant such an honor lightly, and Merlin vanishes. Then a child comes into the hall and tells Arthur to prepare to move against Rion, again requesting the right to carry the standard; Arthur, surmising that it must be Merlin, agrees.

  Merlin sets about gathering Arthur's army. Arthur and his barons ride to Carmelide to rescue Leodagan. The fighting is fierce. Rion, sickened by the slaughter, proposes to Arthur that they spare their men and fight in single combat. Arthur agrees, wins the battle, and beheads Rion. Rion's men become Arthur's liegemen, and Arthur and his men return to Camelot. After five days, the princes return to their lands, and Arthur returns to Logres. Merlin leaves Arthur.

52.   King Flualis's Dream and Roman Claims Against Britain.

Merlin sets out for Jerusalem to find King Flualis, a Saracen, who has gathered many learned men in the hope that someone can interpret his strange dream. An invisible Merlin volunteers to interpret the dream, explaining that the king and queen, under attack by Christians, will convert to Christianity, while their children are slain and their earthly goods are destroyed.

  Merlin then goes directly to Benoic to see Viviane, with whom he lies and to whom he teaches everything he knows. Afterward, he visits Blaise to recount all the adventures, then returns to Logres, where, upon his arrival, a maiden asks Arthur to knight a deformed dwarf. Arthur does so and makes the dwarf the maiden's knight. The two leave, and Merlin explains that the dwarf is the son of a king and a queen. Messengers from Rome bring a letter from Lucius that accuses Arthur of snatching Britain from Rome and orders him to make amends. Arthur tells the messengers that he will take Rome, as is his right of succession and inheritance. Lucius, angered by the message, seizes Burgundy.

53.   The Expedition to Gaul and the Giant of Mont Saint-Michel.

Merlin quickly takes Arthur's message to the barons, who gather at Logres before sailing to Gaunes, where Ban and Bors gather their forces to help. Arthur has a bewildering dream, which Merlin interprets as Arthur fighting a giant.

Indeed, a giant is laying waste the land, and Arthur, Bedivere, and Kay set out to fight it. Bedivere finds an old woman who is condemned to satisfy the giant's lust as she mourns her daughter, whom the giant killed. Arthur goes to fight the giant; after a bloody battle, he kills him. The next day, they all set out for Burgundy and learn that Lucius is laying it waste. Arthur sends him a message: if Lucius does not make amends, Arthur will drive him out of Rome.

54.   Battles with the Romans; Arthur's Victory.

Worried about the messengers, Arthur sends Yder and many other knights after them. Yder and his men find the messengers battling the Romans and help them to defeat the enemy. The Roman emperor's spies tell him about the prisoners, so he sends knights to rescue them. The Romans attack the Britons transporting the prisoners to Benoic, but, upon Merlin's advice, Arthur sends Cleodalis and the men from Carmelide to rescue the Britons. The Britons win and have even more prisoners. In a further battle, Gawainet kills the emperor with Excalibur. The Romans try to avenge Lucius, but eventually the Britons rout them.

55.   The Devil Cat of the Lake of Lausanne; King Claudas's Men Routed.

Merlin tells Arthur that next he must battle a great cat. The animal, which lives in a cave at the Lake of Lausanne, is filled with devils and is laying waste the countryside and killing people. Arthur, Merlin, and the companions go there, and Arthur kills the cat in a bloody fight. Arthur orders that the Hill of the Lake be renamed the Hill of the Cat. Meanwhile, the knights leading the Roman prisoners encounter Claudas's knights, who do battle with them. Claudas's knights almost rout the Britons, but Leonce of Payerne and Pharian of Trebe, along with eight hundred knights, happen upon the battle and rescue the Britons. Claudas's men run off, and Leonce and Pharian accompany the Britons to Benoic.

56.   The Birth of Hector; Flualis's Imprisonment.

After Merlin, Ban, and Bors leave the Castle of the Marshlands (or Fens), a knight named Leriador lodges there. He asks the lord of the castle, Agravadain, for his daughter's hand in marriage, but the maiden protests, telling her father what happened between her and Ban. Her father tells the knight that he must wait two years, but the knight swears to take her by force. He camps outside the Castle of the Fens with his men, who, one by one, come to joust with Agravadain. The latter wins every joust, including the last one against Leriador, and the siege is lifted. His daughter gives birth to her and Ban's son, Hector.

Flualis lives to see Merlin's prophecy come true. His land is destroyed, and he and his wife are taken prisoner and instructed in the tenets of the Christian religion. They have many grandsons, all of whom become Christian knights.

57.   Merlin's Imprisonment.

Arthur and his barons go to Benoic, where they are greeted by Leonce and Pharian, who tell them about the prisoners. Arthur orders Gawainet to destroy the castle called the Borderland, and he does so. Arthur receives news that Leodagan has died, and he immediately returns to Logres to comfort Guenevere.

Merlin leaves Arthur to go to Blaise, telling Arthur that this is for the last time. He tells Blaise all that has happened, then leaves him in order to join Viviane. She has Merlin teach her how to imprison a man through wizardry; she then uses that knowledge against him, imprisoning him for the rest of his life. Arthur sends Gawain and twenty-nine other knights to find out what has become of Merlin.

58.   Evadeam, the Dwarf Knight.

On the way back to their country, the young lady and the dwarf knight encounter another knight, Tradelmant, who unsuccessfully fights the dwarf for the lady. Arthur learns that the dwarf is the son of King Brandegorre of Estrangorre and that a young lady made him a dwarf because he was unwilling to love her.

In his search for Merlin, Yvain encounters the dwarf's grief-stricken lady. He learns that five knights are attacking the dwarf, and, rushing to his rescue, he finds the dwarf successfully fending for himself. He kills one of the knights and sends the other four to be Arthur's prisoners. After a year's time, Yvain and the other knights return to Arthur's court without news of Merlin.

59.   Gawain, Merlin, and the Dwarf Knight.

Gawainet encounters a woman but, deep in thought, does not greet her. She upbraids him for his uncourtly behavior, then tells him he will not find what he is seeking in Logres, but in Little Brittany. She curses him with a spell that will make him look like the first man he meets and retain that appearance until he sees her again. Gawainet meets the dwarf and the maiden; the dwarf returns to his former beauty, and Gawainet turns into a dwarf, though he retains his knightly prowess.

He goes to Little Brittany to look for Merlin but, finding nothing, is on his way home when a voice in a mist calls to him. It is Merlin, and he tells Gawainet about his imprisonment by Viviane. On his way back, Gawainet encounters the same maiden; she pretends that she is being raped, and he fights the would-be rapists until the maiden tells him to stop. She returns Gawainet to his former self in exchange for his promise always to help and greet ladies. Gawainet then returns to Arthur's court to tell everyone about Merlin. Evadeam comes to court and tells how he changed from a dwarf back to his former self when Gawainet passed him in the forest.

60.   The Birth of Lancelot and the Loss of Benoic.

Ban and his wife have a son named Galahad, whose surname is Lancelot, while Bors and his wife have a son named Lionel and another named Bors. King Bors grows ill, but Ban cannot be with him because he must defend his land from Claudas and

Pontius Anthony. The Romans take Benoic, except for the castle of Trebes, which Ban's godson, Banin, defends with all his might.

Volume III

Lancelot, Part I

1. King Ban of Benoic and Queen Elaine Take Flight with Their Infant Son Lancelot.

King Ban resides in Benoic with his queen and their son Lancelot. His neighbor Claudas, lord of Bourges, disregards Aramont as overlord of Bourges and is a vassal to the king of Gaul. After the deaths of Aramont and Uther Pendragon, the land of Logres comes to King Arthur. Claudas lays siege to Ban's castle, Trebe. Ban refuses to be the liegeman of Claudas and departs from Trebe with his wife and son to seek aid from King Arthur. Ban entrusts his castle to his seneschal with instructions not to inform Claudas of his departure.

2. King Ban's Realm, Despite the Efforts of His Godson Banin, Falls into the Hands of King Claudas.

Ban's seneschal goes to Claudas and offers him the castle. Ban's godson, Banin, asks the seneschal where he has been. He replies that he went to Claudas to confirm his father's truce. The men on guard go to sleep when they hear about the truce. Banin stays awake, sees Claudas's soldiers approaching the castle, and raises the cry of "treason," but it is too late. He retreats to a tower with three soldiers, and they fight Claudas's men. Eventually, Banin surrenders under certain terms. He challenges the seneschal and beheads him; Claudas offers him the land if he will become Claudas's liegeman, but Banin refuses and leaves.

3. Lancelot Is Kidnapped by the Lady of the Lake.

King Ban sees his castle burst into flames. He dies; the queen rushes to his side, leaving her son on the ground. After grieving terribly, she remembers her son and runs back toward the lake. She finds her son on the lap of a young lady. She asks the lady to release her son, but the lady jumps into the lake. The queen faints, and when she comes to, she sees no sign of her son. An abbess arrives, and the queen asks to be made a nun. The squire becomes a monk, and the king is buried at the abbey.

4.   Lancelot's Cousins Lionel and Bors of Gaunes Are Entrusted to the Faithful Pharian.

After King Ban's death, Claudas takes over the entire kingdom of Benoic, causing Queen Elaine to flee Montlair with her two sons. Pharian discovers her and forces her to relinquish her two sons to him and then leads the lady to a monastery.

5.   Queen Evaine of Gaunes Joins Her Sister Queen Elaine at the Royal Minster.

Pharian reunites Queen Evaine with Queen Elaine at the convent. They recount their miseries to each other and tell how they lost their sons. Queen Evaine takes the veil and remains at the convent.

6.   Background of Ninianne, the Lady of the Lake.

The story tells of the lady who carried Lancelot off into the lake. Merlin, living in the forest, is attracted to Ninianne. After learning who he is, she asks him to teach her his craft. Merlin agrees. Once she learns his craft, she puts Merlin to sleep and seals him in a pit. She raises Lancelot on her private estate masked by the lake.

7.   Pharian Surrenders Lionel and Bors to King Claudas.

Pharian learns that his wife is having an affair with Claudas, tries to kill him, but fails. He locks his wife in a tower, but she sends word to Claudas, informing him that Pharian is keeping King Bors's two sons. One of Pharian's enemies publicly accuses Pharian of treason and challenges him to combat. Pharian kills the accuser, and Claudas requests that he surrender the children to him. They are kept in the tower of Gaunes with Pharian and his nephew.

8.   Portrayal of King Claudas.

Claudas makes plans to go to war against King Arthur. He first goes disguised as a mercenary to Arthur's court to see if he would be able to defeat him. While returning to his lands, he asks his man-at-arms for counsel; he jokes with the man, calling him a traitor, and they nearly come to blows. Claudas makes peace with him, has him knighted, and names him constable of his court.

9.   Portrayal of Lancelot as a Boy.

While hunting, Lancelot encounters a knight in need of a horse and exchanges his own for a tired one. Then he meets a vavasor and gives him a roebuck he has killed. His tutor reprimands him for giving these gifts, and Lancelot beats him with his bow. When he arrives back at the lake, the Lady of the Lake concedes that he will have the independence due him.

10.   King Arthur Is Rebuked for His Indifference to Queens Elaine and Evaine and Their Children.

While Queen Elaine mourns the loss of her husband and son, a monk arrives and assures her that her son is alive and well. He returns to the convent with her and tells Queen Evaine that her sons too are safe and well provided for. He then goes to King Arthur to make an appeal on their behalf. Arthur agrees that it is his duty to right the wrongs done to Kings Ban and Bors.

11.   A Messenger from the Lady of the Lake Rebukes Claudas for Holding Lionel and Bors in Prison.

A messenger sent by the Lady of the Lake admonishes Claudas for holding King Bors's two sons in prison. He agrees with her charges and sends an escort to release them from prison.

12.   The Messenger of the Lady of the Lake Saves Lionel and Bors from Claudas.

Lionel and Bors arrive at Claudas's feast. The messenger pins a magic clasp on each of them to protect them from all weapons. Lionel strikes Claudas with a cup, and a melee ensues in which Lionel and Bors kill Dorin. By casting a spell on the two boys and transforming them into greyhounds, the messenger successfully kidnaps them.

13.   Lionel and Bors Are Taken to the Lake to Live with Lancelot.

The messenger arrives safely back at the Lake with Lionel and Bors. Lancelot regards them as his most intimate companions.

14.   Pharian in Conflict with Both Claudas and the Knights of Gaunes over the Fate of Lionel and Bors.

Claudas mourns the death of Dorin. Pharian assembles an army to go attack the palace and free Lionel and Bors. Pharian's nephew nearly kills Claudas, but Pharian saves him. Claudas hands over what appears to be the two boys. After they are transformed into greyhounds, the knights of Gaunes are certain that Claudas killed Lionel and Bors. Claudas denies it and claims that they were carried off, and he offers to be taken as Pharian's prisoner. After a first denial, the knights grant this request, having plans for Lambegue and Grayer to kill Claudas. Pharian devises a plan to protect Claudas by sending another knight in his armor. Lambegue tries to kill the knight armed as Claudas. A fight ensues in which Pharian's wife deters Pharian from killing his nephew. Pharian and Lambegue remain wounded in the tower.

15.   Pharian's Nephew Lambegue Is Brought to the Lake and Observes How the Lady Cares for the Three Young Cousins.

In order to cheer up Lionel and Bors, the Lady of the Lake promises to send for their tutors, Pharian and Lambegue. Arriving in Gaunes, the messenger finds Pharian and Lambegue in a tower under attack by the townspeople. The barons demand to see the boys before they will release the tutors. Lambegue and Leonce of Payerne leave with the messenger, while Pharian remains in prison. Leaving Leonce behind, the messenger and Lambegue arrive at the house in the lake.

   Bors is thrilled to see his tutor, but Lionel, distressed upon learning that Pharian is not with him, turns to the wounded maiden who brought him to the lake. Lionel puts all his trust in her as his new tutor. The next morning, the Lady of the Lake, Lancelot, several knights, and Lambegue accompany the two boys to meet Leonce of Payerne, who informs the Lady of the Lake of the importance of the wellbeing of Lionel and Bors. She assures him of the two boys' safety in her care and sends Lambegue and the lord back home.

16.   Pharian and Lambegue Are Caught in the Conflict Between the Men of Gaunes and King Claudas.

While returning to Gaunes, Leonce and Lambegue discuss Lancelot's identity. Leonce tells Lambegue that he is certain that Lancelot is King Ban's son. All rejoice at the news of the two boys, yet many of the townspeople do not wish to see Pharian go free for fear that Claudas will return and attack them. Thus, they capture Pharian and Lambegue.

17.   The Conflict Between Claudas and the Knights of Gaunes Is Resolved, Thanks to Pharian and Lambegue.

Claudas plans revenge. The barons release Pharian and beg him to negotiate a peace settlement with Claudas. Those guilty of treason surrender themselves to Pharian under the guidance of Leonce of Payerne.

   Pharian asks Claudas to enter the city peacefully. Claudas refuses, and Pharian renounces his homage to him. Returning to the city, Claudas's knights pursue Pharian, ready to attack him. Claudas follows them. Meanwhile, Lambegue and others come out to defend Pharian. Lambegue pursues Claudas and knocks him to the ground before he himself is beseiged by Claudas's knights. Pharian manages to bring Lambegue back to the city, then goes to meet Claudas alone. Claudas asks him to remain his vassal, but Pharian refuses.

   Claudas offers a peace settlement, contingent on Lambegue's being released to him, but the barons refuse the offer. Hearing the news, Pharian laments the fate of the city.

   After confession, Lambegue rides to Claudas's tent and relinquishes his arms to him. Claudas releases Lambegue in recognition of his valor and requests that Pharian renew his homage to him. Pharian refuses, objecting that he cannot accept a fief until he has news of King Bors's sons. Pharian and Lambegue leave in quest of Bors and Lionel.

18.   Pharian and Lambegue Rejoin the Boys, and Pharian Dies.

Once peace is made between Claudas and the barons of Gaunes, Lambegue and Pharian rejoin Bors and Lionel at the lake. Lionel does not greet Pharian warmly, but does agree to greet him at his lady's request. The tutors remain with the children, and Pharian dies at the lake.

19.   Reassured in a Dream That the Three Young Cousins Are Alive and Well, Queen Evaine Dies.

The story returns to the two queens, Elaine and Evaine, at the Royal Minster. Queen Elaine lives a severe life following the rules of her order, whereas Queen Evaine falls ill as a result of not hearing any news of her sons. She has a vision of the three boys and awakes seeing the three names Lionel, Bors, and Lancelot on her hand. Queen Evaine reports her vision to her sister, makes her confession, and then dies.

20.   King Arthur, Receiving Banin at Court, Regrets Not Having Come to the Aid of King Ban.

The story turns to King Arthur, who is celebrating Easter at Carhaix. During the jousting, Banin, the godson of King Ban, proves himself to be the best among the visitors and thereby wins the honor of dining at Arthur's table. Upon learning that Banin was King Ban's godson, Arthur starts to brood over the fact that he has not acted on King Ban's behalf. Kay sounds a horn that startles the king, and Gawain tells the king that it is not the appropriate time for such broodings. Banin becomes one of the knights of the Watch.

21.   The Lady of the Lake and Lancelot, Now Eighteen Years Old, Discuss the Meaning of Knighthood and Then Leave for King Arthur's Court at Camelot.

Lancelot turns eighteen. He and the Lady of the Lake discuss his plans to become a knight. The Lady of the Lake explains the concept of knighthood to Lancelot: she tells him of the burden of upholding justice, especially protecting the Holy Church, and she describes the function of the different arms. At Lancelot's request, the Lady of the Lake names some of the knights who upheld all the virtues of knighthood. She then tells Lancelot that they will leave that very week so that he will be knighted on the Feast of St. John. The Lady prepares all that Lancelot will need to be knighted, and then she and a large entourage depart for Arthur's court.

22.   Lancelot at Camelot: Queen Guenevere, Knighthood, the Adventure of the Wounded Knight, and Departure for Nohaut.

King Arthur holds court at Camelot. He and several companions encounter a wounded knight, who asks to be avenged. Arthur considers him reckless but agrees to lodge him. Returning from his hunt, Arthur meets the Lady of the Lake and her party. The Lady requests that Arthur make Lancelot a knight, and Arthur agrees. She presents Lancelot with his horses and arms and instructs him to prove himself in all the feats of chivalry, telling him that he is of noble birth and the cousin of

Lionel and Bors; she does not disclose his name. She gives him a magic ring, and Lancelot joins Arthur. Arthur puts Yvain in charge of Lancelot.

Lancelot makes it known that he wishes to be knighted the following day. Yvain presents Lancelot to the queen. Lancelot meets the wounded knight, and, once he receives his arms and attends mass, he removes the arms from the wounded knight's body. At dinner, a knight arrives to request that Arthur send a knight to defend his lady, the Lady of Nohaut, in combat. At the urging of Gawain and Yvain, Arthur consents to permit Lancelot to undertake this adventure. Upon taking leave of the queen, Lancelot asks to be her knight. Yvain realizes that Lancelot is not yet a knight, since the king did not gird him with a sword. Lancelot leaves without a sword.

23. The New Knight Champions the Lady of Nohaut.

After missing his first challenge, Lancelot separates from his guide, promising to arrive at Nohaut as soon as he has found the lady in the tent. A knight asks him to be his second in a battle to win a maiden on an island. Lancelot wins the lady and the following day fights the tall knight and also wins the lady of the tent. He then sends the knight and the two ladies to the queen. He also sends word to the queen that he wishes her to gird him with a sword so that he will be her knight forever. The queen sends Lancelot a sword, and he presents himself to the Lady of Nohaut. Seeing that Lancelot is wounded, the Lady of Nohaut delays battle until he is healed. News arrives at Arthur's court that the battle has not yet taken place, and Kay requests the right to do battle. To appease both knights, the lady requests a battle with two knights; Kay and Lancelot defeat their opponents, and peace is made. Kay returns to Arthur's court, and Lancelot leaves to seek new adventures.

One day, Lancelot, in deep thought, is disturbed by a knight named Albion, who is guarding a stream. Lancelot refuses to identify himself, and they do battle. Defeated, Albion goes to the queen to learn Lancelot's identity. He reports news of Lancelot to the court but does not learn his name.

24. Lancelot, as the White Knight, Captures the Dolorous Guard and Learns His Identity.

Lancelot encounters a young lady who is weeping about the loss of her lover, and he learns about the adventure of the castle of Dolorous Guard: any newcomer to the castle is put to the test of fighting ten knights consecutively. Lancelot informs the watchman that he wishes to enter the castle, and the fighting begins. Lancelot defeats five knights before nightfall. A maiden sent by the Lady of the Lake gives Lancelot lodging and presents him with several shields. The following morning, Lancelot returns to the castle to resume his battles. Lancelot defeats seven of the ten knights with the aid of the magic shields. The last three knights surrender, and the castle gate opens to reveal ten more knights ready to face Lancelot in combat. The lady gives him a new helmet and the last shield. The knights yield the second gate to Lancelot, but the lord of the castle flees without fighting him.

Lancelot learns his name and his lineage by lifting a large slab in the graveyard; the slab bears an inscription that states that the only knight who can lift the slab will be the one who frees the castle. Thus Lancelot wins Dolorous Guard.

25.   Gawain and Nine Other Knights Go to the Dolorous Guard.

A young man of the castle departs for Arthur's court to tell him of the miraculous news. Ten knights led by Gawain leave for Dolorous Guard to see if the news is true. Gawain and the hermit accompanying him are led into the cemetery, where they learn that the knight who had captured the castle is dead. Gawain encounters a young lady who confirms the death of the captor and tells him that the knight was wearing white arms and was riding a white horse.

26.   King Arthur Goes to the Dolorous Guard but Is Denied Entry.

Upon learning the news of the White Knight, the king departs for Dolorous Guard with the queen and a large party. Once Arthur arrives at the castle, he is instructed to find lodging and to send a knight to the castle at the hours of prime, tierce, midday, nones, and vespers until a knight is granted entrance into the castle. Arthur follows these instructions for three days, but no knight is allowed to enter the castle.

27.   Gawain and His Companions Are Betrayed and Captured.

Gawain and his companions meet a vavasor who promises to reveal to them the truth of the gravestones. He tells them that most of what they saw is a lie and the effect of a spell. He then takes Gawain's party to a castle on an island in the Humber, where they are tricked and taken prisoner. They join many of Arthur's other knights who are also prisoners in an underground strongroom.

28.   Lancelot, Entranced by Guenevere, Neglects to Admit Her to the Dolorous Guard and Then Leaves the Castle Himself.

Lancelot learns that Gawain and the other knights are being held in Dolorous Prison by the man who used to be the lord of Dolorous Guard, Brandin of the Isles. Lancelot has the gates to the castle opened for the queen as he leaves by a hidden gate. The king enters the cemetery and sees the gravestone that says Gawain is dead. The king and his party return to their tents, grieving for Gawain and his companions.

29.   The White Knight Triumphs over the Captor of Gawain and His Companions, Then Admits Arthur and Guenevere to the Dolorous Guard but Once Again Leaves the Castle Himself.

The White Knight arrives at Dolorous Prison and waits there until dark. A hermit tells Lancelot that the men of Dolorous Prison are planning an attack on King Arthur. Lancelot surprises them and heads off their attack. The White Knight pursues the leader of the attackers and makes him his prisoner. Kay approaches the White Knight as he is leading the prisoner to a hermitage and demands that the prisoner be turned over to him. Lancelot refuses; they enter into combat, and Lancelot defeats him. Once at the hermitage, the captive knight has his seneschal bring Gawain and all the other prisoners to him. He then turns all of them over to the White Knight. Returning to Dolorous Guard, Lancelot instructs the gatekeeper to open the gates to no one except Kay. King Arthur, the queen, and the rest of his party enter the castle. Once inside, the king is instructed not to ask the inhabitants any questions. Lancelot asks leave of the king; Arthur grants it and is thereby deprived of further information about the castle. Lancelot leaves to go meet Gawain.

30. The White Knight Frees Gawain and His Companions but Does Not Reveal His Identity.

The White Knight releases Gawain and the other prisoners and tells them to go back to Dolorous Guard to join the king the following day. He then departs and stays the night with a vavasor.

31. The First Tournament Is Arranged, and Gawain Leaves Arthur's Court in Search of His Unknown Liberator.

A lady asks Arthur to help her but tells him that only the White Knight can free her. Gawain promises to search for his liberator until he finds him. King Arthur sends word to the King of the Land Beyond Galone to set a date for battle.

32. Lancelot Is Injured and Requires a Litter.

Lancelot learns that the queen has announced a tournament between Arthur and the King of the Land Beyond Galone. She asks Lancelot if he has news of the knight who captured Dolorous Guard; he assures her that that knight will be present at the tournament but does not reveal that it is he.

   Lancelot rescues a knight who is about to be killed. The freed knight asks his rescuer's name, but Lancelot declines to reveal it. The knight goes to the queen and describes her defender by his shield. The White Knight continues on his way and injures himself in a fall. Once his wounds are healed, Lancelot sets out again, leaving his three-banded shield behind and carrying in its place a red shield with a single white band. Lancelot encounters a knight whom he must engage in battle; he kills his foe but is gravely injured. His squires prepare a litter for him.

33. Gawain Encounters the Knight in the Litter but Does Not Know It Is Lancelot.

Gawain arrives in a meadow before two large pavilions. He meets Lancelot in his litter but does not recognize him or learn his identity. Gawain meets two of the knights of the pavilions and learns that the tents belong to the King of the Hundred Knights and that they are going to fight in the tournament on the side of the King of the Land Beyond the Borders.

   Gawain leaves and comes upon another pavilion, where he meets Helis the Blond. Helis asks him to stay for the night, and he agrees. While the Lady of Nohaut passes by, some of the knights of the King of the Hundred Knights summon her escort to bring her to their king. Gawain and Helis intervene in the ensuing fight and present the lady to the king. The lady then proceeds along her way to the Tournament.

34.   Lancelot, as the Red Knight, Takes Part in the First Tournament.

Lancelot arrives in the city of Orkney and has his wounds looked after. After five days, he continues on to Godorson.

   Arthur arrives at the city and commands that none of his men should bear arms on the first day. Lancelot, wearing red arms, defeats everyone at the tournament, and the King of the Hundred Knights then challenges him. The Red Knight is gravely wounded, and the King of the Hundred Knights is led to believe that he has slain him. The queen comes out to meet Lancelot, and he faints. He then goes away to have his wounds tended. Gawain goes to visit the injured knight in the hope of learning some news about his quest. He learns that Lancelot arrived in a litter. So as not to be recognized, Lancelot slips away in secret during the night.

35.   Gawain Resumes His Search for the Unknown Captor of the Dolorous Guard and His Own Liberator.

Gawain continues to look for Lancelot. Battle commences between the two kings' forces, and Arthur's men defeat those of the King of the Hundred Knights. Arthur arranges another tournament at a later date, then returns to his land. Gawain resumes his quest and encounters a lady who tells him that the Red Knight is the same as the knight who captured Dolorous Guard. They continue to search for Lancelot together.

36.   The Knight in the Litter Goes to Nohaut to Recover from His Wounds.

After slipping away from the tournament, Lancelot encounters the Lady of Nohaut, who convinces him and his doctor to come back to her castle until he is healed. On the way there, they pass Dolorous Guard, the sight of which upsets Lancelot.

37.   Gawain, Helped and Hindered by Brun the Merciless, Pursues His Attempt to Locate and Identify Lancelot.

Gawain and the lady traveling with him meet a squire who tells Gawain that he must send or bring the lady to his lord, Brun the Ruthless. Gawain refuses, and he and Brun do battle. Gawain is victorious, and after the battle, he tells his opponent that they are looking for the Red Knight. Brun says that he will be able to give him news two weeks from that time (in exchange for a future boon). Two weeks later, Brun takes them to the Lady of Nohaut's castle. Lancelot refuses to see Gawain, pretending to be too ill. Yet his doctor allows the lady to see him. She reads him a letter from the lady imprisoned at Dolorous Guard. Giving her his ring to prove his identity, Lancelot sends her back to the castle to tell the lady that she is free.

   Then Gawain, the lady, and Brun go to Dolorous Guard. Seeing the ring, the lady in the tower allows them inside and promises Gawain that, if he stays with her until she finds the Red Knight, he will learn the latter's identity. Brun demands as his reward the lady of the tower, but Gawain objects that she is not his to give. The ladies convince the irate Brun to postpone battle for the present.

38. The Knight in the Litter Leaves Nohaut.

The injured knight leaves the Lady of Nohaut and goes to the house of the Hermit of the Hedged Manor, where he continues to rest and let his wounds heal. Two weeks before the Tournament, the doctor proclaims that he is stronger than ever.

39. Gawain Is Harassed by Brun the Merciless.

Gawain and his party continue their search for the Red Knight. Brun maligns Gawain to a knight who offers them lodging. The following day, two knights attack Gawain. A young lady tells them whom they are attacking, and they apologize to Gawain.

Gawain tells Brun that he can no longer travel with him and says that he may have the battle that he has been awaiting. Brun refuses to fight and leaves. Gawain and the ladies arrive at a river with a narrow bridge that leads to a tower. Challenged by knights, he realizes that once again Brun is behind the attack. The knights learn who Gawain is, and he is once again freed, yet the ladies are not allowed to leave with him.

Gawain comes upon a maiden who is holding a wounded knight in her lap. She takes him to a ford, where they encounter a knight who offers to help Gawain. He tells Gawain that the knights are in a castle that has an evil custom.

40. Lancelot Returns to the Dolorous Guard and Puts an End to Its Enchantments.

Lancelot leaves the hermitage and his doctor. A squire tells him that the queen is being held prisoner at Dolorous Guard and that only the knight who captured that castle will be able to free her. Lancelot arrives at the castle and is taken prisoner. He agrees to do all he can to free the castle from its spells. He then goes into a cellar in the chapel to look for the keys to the spells. After defeating several knights, he finds the keys to a pillar and the Perilous Chest. He opens the chest and thereby frees the castle of its evil spells. Leaving the castle by way of the cemetery, which no longer has any graves, he is greeted enthusiastically by all who see him. Since that time, the castle has been called Joyous Guard.

41. Gawain and the White Knight Both Take Part in the Second Tournament, Where Gawain Learns That the Other Is in Fact Lancelot.

Gawain learns that the knight helping him find the two ladies that were taken from him is his brother Gaheriet. When they leave the castle, Gawain takes the two ladies with him, stating that he believes it to be his right. They later encounter ten armed knights, and Gaheriet challenges Brun to fight him. Brun agrees to do battle with Gaheriet at Arthur's court.

Gawain and his party then go to the tournament but do not bear arms that day. The White Knight wins everything the first day of the tournament, and Gawain assumes that this is the knight he is seeking. Gawain and the maiden who promised to reveal the knight's name to him follow the White Knight to the house where he is staying. The knight refuses to reveal his name; the maiden recounts Lancelot's lineage to Gawain in Lancelot's presence. Lancelot refuses to confirm what she says, but Gawain returns to the castle satisfied with what he has learned.

42.   Gawain Reveals to the Royal Court That the Captor of the Dolorous, Now Joyous, Guard Is Lancelot of the Lake, Son of King Ban of Benoic.

Gawain and Arthur's other knights defeat the King of the Land Beyond the Borders at the tournament. Once back at court, Gawain relates to Arthur the outcome of his search and announces Lancelot's identity.

43.   Lancelot, Bound by Oath, Kills His Host.

Lancelot does not return to the tournament for fear of being recognized. Setting out in the opposite direction, he approaches a tower, where the guard says that he will not allow any knight of Arthur's court to enter. A lady in the tower uncovers Lancelot's shield and invites him to stay as her guest. At dinner, the lady tells the lord of the household that Lancelot is the winner of the tournament and proves it to him by showing him his shield. Lancelot learns that he must fight his host according to his promise to avenge the wounded knight. He defeats the knight in battle and throws him into a stream, where he drowns.

44.   King Arthur Has Strange Dreams Presaging His Fall from Power.

After an uneventful stay at Carduel, Kay asks Arthur if they might go to Camelot. Arthur has two disturbing dreams and sends word to his bishops to meet him at Camelot. The king has ten of his wisest clerics spend nine days trying to interpret his dreams. Even after three delays, the clerics still will not give an explanation to the king. When Arthur threatens them with death, they finally agree to tell him their interpretation of the dreams. Arthur learns that he is to lose all his worldly honor, and he is told that he can be saved only by "the water lion and the drugless doctor at the prompting of the flower."

45.   Lancelot Is Entranced by the Sight of Queen Guenevere at Camelot.

Lancelot learns that the queen is at Camelot. At the sight of the queen at a window, Lancelot falls into a deep trance. A knight brings him out of this state and challenges him to follow him to the queen. He agrees to stay the night with the man and to go see the queen the following day.

46.   King Arthur Receives a Challenge from Galehaut.

An elderly knight approaches Arthur on behalf of Galehaut, who sends word that Arthur should either surrender his land to him or be his liegeman. Arthur refuses this request, and the knight tells him that he will lose his honor and his land and that he must defend his land in battle against Galehaut. Arthur decides to go hunting the next day.

47.   Lancelot, in a Lover's Trance, Is Saved from Drowning by Yvain, Who Does Not Recognize Him but Is Subsequently Impressed by His Prowess in Battle.

Lancelot, on the way to Camelot, catches sight of the queen on a balcony and once again becomes deeply entranced. He loses sight of the knight he is following, and the queen gives him directions. Distracted, Lancelot lets his horse wander into the river. Yvain rescues him from drowning by pulling his horse from the river. Daguenet the Fool takes Lancelot prisoner; Yvain requests to be Lancelot's guarantor and, with the queen's assent, sets Lancelot free.

   Lancelot finally catches up to the knight he was following and, at his instruction, goes to fight two giants who are Arthur's enemies. Lancelot defeats them both; then Yvain gives him his horse and returns to Arthur's court with the other knight. Yvain relates all of these adventures to the queen and Gawain. He also tells them of a perplexing statement made to him by a passing young lady. Gawain understands and tells the queen that the knight who slew the giants is Lancelot.

48.   Lancelot Is Imprisoned by the Lady of Malehaut.

After slaying the giants, Lancelot spends the night with a vavasor. The young lady who approached Yvain joins Lancelot, and they continue to travel together. Lancelot fights and kills a knight in order to avenge the wounded knight. Approaching the city of Malehaut Bluff, he fights furiously and then surrenders to the lady of the city, who happens to be the mother of the knight he has just slain. The lady puts Lancelot in prison, and the lady who was accompanying Lancelot believes him to be dead and enters a nunnery.

Lancelot, Part II

49.   Arthur Is Attacked by Galehaut and Gets Advice from a Wise and Worthy Man.

The lady of the Borderlands sends a messenger to Arthur telling him that Galehaut has attacked her land and that Arthur must come defend it. Upon Arthur's arrival, Galehaut sends the King of the Hundred Knights along with ten thousand knights to go attack Arthur's troops. Gawain and all of Arthur's men do battle against Galehaut's forces, who, superior in number, force Gawain and his men to retreat.

   In the prison of the lady of Malehaut, Lancelot hears word of Gawain's great prowess; he asks the lady to allow him to go fight in the battle on the condition that he return to prison at night. She grants his request, but only after Lancelot pledges to tell her his name as soon as he is able. In battle, the knight with the red armor defeats more knights than anyone else and manages to slip away unnoticed at nightfall. Galehaut decides to grant Arthur a truce for one year, at the end of which they will go to war.

A wise man accuses Arthur of not ruling his land as he should. The man sends him and all of his wisest clerics to go to confession. Afterward, Arthur returns to the wise man and asks him for advice because his men are deserting him. The wise man instructs Arthur to go to all of his cities and to give generously to all, but especially to the poor. Arthur then asks the man if he will interpret what his clerics told him about his dream when they said that nothing could prevent his losing his land except for the lion in water and the doctor without medicine through the advice of the flower. The wise man tells Arthur that the lion and the doctor are Jesus Christ and God, while the flower represents the Virgin Mary. Two of the kings serving Galehaut come to Arthur to offer him a one-year truce. They also tell Arthur that Galehaut will have the knight with red armor in his forces when they meet again in battle in one year's time.

50.   Lancelot and the Lady of Malehaut.

The knight with red armor returns to the lady of Malehaut's prison after battle. The lady asks some of her knights for news of the battle, and they tell her a knight with red armor carried the day. Then the lady and her cousin go to look at Lancelot's horse and his arms to see if their knight was the knight of the day. They are not entirely persuaded that Lancelot is the same knight until they go to see him. He is sleeping, but the lady sees that he is wounded and bruised from his fighting. She wishes to kiss him, but her cousin leads her away. She is determined to learn who the noble lady is to whom Lancelot has given his heart.

51.   Gawain and Thirty-Nine Other Knights Leave Arthur's Court in Quest of Lancelot.

King Arthur goes to Carduel and holds court there as the wise man instructed. On the twenty-third day, Gawain notices that Arthur is deeply troubled. Arthur explains that he was thinking of the best of all knights and how Galehaut had boasted of having him in his household. Gawain, with thirty-nine knights, sets out on a quest for this knight, swearing on relics not to return without the knight or without knowledge of him.

52.   The End of Galehaut's War with Arthur; The Meeting of Lancelot and Guenevere.

The lady of Malehaut asks Lancelot to tell her his name. He refuses, and she promises that he will suffer greatly in the year preceding the battle between Arthur and Galehaut. The lady then goes to meet Arthur at Logres in order to learn Lancelot's identity. Arthur tells her that the knight with red armor is not of his household and informs her of Gawain's quest for him.

The lady allows Lancelot to ransom himself by answering one of three questions. She then asks him to stay in her cell until the battle, saying that she will provide him with whatever arms he desires; he requests black armor.

Gawain and his companions return to Arthur in time for the battle. Arthur's troops win the first day of the battle, but Gawain is gravely wounded, and this news reaches the lady of Malehaut, whom Lancelot reproaches for not allowing him to do battle the first day. She promises him that he may enter the battle in two days' time. With Gawain, the queen, and others, the lady of Malehaut watches Lancelot do battle in his black armor. Asked by the queen to defend the king's honor and his land, Lancelot agrees.

Hearing of Lancelot's incredible feats of arms, Galehaut goes to see him for himself. When he sees Lancelot fighting on foot, he gives him his horse and serves as his squire. At nightfall, Galehaut follows Lancelot, who is leaving as secretly as possible. To persuade Lancelot to stay with him, Galehaut agrees to put himself in Arthur's power as soon as he has overcome him in battle.

Lancelot fights on Galehaut's side, and the latter then places himself in Arthur's power. Noticing Lancelot's great torment at night, Galehaut asks him the cause of his grief, but Lancelot does not reveal it. The queen asks Galehaut to arrange for her to see the Black Knight. Galehaut plans the first tryst between the queen and Lancelot. Lancelot recounts all of his adventures to the queen, and when she asks him for whom he did these things, he reveals his love for her. Galehaut asks the queen to grant her love to Lancelot and to demonstrate it by a kiss. The lady of Malehaut asks the queen if she may be her companion, and Guenevere arranges for Galehaut and the lady of Malehaut to become lovers. After some time, Arthur decides to return to Logres.

53. Lancelot and Galehaut in Sorelois.

Galehaut and Lancelot journey to the former's kingdom of Sorelois. Lancelot is unhappy because he has been separated from the queen. The Lady of the Lake sends Lionel to stay with him until it is time for him to be knighted.

54. Gawain and Nineteen Other Knights Leave Arthur's Court in Quest of Lancelot.

King Arthur continues to visit his cities, giving gifts generously, until he decides to return to Carduel, where he will hold a court of law. There, Arthur starts to brood about his knights' great shame. When Yvain and Gawain learn this, they demand that Arthur explain what he means. Arthur reminds Gawain of the unfulfilled oath he had made to find the knight in red armor. Gawain prepares to recommence this quest, accompanied by fourteen of the original forty knights. Both the queen and the king try to detain Gawain, but to no avail. The queen reveals the Red Knight's identity to Gawain and tells him that he will find him in Galehaut's company. Once the knights depart, Gawain suggests that they separate.

55. The Spring of the Pine.

Gawain enters a heath and sees four knights ready to attack. One of the knights approaches Gawain and is about to attack him when they recognize each other. Gawain learns that the four knights are his friends Sagremor, Yvain, Kay, and Girflet. The five set out together and encounter a knight who is alternately sorrowing and rejoicing. They decide to ask him the source of his joy and sorrow. He manages to unhorse the first four knights; then, before Gawain can approach him, a dwarf beats the knight and leads him away. Gawain, swearing to find out about this knight, retrieves Yvain's horse and leaves all four knights behind.

56.   The Story of Hector; Segurade and the Lady of Roestoc.

Gawain, following the knight and the dwarf, comes to a pavilion, where a beautiful lady calls him a coward for not having defended the knight beaten by the dwarf. The dwarf then tells Gawain that he must do battle with this knight in order to learn his identity. Gawain agrees and learns that the knight is Hector; he also learns why he was both grieving and rejoicing. A maiden asks the dwarf to go to Arthur's court and seek Gawain to fight against Segurade in order to protect her lady's lands.

On the way to the lady's castle at Roestoc, the dwarf repeatedly sends Hector into battle, each time accusing Gawain of cowardice. Gawain prepares for battle, requesting that no one ask him his name for a week. The battle begins between Gawain and Segurade. After the hour of noon, Gawain's strength increases, and he is victorious. The lady of Roestoc leaves for Arthur's court, seeking knowledge of the knight who defended her lands and promising to avenge herself for the base conduct of the dwarf toward Gawain.

57.   Gawain and Helain.

The young man who gave Gawain lodging asks him to make him a knight. The following day, Gawain knights the squire and learns that he is Helain of Channings. At Helain's request, Gawain divulges his own identity and exchanges his arms for Helain's, before departing for Galehaut's land.

58.   The Split Shield; Hector Sets Out in Quest of Gawain.

The lady of Roestoc comes to tell Arthur about the knight who defeated Segurade on her behalf and to ask if they can identify him. The queen tells her that it must be Gawain. The queen tells the dwarf that, in order to make peace with his lady, he must send Hector in search of the knight who won the battle. The dwarf's niece will not allow Hector to depart, even at the queen's request. Hector hears of the plan, and he and the dwarf beg her to allow him to leave. Afterward, when the lady of Malehaut and the queen try to persuade her, the maiden refuses again.

An armed knight comes to court to tell the queen that Gawain will send her his half-repayment for the half-service that she had offered him. A maiden presents a split shield to the queen, sent to her by the Lady of the Lake, promising that it will cure her of her great sorrow. She tells the queen that this shield will be whole again when the best knight outside of Arthur's court has joined his household. The injured knight presents himself to the lady of Roestoc and gives her a message from Gawain, stating that since she forgot him, he would not help her in her hour of need. The dwarf's niece finally allows Hector to leave in search of Gawain. Hector takes leave of the king and queen and departs toward North Wales.

59.   The Lady of Roestoc Learns the Identity of Her Champion.

The lady of Roestoc takes leave of the king and queen, but the dwarf's niece remains behind to hear news of Hector. Before the lady leaves, a squire appears, carrying Gawain's broken shield. The squire brings greetings to the lady of Roestoc from Helain of Channings and tells her that Helain was dubbed a knight by Gawain and that it was Gawain who fought against Segurade. The lady leaves, troubled by the news, and takes the shield from the squire because she feels that Helain hid Gawain from her.

60.   Gawain Helps to Heal His Brother Agravain.

Gawain meets a maiden with a sword hanging from her neck. She tells Gawain that she is seeking the two best knights alive. Gawain follows her and, after several battles, arrives in a great hall with a bed guarded by ten knights. In the bed is a handsome but wounded knight. A maiden takes Gawain prisoner and explains that the wounded knight can be healed only by blood from the two best knights. Gawain consents to give his blood. A young squire starts to grieve bitterly over Gawain. The injured knight's leg is completely healed by Gawain's blood, and he goes to find out why the squire is grieving. The latter tells him that it is their brother Gawain who has healed him. Agravain, the injured knight, goes to greet Gawain and recounts the story of his illness. Gawain explains that he is in quest of Lancelot. Then Gawain departs, and the story relates how he defeats the knight guarding the Heath of the Seven Roads. The knight then directs Gawain to the road to North Wales.

61.   Hector's Adventures During His Quest for Gawain.

Hector encounters a lady lamenting a wounded knight. She offers to lead Hector to the forest of Breckam. Hector defeats the knight, Guinas, who injured the maiden's beloved. On the road to North Wales, Hector meets three knights accompanied reluctantly by a lady. He fights the knights in order to save her. The lady then sends Hector to help her husband, Sinados, in battle; with Hector's help, Sinados and his men are victorious.

Hector leaves the following day and travels to a castle where he is taken prisoner. A squire tells Hector that he must spend the night with the lord of the Castle of the Narrow March. Hector learns of the custom of the castle: every knight errant must spend one night in the castle and swear an oath to be hostile to all who make war against the castle. Hector also learns that Yvain and Sagremor were taken prisoner while fighting against Marganor, who was attacking the castle. The following day, Hector takes several of Marganor's men prisoner, and Marganor accuses Hector of treason. Hector and Marganor do battle, and Hector defeats him.

Hector sends for Yvain and Sagremor and informs them of his quest; they reply that he must be seeking Gawain. Hector arranges peace between Marganor and the lord of the Narrow March. The latter tries to persuade Hector to marry his daughter, but Hector refuses, objecting that he is not free to do so. As Hector prepares to leave, the maiden gives him a magic ring.

Hector, Yvain, and Sagremor separate in order to seek adventures. Hector sees a great company of people carrying a bier. A dwarf tells Hector that the bier contains the body of Mataliz, the knight whom Hector killed when he rescued Sinados. After being attacked and having his horse stolen, Hector comes to the castle known as The Fens. There he is led before Mataliz's father and is accused of murdering Mataliz. He is locked in a chamber, and the following day Mataliz is buried.

62.   Galehaut Sends Lionel with a Message for the Queen.

Lancelot is gravely ill, and Galehaut is greatly distressed as a result. Galehaut tells Lionel of Lancelot's liaison with the queen and sends Lionel with messages to both the lady of Malehaut and the queen.

63.   Gawain's Further Adventures During His Quest for Lancelot.

A hermit relates to Gawain the tales of Alier and his son, Marec, attacked by Segurade. Then Gawain reveals his identity to the hermit and tells him of his quest for Lancelot. In a battle at the castle of Leverzep, Girflet is knocked off his horse by Gawain. Once they discover each other's identity, they embrace and then ride away together.

They encounter two maidens; one of them grants her love to Girflet, but the other refuses her love to Gawain, promising instead to take him to a more beautiful lady. Gawain follows her and comes to a fine pavilion with a beautiful bed; the maiden tells him that all of this is being done by her lady, who loves him more than anyone else. The next day, they ride on, and soon Gawain finds himself doing battle to defend one of the maiden's relatives.

64.   Lionel's Encounter on the Way to Court; Adventures of Gawain and Sagremor.

Lionel comes to the place where Gawain is fighting and quarrels with a knight watching the battle. Hearing Lionel boast of Galehaut, Gawain wishes to see if he has news of Lancelot. A maiden asks Lionel to tell her the name of the knight he serves. When he mentions Lancelot's name, Lionel learns that the maiden is Celise, who once protected him from great harm. Lionel departs, followed soon by Gawain.

The next day, the maiden and Gawain continue their journey toward North Wales. Finding Sagremor the Unruly in battle against three other knights, Gawain assists him, and then the two rejoice at being reunited. Sagremor relates his and Yvain 's adventures and tells how Hector freed them from prison. Gawain then leads him to the maiden, who proclaims her love for Sagremor.

Sagremor falls ill. After caring for him, the maiden instructs Gawain to go meet his lady, who is the daughter of the king of North Wales. Gawain enters the lady's chamber, and she welcomes him with all her love. Seeing them sleeping in each other's arms, her father sends two men into the chamber to kill Gawain, but Gawain kills his attackers and escapes. Sagremor will accompany his lady to Agravain, while Gawain continues his journey to Sorelois.

65. Hector Rescues Elaine the Peerless from Her Imprisonment.

The niece of the Lord of the Fens asks her uncle to deliver Hector to her as her prisoner. Hector accepts this and agrees to fight another knight at her request. The lady explains to Hector that he is to fight on behalf of her sister, Elaine the Peerless, who is being held prisoner by her husband, Persides. Once they arrive at the castle (Gazevilte), Hector defeats Persides in a battle to prove that the lady is more beautiful than her husband is valiant. The maiden who led Hector to the castle sends him in the direction of North Wales to learn news of knights errant.

66. Lionel at Logres; Saxons and Irish Attack Scotland; Guenevere Sends Word to Lancelot.

Lionel arrives at Logres, where the queen and the lady of Malehaut greet him warmly. He gives them news of Gawain. Arthur prepares for battle at Carduel against the Saxons and the Irish. Guenevere sends word to Lancelot and Galehaut that they should go to Carduel and remain there in secret until she gives them further instructions.

67. Gawain Defeats the Defenders of the Bridge into Sorelois.

Gawain stays with the hermit of the Red Mountain, who warns him of the treacherous passage into Sorelois. Gawain arrives at a bridge and learns that he must fight a knight and ten other men before he may cross the bridge. After Gawain defeats the knight, Gawain's squire rushes to the battle scene and announces to the ten others that they are fighting against Sir Gawain. Learning who he is, they surrender and give Gawain the keys to the castle.

68. Hector Achieves His Quest for Sir Gawain.

Hector encounters Gawain's squire, who gives him news of Gawain and tells him about the battle on the causeway. The next day, Hector does battle with Gawain at the causeway. During a pause in the battle, Gawain learns who his opponent is and immediately declares himself defeated.

69. Galehaut Takes Lancelot to the Lost Island.

Galehaut and Lancelot hear news of a knight crossing the causeway; they are unaware that it is Gawain. Galehaut takes Lancelot to the Lost Island. Gawain sends the injured knight to Arthur's court, and he and Hector leave to seek Galehaut and Lancelot.

70. Gawain and Hector Find Lancelot; The Battle of Saxon Rock.

A maiden leads Gawain and Hector to the Lost Island.
Told that Galehaut is not there, Gawain insists that they wait until they see him. Galehaut sends two knights to fight Gawain and Hector, who promptly defeat them. Lancelot and the King of the Hundred Knights then challenge them. Hector defeats the king, but Lancelot and Gawain are evenly matched, and their battle continues.

Lionel arrives and tells Lancelot that the queen requests that he do what Gawain wishes. Galehaut reunites Gawain and Lancelot.

A maiden tells Gawain about the battle to take place in Scotland. Gawain, Hector, Lancelot, and Galehaut depart for Scotland, bearing unfamiliar arms. After driving away Arthur's enemies, Lancelot and Galehaut go to greet the queen and the lady of Malehaut. With Lionel's help the queen arranges for Galehaut and Lancelot to come to her residence that night. While Arthur is lying with a maiden elsewhere, he is taken prisoner. After the tryst of Lancelot and Guenevere, the queen goes to check the split shield and finds it whole.

The maiden who earlier led the four knights to King Arthur arrives and summons them to keep their promise, telling them also that they will be able to free Arthur in secret. She betrays them, and all four knights are taken prisoner. Yvain takes the place of Arthur, while the Irish and Saxons attack his forces. With King Yder prevailing in battle, Arthur's men drive the enemy back to Malaguire.

71. Lancelot's Madness and Cure; Defeat of the Saxons and Irish; Lancelot, Galehaut, and Hector Become Companions of the Round Table.

Lancelot goes mad in the Saxon prison. The lady of the Rock has him released, and the queen brings him to her chambers; the Lady of the Lake arrives and cures him. Before she departs, the Lady of the Lake instructs Guenevere to have Lancelot wear the shield that was recently made whole and to love Lancelot as fully as possible. Healed, Lancelot enters the battle against the Saxons, performing great feats of arms and pushing the enemy back. He then enters the castle and frees Arthur, Gawain, Hector, and Galehaut from prison, forcing the lady of the Rock to surrender the tower to him.

With the queen's help, the king persuades Lancelot to join his household. Galehaut requests that the king retain him as well, in order that he may remain with Lancelot. After holding a great celebration in Lancelot's honor, Arthur returns to Britain, while Galehaut and Lancelot go to their land, promising to come to Arthur's court at Christmas.

LANCELOT, PART III

72.   The Nobility of Galehaut.

Galehaut and Lancelot leave Arthur's court, full of concern for each other. The text
praises Galehaut's nobility of spirit and manners.

73.   Galehaut and Lancelot Return to Sorelois, Where Galehaut Hears Alarming
News.

Galehaut explains that he has had two dreams that are troubling him: the first one
has him attacked by a serpent coming from the queen's room; in the second, he has
two hearts in his chest, but one of them leaves him and turns into a leopard.
   Lancelot and Galehaut arrive at Galehaut's Proud Fortress, and part of the castle
crumbles before them. Approaching Alantine, one of Galehaut's stewards informs
him that half of every castle throughout Sorelois has collapsed. Galehaut sends a
letter to Arthur, urging him to send him the wisest men of his land.

74.   Guenevere Is Accused of Imposture.

King Arthur receives Galehaut's messenger and then a messenger named Clice.
The latter brings a letter, purportedly from Guenevere, to be read before the entire
court. It states that its sender is the real Queen Guenevere and that King Arthur
has been living in mortal sin. She requests that Arthur invite her back to live as his
rightful spouse. Arthur asks the queen to defend herself, and Gawain offers himself
as the queen's champion. Arthur postpones a battle between Gawain and Bertelay
until Candlemas at Bredigan.

75.   Galehaut's Plans and the Interpretation of His Dreams: Lovesickness and
Destiny.

Galehaut's messenger returns with the news of the accusation against the queen.
When Lancelot learns this, he is despondent, and Galehaut tries to cheer him up by
devising a plan that would enable Lancelot and Guenevere to be together always.
Galehaut and Lancelot meet with wise men who are to explain the significance of

the former's dreams. Finally, Master Elias asks to speak with Galehaut alone. He predicts that there will be a knight, greater than Lancelot, who will complete the adventures of Britain. Galehaut convinces Elias to tell him when he will die. Elias shows him that he will live for at least three years and tells him not to disclose this to anyone.

76.   Galehaut Makes Plans to Leave Sorelois in the Hands of Bademagu; Portrayal of Bademagu's Son Meleagant.

Galehaut proposes that he and Lancelot be crowned kings and avenge Lancelot's father's death. Meeting with the barons, Galehaut informs them that he will be living at Arthur's court for a while and requests that they appoint a steward. King Bademagu of Gorre is appointed. The adventures of the kingdom of Gorre are introduced, and Galehaut departs with his selected barons for Arthur's court.

77.   Lancelot Is Wounded by Meleagant; Guenevere Is Confronted by Her Accusers; Arthur Is Captured and Succumbs to the Wiles of the False Guenevere.

Galehaut and his retinue are met at Carduel by Arthur. The king holds court at Camelot, and on Christmas day Meleagant wounds Lancelot in a joust. A week before Candlemas, the king goes to Bredigan to await news of the maiden of Carmelide. She takes him prisoner, and at Easter the king asks her to release him from prison. He proclaims his love for her and agrees to swear on relics that he will regard her as queen, and she relents. Arthur sends word to Gawain and the other barons to come to Zelegebre on Ascension Day.

78.   Arthur Returns to Court and Proclaims the False Guenevere Queen.

The barons of Britain, telling Gawain that they must find a protector, ask him to accept the honor of being proclaimed king. He accepts, though reluctantly. Shortly thereafter, the king's messengers arrive from Carmelide with his request that the barons meet him at Zelegebre on Ascension Day. Galehaut promises the queen that he will protect her. When everyone is convened, the king proclaims that he has sinned out of ignorance and asks the barons of both lands to decide who will be queen. Bertelay and other barons swear that their lady is the rightful queen. Casting aside the true queen, the king asks what should be done with her, and Galehaut asks that the decision be made at Pentecost. Until then, she is put in the care of Gawain.

79.   Lancelot, as Guenevere's Champion, Defeats Three Foes; He Breaks with Arthur.

At Pentecost, the king asks the barons to pronounce sentence on the queen, and they proclaim that she is to be stripped of her royal rank and severely punished. In response, Lancelot proclaims that he will fight to prove his lady's innocence. He fights against three of the best knights of Carmelide. Gawain speaks to the king about the shame that has befallen the Round Table since Lancelot's withdrawal and says that he must try to reestablish good terms with him. Lancelot refuses the king's plea to stay, and Guenevere refuses to try to convince him.

80. The Imposture Is Revealed; the False Guenevere Dies; Arthur Repents and Is Reconciled First with Guenevere, Then with Lancelot.

Gawain leaves as soon as Galehaut has Guenevere properly settled in Sorelois. The pope hears of the king's offense against the Church and places his land under interdict. The queen and Bertelay fall sick, and Gawain chides the king for his listless behavior.

One day, the king asks a white-robed man for a meal; he falls sick while eating, and Gawain fears he is dead. The bedridden Guenevere calls the king back to her. In Bredigan, Berteley and the queen confess all of their traitorous behavior. The barons go to ask forgiveness of the queen in Sorelois. Three weeks after Christmas, the False Guenevere dies, and the queen returns to Arthur in Carduel. At Easter Lancelot is reconciled with the king.

81. Gawain Is Abducted by Caradoc; Lancelot, Yvain, and the Duke of Clarence Set out in Quest of Him.

At the king's court at Pentecost, Gawain, Lancelot, Yvain, and Galescalain go walking in the forest and decide that they will go seeking adventures there. As they are speaking, a knight comes and abducts Gawain. After arming themselves, the remaining three knights separate and set off in an effort to rescue him.

82. The Duke of Clarence Learns About Caradoc from His Cousin.

When Galescalain stops for shelter, it happens that he is staying with his long-lost first cousin. She tells him about the knight, Caradoc, who abducted Gawain. Realizing that she cannot stop him from seeking Caradoc, she offers him an escort to his castle and advice on how to enter it.

83. Yvain Rescues a Young Man and His Family from a Band of Thieves.

Yvain encounters a lady crying over her wounded knight in a coffin. She challenges Yvain to remove the knight from the coffin. He fails and continues on his way. Hearing a horn being blown and fearing that someone is in danger, he helps a man defend his castle from a group of thieves and is lodged there that night.

84. Lancelot Extricates Drian from an Enchanted Coffin and Is Warmly Received at Gay Castle.

Lancelot encounters the same wounded man and successfully removes him from the coffin. He learns that he has aided a whole family in their troubles, which were caused by Caradoc. Lancelot reveals that it is Caradoc he is seeking, and one of the brothers tries to convince him to give up his search. He explains Caradoc's plan to overtake all the good knights of Arthur's court. Lancelot refuses to abandon his quest.

85.   Gawain, in Caradoc's Prison, Is Helped by a Resourceful Damsel.

Caradoc takes Gawain to the Dolorous Tower and has his mother watch over him. She poisons his wounds and has him thrown into a prison full of vermin. A young lady being held captive by Caradoc relieves Gawain of all his torments in prison.

86.   Galehaut Stops Lionel from Setting out After Lancelot.

Galehaut, after unsuccessfully seeking news of Gawain, sees Lionel, Lancelot's cousin, trying to follow the four knights into the forest. He forces Lionel to give up the pursuit, pointing out that the knights are sufficiently valiant to take care of themselves and that he, Lionel, is not yet a knight—the dubbing is to occur the next day.

87.   The Duke of Clarence Rescues a Damsel, Defeats Four Fighters at Pintadol, and Fails at Escalon the Dark.

The duke of Clarence performs several valiant deeds on his quest for Gawain: he defends a damsel and frees a castle from its woeful customs. He fails at the church adventure of the castle of Escalon the Dark. He learns that only the knight who will put an end to the evil customs of the Dolorous Tower will be able to open the door to the church.

88.   Yvain Attempts to Rescue Sagremor and a Damsel.

Coming to a pavilion, Yvain finds a maiden hanging by her braids and a knight bound to a stake. In trying to untie her, Yvain is subject to a series of attacks. In an uneven battle, one knight in the throng tries inconspicuously to aid Yvain.

89.   Melian Brings News of Lancelot to the Royal Court; Arthur and Galehaut Set out to Rescue Gawain.

Lancelot takes leave of Melian, his father, and his brother, and starts down the road taken by Yvain. Melian leaves for Arthur's court, where he is welcomed for bringing word from Lancelot and news of Gawain's capture. Guenevere becomes inconsolable when she hears that Lancelot departed without taking leave from her. Arthur and Galehaut, with Melian as guide, set out to rescue Gawain.

90.   Lancelot Comes to the Rescue of Yvain and Sagremor.

Lancelot aids Yvain in battle, vanquishing all the knights except the one who helped Yvain. He then unties Sagremor and the maiden. Sagremor explains his ordeal, and Lancelot tells of their quest for Gawain. They part and go separate ways: Sagremor leaves for London, and Yvain and Lancelot set out to follow Gawain.

91.   Lancelot and Yvain, en Route to Caradoc's Dolorous Tower, Stop at Escalon the Dark; Yvain Fails, but Lancelot Succeeds.

Lancelot and Yvain encounter the sister of the maiden who led the duke to Escalon the Dark. She challenges their ability to put an end to the evil customs of the

Dolorous Tower. She leads them to the church of great darkness and tells them of its adventure. Yvain enters the church first and fails. Lancelot succeeds in opening the church door and liberates all the people of the castle. The next day, the maiden leads Lancelot and Yvain along their way.

92. The Duke of Clarence, Despite Warnings, Enters the Valley of No Return.

The duke and the squire continue along the Devil's Road in search of Gawain. They spend the night at a manor, and the following day, the vavasor warns the duke about the terrible dangers he will encounter if he continues on this road. He explains that for the past three years, no one who has entered the valley has come out; for that reason it is called the Valley of No Return. Refusing to turn back, because that would bring him shame, the duke starts down the valley road.

93. Description of the Valley of No Return.

The story recounts how Morgan cast a spell on the Valley of No Return, otherwise known as the Valley of False Lovers. She formerly loved a knight who loved another woman. Her jealousy led her to keep him there, and she used her powers to imprison any knight who came there and had been unfaithful. Ladies, however, could leave at will. The spell would end if a knight came there who had never been unfaithful to his lady.

94. The Duke of Clarence Is Held Prisoner in the Valley of No Return.

The duke enters the valley and undergoes a series of trials, involving battles with dragons and knights, before being carried into a beautiful garden. There he finds himself among many knights, including three from Arthur's court. These knights ask him about his travels and explain the spell of the valley to him.

95. Lancelot Liberates the Valley's Prisoners but Is Abducted by Morgan the Fay.

Lancelot, Yvain, and the maiden arrive at the Valley of False Lovers. The maiden suggests that Yvain enter first. He accepts and fails at the adventure, thus being carried off in the same way as the duke. Then Lancelot enters and succeeds in many adventures. He and Morgan meet, and as they are talking, a maiden comes in to announce that the spell on the valley is broken. Morgan is angry because, once freed from the valley, the knights will never again be as attentive to their ladies. When Morgan learns Lancelot's identity, she guesses that he is in love with the queen, and she plots to deprive Guenevere of any further happiness. The story then recounts how the hatred developed between Morgan and the queen: the latter once put an end to an affair between Morgan and Guyamor (the queen's nephew). Morgan places on Lancelot's finger a ring that induces sleep. This deception enables her to kidnap and imprison him.

96.   The Valley's Newly Liberated Prisoners Are Received by Kay of Estral; News of Lancelot Arrives.

Astonished to find Lancelot missing, Yvain and the duke realize that Morgan has taken him away. The duke suggests that they continue the quest to rescue Gawain. Kehedin the Fair leads them and all the liberated knights to his uncle's castle for lodging. His uncle, Kay of Estral, is overjoyed by the news of the valley, as it also frees him from his pledged imprisonment to his wife.

The squire who led the duke arrives, along with the maiden who led Lancelot and Yvain. She tells Yvain that Morgan gave assurances that they would see Lancelot unharmed at the Dolorous Tower the following night.

97.   Lancelot, Released Provisionally, Resists Seduction by Morgan's Damsel; He Recovers Two Bodies from a Riverbed, Then Rejoins Yvain and the Duke of Clarence.

Imprisoned, Lancelot tells Morgan that he will give her anything if he is able. She asks him to tell her whom he loves. He refuses to tell her, but he pledges to return to her prison after rescuing Gawain. Morgan sends one of her maidens to accompany Lancelot; she tries in vain to seduce him along the way and finally promises to leave him in peace if he will tell her that he is in love. He proclaims his love. The following day, after passing through a wasteland with another adventure, Lancelot and the woman meet the duke and Yvain. The duke suggests that they attack Caradoc's unguarded castle, but Lancelot refuses, objecting that the plan is dishonorable and that Gawain deserves to be rescued through an act of genuine prowess. The duke of Clarence and Yvain leave Lancelot and the rest of the knights.

98.   Lancelot Confronts Caradoc's Men at the Wicked Pass While Yvain and the Duke of Clarence Go Directly to the Dolorous Tower, Where They Are Captured.

Yvain and the duke approach the castle. In order to enter, they must fight ten knights. The duke proposes another way to enter, but Yvain remains and takes on the ten knights. They defeat him and put him in prison. The duke tries to enter through another door but is also defeated and imprisoned with Yvain.

99.   Lancelot Triumphs over Caradoc, Liberates Gawain and the Others, and Is Then Recalled to Prison by Morgan the Fay.

Lancelot and his companions arrive at the Wicked Pass, where Arthur's troops are doing battle against those of Caradoc. Caradoc tries to escape unnoticed, but Lancelot follows him. While fighting, they enter Caradoc's castle, where a woman gives Lancelot an enchanted sword, with which he beheads Caradoc and frees Gawain. Caradoc's knights beg for mercy from Lancelot and free Yvain and the duke. Morgan's messenger summons Lancelot to honor his agreement and return to her prison. After informing Gawain of his departure, he leaves. The king rebukes Gawain, and Galehaut is grieved that Lancelot disclosed his plan to someone else. The king gives the Dolorous Tower to the woman who helped Gawain; then he departs. When the queen hears the news, her suffering is renewed.

100. Morgan the Fay Sends a Messenger to the Royal Court to Denounce the Love of Lancelot and Guenevere; Galehaut, Lionel, and Gawain Set out in Quest of Lancelot.

Morgan tries in vain to get Lancelot to give her his ring. She resorts to deceitful means and, without his knowledge, exchanges the ring with one similar to it. She then sends a woman to Arthur's court to return his ring to Guenevere and to announce that they will never see Lancelot take arms again. Galehaut, Gawain, and Lionel follow the messenger and Yvain. She tricks them and returns to Morgan, who is distressed by the fact that the queen was not disgraced.

101. Galehaut Discovers Lancelot's Shield and Battles Successfully, Though Not Without Being Wounded, to Gain Possession of It.

Galehaut and his companions separate in order to search for Lancelot. Galehaut, worried and distraught over his friend, has a troublesome dream, and then he encounters a woman who tells him Lancelot is in prison. He arrives at a castle where he finds Lancelot's shield. Against the warning of an old knight, he steals the shield; attacked by many knights, he defeats most of them. He stays at a religious house until his wounds heal, and afterward he decides to return to his land and found churches and hospitals.

102. Morgan the Fay Releases Lancelot, but on Condition that He Not See the Queen Before Christmas.

In prison, Lancelot, unwilling to tell Morgan what she wants to hear, stops eating and risks dying. She asks him to make an oath that before Christmas he will not go where he might find the queen. He refuses, but then, owing to a potion given him by Morgan, he has a dream in which the queen is in bed with another knight. Taking the dream as real, he now agrees to take the oath. After recovering his strength, he leaves.

103. Lionel Is Led to Believe that Lancelot Is Dead, but Then Learns the Truth by Catching Sight of Him Himself; Lionel Rejoins Galehaut and They Both Go to Sorelois.

Lionel learns news of Galehaut and asks to be directed to him. He inquires about his wounds and leaves seeking adventures. Lionel fights Swagar of Hungary, thinking he killed Lancelot. A young lady approaches and saves Swagar's life by promising to lead Lionel to Lancelot. He sees Lancelot walking in a garden and goes to share this news with Galehaut. They both go to Sorelois, where Galehaut distributes alms and builds churches.

104. Yvain Comes upon Gawain in Combat and Helps Him; They Discover Lancelot in a Tournament, but He Refuses to Return to Court with Them.

Gawain fights with a knight who is guarding Morgan's heath. The knight tramples Gawain and tries to steal his horse but is stopped by Yvain. Gawain and Yvain find Lancelot in a tournament. He retreats into the woods, and Gawain and Yvain follow him. Explaining to them that he cannot return to the court, he rides away, and they set out for the court.

105. Lancelot Goes to Sorelois, Only to Find that Galehaut Has Departed; He Too Leaves, but in Circumstances That Suggest Suicide.

Lancelot goes to Sorelois to find Galehaut, who is away looking for him. Lancelot steals away, and because he had suffered a nosebleed during the night, the people of Sorelois, seeing the blood, think he is dead.

106. Galehaut, at Court, Hears that Lancelot Is Back in Sorelois; He Returns, Only to Hear the News of Lancelot's Apparent Suicide, and Dies Heartbroken.

Galehaut returns to Sorelois; hearing of the blood in Lancelot's bed, he believes him to be dead. Galehaut stops eating. His wound festers; he falls ill and then, at the end of September, dies.

LANCELOT, PART IV

107. Meleagant Abducts Guenevere; Lancelot, in Quest of the Queen, Rides in a Cart.

Lancelot goes mad. The Lady of the Lake finds him and cares for him; she informs him that he must go to Arthur's court to rescue the queen. Meleagant arrives at court and dares King Arthur to entrust the queen to one of his knights. Kay escorts the queen, and Lancelot follows them. Meleagant defeats Kay; Lancelot attacks Meleagant, only to have his horse killed. Lancelot pursues them on foot until he comes upon a cart and, promised news of the queen, jumps into it; Gawain follows the cart. At a castle, ladies tell Lancelot he is disgraced for having ridden in the cart. He survives the marvel of the perilous lance while he is sleeping.

The next day, Lancelot sees the queen being led away by Meleagant's entourage. Lancelot and Gawain leave the castle and meet a woman who tells them of the two bridges that lead into Meleagant's land. Gawain goes toward the Lost Bridge; Lancelot, toward the Sword Bridge.

108. Lancelot and an Amorous Young Lady; Lancelot at the Holy Cemetery.

A young woman who has offered Lancelot lodging asks him to sleep with her. He first saves her from rape and then lies next to her; unable to arouse him, the woman leaves him in peace. The following morning, the two of them ride to a castle near Bademagu's land. They encounter a knight who wishes to take her against her will. The two men prepare to do battle, but the knight's father intervenes.

The following day, an abbot informs Lancelot that if he wishes to rescue the queen he must first undergo a test in the cemetery. Lancelot lifts the stone from Galahad's tomb, and monks arrive to take the high king's body to Wales. Lancelot then descends into the cave of Simeon's tomb. A voice tells him that his deliverer will come from his own lineage. Before leaving the cave, Lancelot tries unsuccessfully to raise that tombstone.

109. Lancelot Crosses the Stony Pass; Lancelot and Meleagant's Sister; The Sword Bridge.

From a vavasor, Lancelot learns about the customs of the land of Gorre; he is told that his quest to rescue the queen will be successful and that he will free the prisoners from the kingdom of Gorre. Lancelot and the vavasor's son go to the Stony Pass, which they cross. Then they enter a battle to help the exiles from Logres rout Meleagant's men.

During a dinner, a knight enters and challenges the knight who dares to cross the Sword Bridge. He and Lancelot do battle, and when Lancelot is prepared to behead him, Meleagant's sister arrives and asks for the knight's head; the request is granted. Lancelot and his men arrive at the Sword Bridge; with Guenevere and Bademagu watching from a tower, Lancelot crosses the bridge.

110. Lancelot in Gorre; Guenevere's Rejection and Pardon of Lancelot; Lancelot Captured by Meleagant's Seneschal.

At Bademagu's request, the battle between Lancelot and Meleagant ends in a truce, which Meleagant accepts on the condition that Lancelot will fight him later at Arthur's court. Guenevere refuses to speak to Lancelot, telling Bademagu that Lancelot has greatly wronged her.

Lancelot leaves in quest of Gawain, whereupon rumors cause the queen and Lancelot to believe each other dead. Upon Lancelot's return to Bademagu's castle, the queen rushes to greet and forgive him.

Later, Lancelot enters the queen's room through a window and spends the night with her. The next day, Meleagant finds blood on the queen's sheets and accuses her of sleeping with Kay. Lancelot does battle with Meleagant to prove the queen's innocence. Again the battle ends in a truce requested by Bademagu. Lancelot leaves to find Gawain. A dwarf tricks Lancelot into following him into the woods, where he is captured and imprisoned in a tower.

111. Guenevere and Gawain Return to Arthur's Court; Bors Is Shunned at Court; Gawain, Arthur, and Guenevere Ride in the Cart.

Lancelot's companions find Gawain and explain to him how the dwarf led Lancelot away. Meleagant forges a letter to Guenevere, telling her that Lancelot is at court and that she and Gawain should return. Once at Camelot, the queen grieves when she learns that Lancelot is not there. Arthur declares that no feats of arms will take place until he hears word of Lancelot.

On a feast day, a knight who was seen riding in a cart is rejected by all except Gawain. The cart then passes by with a young lady sitting inside. Gawain frees her by replacing her in the cart. After the young woman's departure, Arthur learns that she was the Lady of the Lake. Guenevere rides after her and learns that Lancelot is in prison but that she can see him at the next tournament.

112. Lancelot at the Tournament of Pomeglai; Meleagant Locks Lancelot in a Tower.

Lancelot is imprisoned at the castle of the seneschal of Gorre. Hearing news of the tournament, Lancelot becomes pensive, and the seneschal's wife allows him to leave and participate. In the tournament, Lancelot defeats many knights, jousting so well that many believe that he must be Lancelot. At the queen's request, he performs in a cowardly fashion for the remainder of the afternoon. The following day, Lancelot repeats his poor performance until the queen asks him to fight his best.

Lancelot returns to the seneschal's castle, but Meleagant hears that he was present at the tournament and therefore decides to build a tower in which to imprison him. Meleagant goes to Arthur's court and informs the king of Lancelot's agreement to fight against him at his request. The king tells Meleagant that he must wait forty days.

113. Meleagant's Sister Frees Lancelot; Lancelot Kills Meleagant at Arthur's Court.

Meleagant's sister goes to the tower and provides Lancelot with the necessary tools to escape. She takes Lancelot off to her land and sends a messenger to obtain news of Meleagant at Arthur's court. After staying with Meleagant's sister for a week, Lancelot returns to court on the fortieth day and does battle with Meleagant. Lancelot defeats him and, at a sign from the queen, cuts off his head. Afterward, the king invites Lancelot to sit at his table for a celebratory feast in his honor.

114. Lancelot Agrees to Fight at Bademagu's Court, Defends Guenevere, and Rediscovers Lionel and Hector at the Castle of Maidens.

Lancelot, accused of murdering Meleagant, agrees to go to Bademagu's court in one month's time to prove his innocence. Lancelot leaves and encounters Margondre, who accuses Guenevere of infidelity. To defend her name, Lancelot fights and defeats Margondre, who begs for mercy.

Lancelot then meets Dodinel the Wildman, who was wounded by the knight of the Hedged Manor. Lancelot goes to the manor and does battle with many knights. Meliaduc the Black then challenges Lancelot, who defeats him.

Lancelot arrives at the tournament between the knights of the Castle of Ladies and the knights of the Castle of Maidens. He joins the former and accomplishes such feats of arms that all are amazed. He learns that two of the knights he has injured from the Castle of Maidens are Hector and his cousin Lionel. All three knights return to the Castle of Ladies, where they celebrate their reunion.

115. Hector and Lionel Reunited with Bors at Court: Bors Defends the Maiden of Hungerford Castle Against a Wicked Seneschal.

At Lancelot's request, Margondre goes to Guenevere and describes Lancelot's armor; she knows that it was Lancelot. Meliaduc arrives at court and relates Lancelot's feats at the Hedged Manor. Hector and Lionel return to court and recount the news of the tournament of Maidens and Ladies. Lionel is reunited with Bors and tells him on behalf of Lancelot that he, Bors, must leave to seek adventures.

Setting out, Bors encounters a young lady and, at her request, follows her to a castle. He learns that she and her sister lost this castle and most of their property to their uncle, Gallides. To save their remaining castle, Bors defeats the uncle's seneschal, who tries to imprison the young lady (Amide), and kills the seneschal and his knight. Gallides swears that he will give his niece the same punishment.

116. Bors Defeats Gallides and His Men Before Hungerford Castle.

Bors meets and defeats Gallides's nephew. Gallides wishes to do battle against Bors, but his men detain him. Six knights are sent to attack Bors; he defeats or kills all of them, sending the last one to Gallides with a message challenging him to battle. Gallides accepts, and the battle lasts many hours. A lady asks Bors to give her his sword in the name of the Lady of the Lake and Lancelot. Bors does so, but manages to seize Gallides's sword and defeat him with it, after which he forces Gallides to return to his niece all the land that he took from her. Bors then approaches the woman who was holding his sword and learns that she is the one who escorted him and Lionel from Gaunes. She gives Bors a message from the Lady of the Lake instructing him to go to the forest of Roevent.

117. Gallides Makes Peace with the Lady of Hungerford Castle, Who Learns that Bors Despises Her.

Gallides goes to his niece and surrenders to her, promising to return her land and to help defend her at all times. As his niece is preparing a celebration in honor of Bors, Gallides gives her a message from Bors himself, who rebukes her for her treatment of the seneschal. The lady is distraught by the fact that she has dishonored Bors and promises never to remain in a city for more than one night until she finds him.

118. Bors Removes the Iron Bands from King Agrippes's Daughter; Bors Wins King Brandegorre's Tournament.

Bors arrives at two beautiful tents and meets a young woman in terrible pain. The woman, King Agrippes's daughter, suffers because of iron bands bound around her chest and her waist. Bors learns that this punishment was imposed on her by King Vadalon in revenge for her having poisoned his soldiers. Bors breaks the bands and agrees to avenge her against Vadalon.

Leaving the next morning, Bors encounters a squire who asks him to go participate in a tournament held in honor of the anniversary of King Brandegorre's coronation. A woman challenges him to follow her and to try to complete a marvelous adventure. They meet another young lady and another knight, Agravain. Both knights are challenged to remove a sword from the hands of a knight who is holding it against his will. Agravain fails, but Bors refuses to try, since only the very best knight will be able to succeed. He and Agravain do combat to prove whether Lancelot or Gawain is the best knight. Bors defeats Agravain and grants him mercy once he swears to find Lancelot and apologize to him. The next day Bors takes leave of the knight with the sword and goes to the Castle of the Borderlands to participate in the tournament. Bors defeats all his opponents and is proclaimed the best knight in the tournament.

119. Bors Spurns King Brandegorre's Daughter; Twelve Knights Take Vows of Service to the Lady.

Custom dictates that the winner of the tournament take a wife and select wives for the dozen best knights. Bors refuses to do the former and leaves to the king the right to do the latter; however, he forbids the king to give away his own daughter, and the young woman herself is upset at not being chosen by Bors. She goes before the twelve peers and asks them how they will reward her for her service. After all twelve vow to serve her, the lady asks Bors what reward she may expect from him. Bors promises to be her knight, to defend her and to remove Queen Guenevere from an escort of four knights, provided one of the knights is not Lancelot.

Once everyone is in bed, the lady confesses to her governess that she loves Bors; the latter agrees to use her enchantments to make Bors fall in love. The governess convinces Bors to wear an enchanted ring, and once he does so, he has a change of heart and goes to the lady. He sleeps with her and fathers Helain the White. Later, the ring falls off Bors's finger, and he realizes that he has been deceived. He asks permission to leave, agreeing to return in six months.

Bors encounters the lady of Hungerford Castle but does not reveal his identity to her. He continues to ride until he reaches a castle where he sees a beautiful woman being beaten by a group of peasants. He rescues the lady, after which a knight emerges from the castle and challenges Bors to fight; Bors kills him.

The lady, Blevine of Glocedun, learns that her cousin, the lady of Hungerford Castle, is arriving, and when she goes to greet her, Bors escapes from the castle. Once the cousins meet, they discuss their adventures, and the lady of Hungerford Castle is certain that the knight who rescued her cousin is the knight she is seeking. Returning to the castle, they find that Bors has tricked them, and Blevine asks to accompany her cousin until they find him.

120. Lancelot Discovers Galehaut's Casket and Defends It; Lancelot Rescues Meleagant's Sister.

Lancelot learns that Meleagant's sister will be burned at the stake the following day, having been accused of murder for freeing him to kill Meleagant. Lancelot leaves for Floego Castle to try to rescue her. At a church, he sees five armed knights guarding Galehaut's tomb. Distraught at Galehaut's death, he intends to commit suicide. A lady stops him and gives him a message from the Lady of the Lake telling him that he must take Galehaut's tomb by force and have it carried to

Dolorous Guard. Lancelot vanquishes the five knights and sends one to take the tomb to Dolorous Guard.

The next day after mass, Lancelot sends the lady to find Bors and to give him Galehaut's sword. Lancelot then continues to Floego Castle, arriving just as Meleagant's sister is being led to the fire. He fights and defeats the knight who accused the sister of murder. Lancelot accompanies Meleagant's sister back to her castle; then he continues on his way to King Bademagu's court, stopping for lodging at a fine tent, where his host's lady falls in love with him.

121. Lancelot Vanquishes Arramant and Kills His Accuser at Bademagu's Court; Lancelot Defeats Parides and Buries Galehaut at the Dolorous Guard.

Arramant enters the tent and abducts a squire. Lancelot's host asks him to help defend the squire, who is his brother. Lancelot follows Arramant to the Forest of Three Perils, where he asks a lady for directions. After Lancelot promises that he will be her knight whenever she summons him, she tells him which road to follow. Lancelot overtakes Arramant and defeats him.

Lancelot arrives at King Bademagu's Court at Windesant. He proclaims that he has come to defend himself against accusations made by Argodras. After a great fight, Lancelot defeats Argodras. Bademagu starts to welcome Lancelot joyously, but the latter explains that Bademagu has greatly wronged him. The following day Bademagu escorts Lancelot on his way and asks him to send him word of the way he has wronged him.

Lancelot stays the night at a convent, where a young lady asks him to escort her to Dolorous Guard. They come upon a knight who tries to kiss the lady against her will. Lancelot challenges the knight, Patrides, defeats him, and learns about the vows made to King Brandegorre's daughter and the fact that Bors was the victorious knight of the tournament. Lancelot returns to Dolorous Guard, where he finds a tomb made of precious stones; he has Galehaut laid to rest in it. He then returns to Arthur's Court, where he relates all his adventures.

122. Bors Rescues Lambegue and Pardons the Lady of Hungerford Castle.

Bors arrives at the forest of Roevent on the day indicated by the Lady of the Lake. He hears a great lamentation and sees twenty knights arriving with a knight on a litter. Bors then sees Lambegue being accused of the death of this knight. Bors kills several knights and rescues Lambegue.

At a castle where they have sought lodging, the maidservant of the Lady of the Lake enters and presents Galehaut's sword to Bors at Lancelot's request. The lady of Hungerford Castle and the lady of Glocedun arrive. The former kneels before Bors to ask and receive his forgiveness. Departing the next morning, Bors encounters a knight who tells him that Lancelot is on his way to Dolorous Guard and that he should be able to find him there. Bors, however, is delayed, and when he arrives at Dolorous Guard, Lancelot has already left. He continues his journey alone.

123. Bademagu Learns that Lancelot Has Killed Meleagant and Mourns.

Patrides arrives at the abbey where Lancelot stayed, and a monk treats his wounds. The next day, he continues his journey to Windesant and delivers the message to King Bademagu that Lancelot killed his son Meleagant. Bademagu grieves bitterly and goes to see Meleagant's body at the Castle of Four Stones. The king buries his son at a hermitage and returns to Windesant, where he continues to mourn.

124. Lancelot Defends Guenevere Against Bors; Guenevere Sends Sagremor and Dodinel to Mathamas's.

The queen, accompanied by Kay, Sagremor, Dodinel the Wildman, and Lancelot, meet a knight who tells her that he must take her, although it is against his will. After defeating the other three knights accompanying the queen, the knight prepares to joust against Lancelot. As that moment, the Maiden of Many Years appears and tells Lancelot that he must uphold his pledge and follow her immediately. Lancelot knocks the knight to the ground and follows the old woman. The queen asks Kay to follow Lancelot.

   Kay arrives at a valley where he sees Lancelot fighting on foot against two knights. Lancelot tells Kay to ask the queen to look after the knight he wounded. The queen cares for the knight and asks that his identity remain unknown for the present.

   Dodinel mentions that Mathamas's tower is nearby but that Mathamas hates King Arthur. He and Sagremor depart toward the tower. They encounter an armed knight, and Sagremor charges him. A young woman approaches Dodinel during the joust and challenges him to follow her. He agrees.

125. The Adventures of Sagremor at Mathamas's.

The knight flees from Sagremor, who then proceeds along the path until he arrives at a tent, where a dwarf strikes his horse. Sagremor throws the dwarf to the ground and tramples him. Entering the tent, he finds Calogrenant a prisoner there and does battle with a knight to free him. Meanwhile, another knight seizes the lady, causing distress to the knight with whom Sagremor is fighting. Surrendering to Sagremor, the knight promises to free Calogrenant if Sagremor will seek his lady.

   Sagremor pursues the abductor and finds the woman with three knights. He rescues her, but when they return to the tent, both her knight and Calogrenant have disappeared. Sagremor goes on to Mathamas's house, where he is jailed. Mathamas's daughter sees Sagremor and is enamored of him.

126. The Adventures of Dodinel, Who Defends a Maiden.

Dodinel and the young lady he is following encounter a dwarf, who kisses the lady against her will. The lady slaps the dwarf, and the dwarf's knight throws his lance at the lady. This infuriates Dodinel; he challenges and defeats the knight, who is Maruc the Red. He then sends him to Guenevere to tell her that he, Dodinel, has been diverted and will be unable to go to Mathamas's.

127. Griffon of the Treacherous Pass Demands Lancelot's Armor; Kay Is Captured by Griffon.

While Lancelot is following the Maiden of Many Years, Griffon appears and demands that Lancelot give him his armor. Lancelot first refuses, but Griffon convinces him that he must concede or else he will break the pledge he has made. Lancelot relinquishes his armor. Griffon notices that Lancelot is badly injured and tries to replace him as the knight following the old lady, but she refuses to have any knight other than Lancelot escort her. Griffon approaches the Fairies' Fountain, where those in the queen's retinue first mistake him for Lancelot, then, realizing their error, conclude that he must have killed Lancelot. The queen sends Kay and the imprisoned knight, Maruc, to pursue Griffon. Griffon kills Maruc and defeats and imprisons Kay.

128. The Queen and Her Retinue Mourn Lancelot at the Fairies' Fountain.

The queen and her ladies weep bitterly, thinking Lancelot dead. The knight whom Lancelot injured faints several times and causes his wounds to reopen. The queen returns to Camelot and forbids anyone to speak about Lancelot until she announces the news to the members of the Round Table at dinner.

129. Lancelot and the Old Woman Stay with a Forester.

Lancelot, following the old woman, encounters a young lady who praises him as the most desirable knight in the world. She tells him that the people of Estrangort long to see him. Lancelot and the old woman arrive at a forester's house, where the old woman removes the lance stump from his body and where he stays until his wound heals.

130. Dodinel Imprisoned.

Dodinel and the maiden he is following arrive at a deep, black river. They abandon their horses, as they must cross the river on a narrow plank. Dodinel falls into the water and nearly drowns, barely saving himself by holding to the plank. He begs a peasant to help him, but the peasant refuses. Using all his strength, Dodinel manages to pull himself up onto the plank. A knight arrives and takes him to his castle, Langree, where he imprisons him.

131. The Queen Recounts Lancelot's Death at Court, and Gawain Makes a Vow; The Story of King Agrestes and the Black Cross.

The queen goes into Lancelot's room and mourns bitterly. The king returns from hunting and asks after the queen. She comes before him, and he demands to know what is troubling her. After they dine, the queen recounts the events at the Fairies' Fountain and says that she believes Lancelot to be dead. Gawain announces that he will set off the next morning in quest of Lancelot. With nine other knights, he leaves and rides to the Black Cross at the entrance of the forest of Camelot. The story then relates the history of the Black Cross, explaining that it was blackened by blood long ago when Agrestes pretended to be converted and then killed twelve disciples of Joseph of Arimathea.

132. Gawain Fails to Join Together the Broken Sword of Joseph of Arimathea; The Story of the Sword.

As Gawain suggests that he and his companions separate for a week and then meet at the White Cross, they hear a voice cry out and ride off toward it. They find a knight who is carrying two swords and fighting ten other men. Gawain, Yvain, and Hector attack the ten knights, knocking three to the ground; the others flee. Gawain asks the knight why he is carrying two swords, and the latter shows Gawain a sword broken in two, half of it bleeding from the tip. Asked about the broken sword, the knight tells Gawain that he must first try to join the two parts. Gawain and all of his companions are unable to do so. The knight, Eliezer, explains that only the knight who will achieve the adventures of the Holy Grail will be able to repair the sword. Eliezer says that Joseph of Arimathea, who was injured by the sword, announced that the sword would by joined only by the chosen knight. Eliezer is certain that, since Gawain failed, no knight can succeed at this task; he tells Gawain that, if Lancelot wishes to seek the sword, he should come to the Fisher King. Gawain and his companions take leave of Eliezer and of one another.

133. The Adventures of Agloval.

Agloval meets a knight whose armor is shattered and who asks for protection from a knight who is pursuing him. Agloval agrees and defeats the knight, Griffon. The latter invites both knights to lodge with him nearby. Agloval explains to Griffon that he is on a quest for Lancelot, and Griffon fears that Agloval will think he killed Lancelot. Griffon decides to free Kay but forbids him to tell Agloval where he has been. Kay agrees to undertake the quest for Lancelot, and he and Agloval resume their travels together.

134. Sir Gawain Defeats Mathamas and Frees Sagremor.

Gawain, engrossed by the adventures of the sword, neglects to return a greeting given him by Mathamas. Mathamas rushes to arm himself, follows Gawain's tracks until he reaches him, and challenges him to fight. Gawain awakens, sees Mathamas charging at him, and knocks Mathamas from his horse. The attacker surrenders to Gawain and tells him his name, causing Gawain to ask him what has become of Sagremor and Dodinel. Mathamas releases Sagremor from prison and departs to surrender himself to Arthur on Gawain's behalf.

135. Hector Kills Dodinel's Captor and Frees Dodinel; The Ten Companions Converse at the White Cross.

Hector wanders aimlessly until he arrives at the plank where Dodinel fell into the river. He crosses the plank, defeats and beheads a knight who has emerged from the castle to attack him, and thus frees Dodinel from prison. Hector explains how the knights of Arthur's court have set off in quest of Lancelot, and Dodinel becomes a companion of the quest. They arrive at the White Cross at the appointed hour and meet all the companions there. Each one recounts his adventures, and all are sorry to learn that no one has news of Lancelot. Gawain announces that they must at once depart to continue the quest.

136. Sir Gawain Champions the Friend of Tanaguin the Blond; Hector Defeats Sir Gawain; Hector and Sir Gawain Are Overcome at the Cemetery of the Burning Tomb.

When Gawain comes to a castle, a lady asks him if he will assist her knight, Tanaguin, in a tournament. Gawain and Tanaguin enter the tournament, and Gawain leads it until a knight in red armor (Hector) joins the fray and defeats him. Gawain follows the red knight and arrives at a large house, where Hector greets him and apologizes for having knocked him from his horse, explaining that he did not recognize him.

The next day, they depart together. They come to a decrepit chapel where they find a burning tomb surrounded by twelve other tombs, a sword erected at each one. Gawain tells Hector that he will attempt the adventure; he tries to approach the tomb but is beaten by the swords. Hector then makes an attempt and is beaten even worse than Gawain. Then he reads an inscription that says that no one will enter the cemetery without shame until the son of the sorrowful queen arrives. Gawain and Hector depart, full of shame for having failed at the adventure. They find a wooden cross with an inscription warning knights not to take the road on the left. Hector insists on taking the left road, and Gawain takes the one on the right.

137. Sir Gawain Fails at the Grail Castle and Learns the Significance of His Adventure from a Hermit.

Coming to a castle, Gawain hears a call for help. He rushes into the hall, where he finds a woman in a tub. He tries to remove her but fails, and she explains that she has been left to suffer in the boiling water for a sin she committed and that she will be freed only by the best knight in the world.

Gawain leaves the woman and enters the great hall, where he observes the adventures of the Grail. He sees a magnificent dove, watches a beautiful maiden carry a wondrous vessel, and sees that every knight, other than himself, is served an abundance of food. Later, he undergoes many trials, including the Adventurous Bed. He also sees many events, such as a battle between a serpent and a leopard, that he does not understand. He then hears celestial voices and again sees the vessel; he finds all his wounds healed. The next day, Gawain finds himself tied to a cart and subjected to abuse and ridicule. Freed from the cart, he comes to a hermitage; the hermit explains that Gawain was refused food because he saw the Holy Grail without recognizing it. The hermit also explains the meaning of the battle between the serpent and the leopard and makes Gawain swear to tell no one what he has learned. The next day, Gawain continues on his way.

138. Hector Defeats Marigart the Red at Raguidel Castle.

Hector comes to a castle guarded by a knight who throws all comers into the water; Hector knocks the knight into the water. Then the castle gate slams closed in his face. After the people of the castle explain the evil customs of the castle, Hector first fights and defeats the lord of the castle, then rescues the lady of the castle from two lions.

During a great celebration, the lady of the castle, Angale of Raguidel, explains how her lord, Marigart the Red, put her to such shame. Then she asks Hector to identify himself and asks him for news of Lancelot, explaining that she is Lancelot's first cousin and that she loves him more than anyone in the world. Hector tells her he has no news of Lancelot, and he resumes his journey the next day.

139. Yvain 's Adventures in Quest of Lancelot.

Yvain defeats a knight and recovers a horse for a woman. Then he recovers a sparrowhawk for another woman, but he himself is wounded in the battle. For two weeks, he stays at a hermitage, where his wound is treated.

140. Sir Gawain and His Brothers Described; The Adventures of Mordred.

After describing Agravain, Gaheriet, and Guerrehet, the text introduces Mordred as the youngest and the most wicked of Gawain's brothers. Mordred arrives at a tent where a dwarf kills his horse and he kills a knight who defends the dwarf.

Mordred is greeted by a woman and, later, by her husband. That evening, Mordred asks the lady to come sleep with him after her husband has fallen asleep. After Mordred and the lady had been together for some time, her husband wakes up and accuses Mordred of being a traitor. They do battle, and Mordred forces the knight to surrender and to forgive him and his lady. The next morning, Mordred departs.

Volume V

Lancelot, Part V

141. Agravain Kills Druas the Cruel and Is Imprisoned by Sorneham of Newcastle.

Agravain finds a knight and a woman weeping bitterly. The knight explains to Agravain that he is mourning the death of his brother, killed by Druas the Cruel. Agravain challenges and defeats Druas and brings his head to the grieving knight. Then a dwarf, grieving over Druas's body, challenges Agravain to blow a horn. Druas's brother, Sorneham of Newcastle, hears the horn and thus learns of Druas's death. He arms himself and challenges Agravain. Sorneham knocks Agravain to the ground, but before he can cut off Agravain's head, a maiden asks him to spare his opponent's life. Sorneham agrees but determines to keep him in prison until Gawain comes to look for him. Sorneham has Agravain put in prison and buries Druas.

142. Adventures of Guerrehet in the Company of Various Ladies; He Too Is Imprisoned by Sorneham.

Guerrehet rescues a knight about to be killed by his nephews. That night, he helps the men of the castle defend it against attackers.

Guerrehet arrives and meets a sorrowing maiden, who explains how her husband has forced her to live as a chambermaid instead of as his wife. He goes to the castle, and the husband welcomes him but is jealous and suspicious. Sagremor arrives, and the lady grants him lodging. Learning that two of Arthur's knights are in his house, the husband fears that his wife is trying to have him killed. He summons ten men-at-arms to protect him. When the jealous husband strikes his wife, Sagremor knocks him down. The men-at-arms attack Sagremor, but he and Guerrehet kill the husband, his brother, and his two nephews.

Sagremor and Guerrehet depart and come to twelve tents where they are forced to joust. Afterward, they meet a maiden who is seeking Agloval; Sagremor departs with her. Guerrehet stops at a group of tents, where he finds a beautiful woman and has his pleasure with her, unaware of the fact that her husband is asleep next to her. The husband awakens and assaults Guerrehet but is killed by him. The woman grieves bitterly, but Guerrehet proclaims his love to her and forces her to accompany him. When they stop at a Cistercian abbey, the lady asks the abbess to accept her into the religious life.

Learning that she has become a nun (and that she is Lancelot's first cousin), Guerrehet sets out again and soon does battle with Sorneham. Sorneham wounds him and places him in prison with Agravain. Sorneham's niece comes to bring them food and tells Guerrehet that she will do all in her power to free him.

143. Adventures of Gaheriet, Who Rescues His Brothers from Sorneham; The Three Brothers Aid Duke Calles.

Gaheriet meets a maiden who is seeking Sir Lancelot to fight on her behalf because her brother-in-law has wrongfully taken her land from her. Gaheriet agrees to fight for her. He jousts with Guinas and defeats him. The following day, Gaheriet and the maiden see a knight and a woman being beaten by six knights. The six knights separate, three leading Brandeliz and the other three leading the woman. Gaheriet rescues Brandeliz, and Gaswain of Estrangort returns with the woman who was beaten.

At a tent, a dwarf offers lodging to Gaheriet and the maiden. When the lord returns, he is furious with the dwarf and throws him to the ground. Gaheriet forces the knight to ask the dwarf's pardon.

Later, Gaheriet and the maiden arrive at the court of the lady of Roestoc, where he is to fight against Guiden to reclaim the maiden's land. The combat between Gaheriet and Guidan is long and grueling. Guidan, seeing that he will die, jumps in the river.

Gaheriet continues his journey and meets a woman who accuses him of being the most wicked of all knights for not trying to free his brothers from prison. He tells her that he was not aware that they were in prison. He sets out to rescue them. He defeats Sorneham and has him release Agravain and Guerrehet. Gaheriet sends Sorneham to constitute himself prisoner to the lady of Roestoc in his name.

The three brothers fight on the side of a duke whose sons are robbing him of his land. They kill four of the sons and take the remaining two prisoner, but Agravain is also captured. The duke exchanges his two sons for Agravain.

144. Bors Will Champion the Lady of Galway.

Lionel arrives at Arthur's court, where Queen Guenevere informs him of Lancelot's purported death. She then takes Lionel to see the injured knight who jousted against Lancelot. Lionel recognizes the knight as Bors. Guenevere lies in bed, grieving over Lancelot, for over two weeks. A maiden comes to speak to King Arthur on behalf of the lady of Galway and requests that he send either Sir Gawain or Sir Lancelot to settle a quarrel for her. Since neither is present, Bors will go in their place to fight for the lady of Galway. Bors and Lionel take leave of the queen, who gives Bors a ring to give to Lancelot. Bors and Lionel depart with the maiden of the lady of Galway.

145. Guenevere Sends a Message to the Lady of the Lake.

After Bors and Lionel depart, the queen is very sad and feels that there is no one in whom she may confide. She has a distressing dream about Lancelot and imagines a wooden statue to be him. Her cousin, seeing the queen embrace the statue, throws holy water on her and frightens her into returning to bed. Guenevere sends the cousin to the Lady of the Lake to ask her to come to Guenevere at once.

146. Lancelot Rescues a Maiden.

Lancelot leaves the lodging where he has had his wounds tended. He and the old woman accompanying him encounter a maiden who has been crying. She explains that since she has learned of Lancelot's death, she fears that no knight can free her sister, who has been abducted. Lancelot is distressed to learn the rumors of his death, and he wishes to put the queen at ease. He tells the maiden that he will rescue her sister if she will deliver a message for him. They enter the castle, but the knight who abducted the sister is wounded and thus unable to challenge Lancelot. He warns Lancelot that when the opportunity arises he will avenge himself. As Lancelot requested, the maiden goes to Camelot and tells Guenevere that Lancelot is alive. Guenevere rejoices greatly at the news.

147. Lancelot Is Poisoned and Healed; He Slays Duke Calles.

Lancelot and the old lady come upon a knight and two young women beside a spring. Lancelot drinks from the spring and becomes violently ill. The old woman reveals his identity to the knight and the maidens. The knight's sister tends to Lancelot, but he is very ill, and he loses his skin, fingernails, toenails, and hair. The maiden realizes that she is in love with him but knows that he will never love her.

Bors and Lionel arrive. Lancelot asks that one of them return to the queen and take her the hair from his head to prove his latest adventure to her. Bors leaves to go to the lady of Galway. Lionel goes directly to Arthur's court. The queen asks Lionel how she can see Lancelot, and he advises her to have the king announce a tournament. He returns to Lancelot and gives him news of the planned tournament.

The maiden who treated Lancelot is dying of lovesickness. Lionel persuades Lancelot to proclaim himself the maiden's knight in order to save his own life, the maiden's life, and the queen's. He does so, and the maiden heals him, but thereafter, Lancelot explains that he is not free to bestow his love upon another.

Lancelot, Lionel, and the old woman arrive at the castle held by the five brothers who are fighting against their father, Duke Calles. Joining the brothers' ranks, Lancelot knocks Gaheriet from his horse, kills the duke, and helps capture Guerrehet and Agravain. Learning the identity of the prisoners, he orders their release, and then he and Lionel leave. The three brothers soon leave as well, searching for the knight who defeated them. When Lancelot is sleeping, Lionel sees a knight kill two other knights and abduct a young woman. Lionel overtakes the knight and is defeated and taken away along with the maiden.

148. Hector Is Imprisoned by Tericam.

Hector enters the forest of Terique and encounters a young woman weeping. She informs him that Tericam has taken Lionel prisoner. Seeking Lionel, Hector approaches a spring surrounded by shields, helmets, and swords. He reads an inscription that states that Tericam has defeated all the knights whose names are found there. Tericam comes out to challenge him. Hector manages to throw Tericam from his horse, but Tericam, uninjured, puts Hector in prison with other knights of King Arthur's court.

149. Lancelot Is Captured by Three Sorceresses; At a Tournament He Fights for King Bademagu; At the Castle of Corbenic He Witnesses the Grail Procession and Fathers Galahad at Case Castle.

Three sorceresses, the queen of the land of Sorestan, Morgan, and Queen Sedile, cast a spell on Lancelot and take him to Cart Castle. They tell him that to be freed he must choose one of the ladies as his mistress. Lancelot refuses. The maiden serving him in prison agrees to free him if he will return and prevent her from being married against her will. Once free from prison, Lancelot goes to help King Bademagu and his men in a tournament against the king of North Wales. He defeats so many men that those from North Wales begin to retreat. Lancelot distinguishes himself in battle, then disappears into the forest so that no one can find him. Galehodin, the nephew of Galehaut, swears to find Lancelot.

Lancelot meets a lady who praises Lancelot's prowess. She takes him to Corbenic, where he frees the maiden from the basin, succeeding where Gawain failed. He then goes to a cemetery where an inscription on a tomb predicts his arrival and the birth of his son. Lancelot lifts the tombstone; a dragon escapes, and Lancelot kills it. King Pelles explains how his land has been destroyed, saying that he thinks Lancelot will deliver them from the adventures. At dinner Lancelot watches the same procession that Gawain saw previously. The king sends his daughter to Case Castle, and Lancelot follows, thinking he is going to see Guenevere. There he is given a potion, and thus he engenders Galahad with King Pelles's daughter, all the while believing that he is in bed with Guenevere.

150. After Further Adventures Lancelot Is Entrapped in a Magic Dance.

Sad and angry, Lancelot leaves Case Castle. Soon he sees the maiden who saved him from the poison. A knight tries to rape her, and Lancelot strikes him, then kills three knights who try to come to the knight's aid. The maiden takes Lancelot to the house of her cousin, who warns Lancelot about the danger of going to the castle on the mountain: every knight who has entered in the last five years has been killed or imprisoned. Lancelot is determined to go. On the way, he is told how King Ban engendered Hector in this castle. Entering the castle, he meets Hector's mother, who confirms that account of events.

The next day, Lancelot comes to a cemetery and reads an inscription warning knights errant not to enter the forest; he does so, along with one of King Pelles's squires. They come to a group of thirty beautiful tents where they see knights and ladies dancing. Lancelot goes to see why they are so happy, dismounts, and joins in the dancing. The squire tries to lure Lancelot away, but seeing that Lancelot has been overcome by folly and enchantment, he leaves, lamenting Lancelot's fate.

151. Adventures of Yvain with Malduit the Giant.

After Yvain's wounds heal, he continues his search for Lancelot. He does battle with a knight, who turns out to be Bors. They greet each other, and Yvain learns news of Lancelot and of the tournament that King Arthur will hold at Camelot. Bors takes leave of Yvain; the latter, gravely wounded, goes to a Cistercian convent, where a maiden tends his wounds.

Yvain leaves as soon as he is able. A woman asks him to take a sword and helmet from a tent. She then tells him to batter a shield and to exchange his shield for the one he has hit. The old woman leaves, and twelve women come and accuse Yvain of condemning them to permanent slavery. He leaves and comes to a hermit's house. The hermit explains the seriousness of Yvain's act: Malduit the Giant will be freed from prison and lay waste the land.

Later, a knight challenges Yvain to fight. Yvain defeats him and sends him to Hill Castle to ask Malduit to come fight against Yvain instead of devastating the land. Malduit arms himself and sets out. Yvain is denied lodging several times, as the people are angry about his having endangered their land. He comes to Castle Passing, where he is taken prisoner. Learning that he is Urien's son, the lady of the castle agrees to protect him in every way she can in honor of his father.

152. Bors at Corbenic and Other Adventures.

Bors and the maiden leading him arrive at Galway Castle. The lady of the castle explains to Bors that she sent for help from King Arthur's court because of a dispute (concerning the ownership of a castle) between her and Mariale, son of Duke Galenin. The lady of Galway takes Bors to King Pelles, who learns that Bors is Lancelot's cousin and welcomes him warmly. Bors enters into battle against Mariale and defeats him. Bors dines at King Pelles's castle and adores the Holy Grail during the procession.

Later, he meets a woman who accuses him of cowardice for not staying in the Palace of Adventures. Then he fights two knights in order to rescue a maiden's brother and protect her land. He then departs for Camelot, hoping to arrive in time for the tournament.

153. News of Lancelot.

Gawain meets the maiden who healed Lancelot from the poison; she tells him that she recently saw Lancelot at Corbenic. She also tells Gawain that she is on her way to the tournament at Camelot, and Gawain decides to go in hope of finding Lancelot there.

154. Lancelot Escapes from the Magic Dance; His Adventures with the Maiden Who Rescues Him from a Well Filled with Poisonous Snakes.

Lancelot puts an end to the Enchantment of the Magic Dance by sitting in a throne and putting a crown on his head. He then learns of a chessboard that plays against a challenger by itself; only one knight will be able to win the game. Lancelot has the chessboard brought forward and wins. Lancelot sets off and meets a knight who tells him that he will die before the day is through. The knight challenges Lancelot but then flees. Lancelot is then attacked by thirty knights; they strip him, beat him, and throw him into a well full of vermin and poisonous snakes. Lancelot is certain he will die and begins to lament to God. A maiden hears him, learns who he is, and brings him a rope; she also returns to the castle to get him some clothes. The maiden's actions are reported to her father, and when she brings Lancelot back to the castle, they are attacked by the lord's men. Lancelot kills them and then kills everyone he can find in the castle.

The next morning, he and the maiden leave. He finds a knight who beats and kills a beautiful woman and then flees. Lancelot chases him to a castle, where he defeats the knight. Lancelot returns to where he had left the maiden and does not find her. She has been abducted and is to be burned; he rescues her. He and the maiden ride to Cart Castle, arriving on the day appointed to rescue the maiden who had freed him from prison. When he challenges the knight who is preparing to marry the maiden, the knight flees. Just as Lancelot is leaving, Morgan demands to know his identity and threatens him. Lancelot and the maiden who was waiting for him depart for Camelot.

155. Lancelot Gives Proof of His Love for Guenevere at the Tournament at Camelot.

Lancelot composes a letter to be taken to Queen Guenevere by the maiden accompanying him. Bors and Sir Gawain return to Arthur's court, and the king welcomes them, saying that he only wishes Lancelot were there. King Yder is offended that the king and queen consider Lancelot superior to other knights. Over one hundred knights agree to disguise themselves and fight against Lancelot if he comes to the tournament. Guenevere decides to forewarn Lancelot by sending him a letter to inform him of the knights' plans. Lancelot sends back a messenger to tell the queen that he will do all in his power to obey her by fighting against the knights of the Round Table. He also promises Bademagu that he will fight on his side and against King Arthur's men.

The knights of the Round Table take the lead in the tournament, with Gawain and Bors as their example. Then Lancelot enters and slays every knight and horse he encounters. His opponents cannot withstand him until he gazes at Guenevere and falls ill. Bademagu carries him off the field, and with him gone, the knights of the Round Table win.

Guenevere sends word to Lancelot to come see her that night. At the feast that evening, Yder speaks of the way the "Red Knight" left the tournament; Guenevere then sends a message to Lancelot that the tournament should recommence in three days. King Bademagu challenges King Arthur's men to a tournament in three days. At Guenevere's request, Lancelot spends two nights with her. The morning of the tournament Guenevere gives Lancelot white armor to wear and Bors red armor so that Lancelot will not be recognized. With Gawain and Gaheriet leading King Arthur's knights, they cause their enemy to flee, but then Lancelot, Bors, and Bademagu enter the battle. Bors unhorses Gaheriet and Lancelot defeats Gawain. Eventually, the knights of the Round Table flee.

King Arthur stops Lancelot and asks him to identify himself. Lancelot removes his helmet, and Arthur greets him happily, then announces a great feast. After dinner, the king has the magic chessboard brought in; many kings try their hand but are defeated; only Lancelot checkmates the set. King Arthur summons clerks to come forward and they write down all of Lancelot's adventures as he recounts them. The king counts the knights of the Round Table who were defeated by Lancelot; they number sixty-four.

156. Bors Frees Yvain; Lancelot Kills Tericam, Freeing Hector, Lionel, and Many Others.

Arthur proposes to commence a quest for the knights who sought Lancelot. King Bademagu is chosen to become a knight of the Round Table; then Lancelot, Bors, Gaheriet, and Bademagu set off on the quest. They come to White Thorn Castle, where they see people insulting and degrading Mordred. The latter explains that the people of the castle treat all the knights of King Arthur's court in the same manner. They do battle against more than sixty armed men, Lancelot beheads the lord of the castle, and they burn the city.

Lancelot and his companions arrive at Castle Passing, where Yvain is imprisoned. Gaheriet releases Yvain. The lord of the castle explains that he was holding Yvain prisoner until the giant Malduit arrived, which should happen the following day. Bors is chosen to fight against the giant, and he kills him.

The six companions decide to separate, agreeing to meet at Castle Passing. Lancelot meets a maiden who promises to give him news of Lionel in exchange for a boon. She tells him that Lionel had been imprisoned by Tericam. The maiden shows him the fountain where some sixty shields of imprisoned knights were hanging. Tericam arrives, and Lancelot challenges him to battle. He kills Tericam and sends Gaheriet to set the prisoners free. Gaheriet tells his companions to go to Castle Passing on the feast of All Saints, and they go their separate ways.

157. Imprisoned by Morgan, Lancelot Paints the Walls of His Room with Scenes of His Love for Guenevere.

Lancelot continues to search for Hector for a month. He comes to a castle that he enters after killing two giants guarding it. An old lady brings Lancelot the keys to the castle, and the people rejoice in welcoming him as their lord. Lancelot escapes. He then encounters a maiden who takes him to a fortified house where Morgan gives him a potion and imprisons him. While in prison, Lancelot paints a mural depicting all the deeds of his lady. Upon seeing the images, Morgan allows Lancelot to finish his painting so that she may one day show it to King Arthur and thereby betray Lancelot and Queen Guenevere.

Lancelot, Part VI

158. Lancelot Is Still Missing; The Quest Continues.

His wounds healed, Gawain leaves Arthur's court in quest for Lancelot. He learns that Lancelot killed Tericam and freed all the knights imprisoned by him. Then Gawain finds Bademagu recovering from wounds he received while rescuing Guerrehet. On the appointed day, all the companions except Lancelot and Bors meet at Castle Passing. At Gawain's request, they all agree to continue seeking Lancelot until the feast of Mary Magdalene and to meet again at Castle Passing at that time. But on that day, only three knights arrive at Castle Passing: Mordred, Agloval, and Bademagu. They send a squire to Arthur's court to ask if the king has any news of Lancelot and their other companions. The squire returns without news, and the three knights set out the next day to begin their search anew.

159. Lancelot Escapes from Morgan's Prison and Rescues Lionel from King Vagor.

Lancelot spends two winters in Morgan's prison and then escapes by pulling the bars from his window. Leaving Morgan's manor, Lancelot meets a maiden who informs him that Lionel is imprisoned at the castle of Strange Island and is supposed to defend himself in battle on Tuesday. On his way to this castle, Lancelot meets a knight in a litter; there is an arrow in his thigh. He tells Lancelot that only the best knight in the world will be able to remove the arrow; Lancelot is not allowed to try. Lancelot finds Bademagu, tells him about his experiences in Morgan's prison, and learns from Bademagu how he and the other knights began the quest anew when Lancelot did not appear at Castle Passing.

Lancelot goes to the castle called Strange Island, where he finds the imprisoned Lionel. The latter explains that Marabron, the king's son, has accused him of killing his brother. Lancelot defeats Marabron in battle and departs with Lionel.

160. The Story of the Abbey of Small Charity.

Lancelot and Lionel arrive at an abbey named Small Charity. The story then recounts how King Eliezer, a servant of God, went into exile for more than thirty years. One day, famished, he stopped at a small abbey that was called Help for the Poor. He received a tiny amount of bread and slept outside the abbey gate. He had a vision in which God told him that he would find his son (Lanvalet) before him when he awoke and that he should return to his life of earthly splendor for the final days of his life.

161. The Story of the Abbey of Small Charity (Continued).

Having returned home, Eliezer set about feeding and caring for the poor. One day Eliezer's wife asked where their son found him; he told her about the abbey and changed its name to Small Charity, as they had so little to give to the poor.

162. Lancelot Frees the Companions Imprisoned at the Forbidden Hill; Lancelot's Grandfather Appears to Him in a Dream.

Four friars at the abbey welcome Lancelot and attend to Lionel's wound. One of the friars explains to Lancelot that all knights who climb the Forbidden Hill are killed, except that the knights of the Round Table are imprisoned instead. Lancelot climbs the hill and challenges the lord of the castle; during the combat, Lancelot sees that his opponent's sword is the one Galehaut had given him. Lancelot asks the knight to identify himself and learns that it is his cousin Bors. Bors explains to Lancelot that he swore an oath that, if he killed Eloides, he would imprison knights of the Round Table and kill all others who came to the Forbidden Hill until a knight came and defeated him. Bors begs all the imprisoned knights to forgive him. Lancelot and Hector rejoice at being reunited. That night, Lancelot has a vision in which his grandfather tells him to go to the Perilous Forest, where a marvelous adventure awaits him.

163. Lionel Arrives at the Forbidden Hill.

The companions of the hill are distressed to find Lancelot gone when they awaken. The squire tells them that Lancelot hopes to return that evening if possible. Lionel hears that Lancelot conquered the hill and goes to join his companions there.

164. In the Perilous Forest, Lancelot Learns the Story of His Grandfather, Hears of Galahad's Birth, and Sends a Message to Court.

Lancelot enters the Perilous Forest and finds his grandfather's tomb. He takes the body into the chapel and buries him beside his grandmother's body. From a hermit he learns how his grandfather was killed. Later, in the forest, he encounters a youth being chased by a bear, which Lancelot kills. He then sees a stag being guarded by lions, and he promises to learn the meaning of this adventure. At a pavilion, a knight says that Lancelot must joust with him before he may receive lodging. Lancelot kills the knight and is then told that he has killed a great king. Lancelot wants to learn who he is.

   Sarras, a knight from Arthur's household, arrives and tells Lancelot that the Fisher King's daughter gave birth to the one who would accomplish the adventures of the Holy Grail. Sarras departs to challenge Beylas, a knight who unhorsed Gawain; Lancelot follows. Sarras is defeated, and Lancelot then challenges Belyas and wins.

165. Claudas Imprisons Guenevere's Messenger and Sends Two Youths to Spy on Arthur.

Guenevere's cousin, on her way to deliver a message to the Lady of the Lake, is stopped by Claudas, who fears that she is spying for Bors and Lionel and attempting to learn how many knights he has. Claudas imprisons the maiden and her retinue, then sends two messengers to Arthur's court to bring him news of Arthur, Lancelot, and his cousins. Learning why the messengers are there and hearing of her cousin's imprisonment, the queen sends the squire to Claudas with a threatening letter. She laments Lancelot's absence.

166. Lancelot Frees Mordred; The Knight in the Litter Finds Lancelot and Is Healed.

Belyas's brother, Briadas, challenges Lancelot to fight. After jousting, Briadas flees for his life, and other knights come to his aid and try to kill Lancelot. Lancelot reaches a garden where Mordred is being held prisoner; he frees him, and they ride away.

The knight in the litter meets Lancelot, who removes the arrow from his thigh. Lancelot sends messages to Bademagu and to the knights at the Forbidden Hill, asking them to go to Arthur's court at Pentecost. At Penning, where Galehodin is lord, they learn that a tournament is to be held. Seeing Agloval being chased by many knights, Gawain and his companions rescue Agloval from his pursuers. The lord of the manor tells Gawain that Galehodin will certainly kill him and his kin for the harm they inflicted on the knights, but when Galehodin learns that they are Gawain and his companions from Arthur's court, he offers them hospitality. Galehodin asks if Lancelot is with them; Gawain says no, but that he believes he will come to the tournament.

167. A Vision, a Prophecy, a Murder; The Tournament at Penning.

Seeing the white stag escorted by six lions, Lancelot and Mordred follow them in the hope of learning more about this adventure. Lancelot and Mordred lodge with a hermit who tells them that only the good knight who will surpass all others in goodness and in chivalry will accomplish the adventure of the stag. Lancelot also learns that the king he killed was Marian the Accursed and that the people of the land were freed from much pain and poverty by his death. A vavasor informs them of the tournament at Penning Castle the following day. On their way there, they meet an old man who prophesies that Mordred will cause the downfall of Arthur's kingdom and tells him that he is not the son of King Lot of Orkney. Mordred accuses the man of lying and kills him. Lancelot accuses Mordred of committing a mortal sin and manages secretly to retrieve a letter the old man was holding.

Lancelot dons red armor, Mordred white, and they head for the tournament. Lancelot and Mordred fight for the side opposing Galehodin and the knights of the quest. Lancelot carries the day, and Bors, having recognized him, follows him into the forest. Lancelot welcomes him.

168. The Aftermath of the Tournament; the Companions Leave for Court.

After the tournament, Lionel and Hector return to the field to look for Bors. They find Mordred injured on the field, and he tells them that Lancelot was wearing red armor. All the companions are sad to learn that they did not recognize Lancelot. Galehodin is so upset at having missed Lancelot that he promises to join the knights at Arthur's court for Pentecost. The knights have a litter prepared for Mordred; Yvain will accompany him back to court.

169. Bors in the Palace of Adventures at Corbenic, Sees Galahad, the Grail, and the Lance.

Bors and Lancelot hear a woman cry out in distress. Bors goes to investigate and rescues Landoine and Maranz, the daughter and son of the King of the Hundred Knights, who were being beaten. Maranz and Bors search for Lancelot but do not find him. Continuing his search, Bors arrives at Corbenic, where King Pelles and his daughter greet him graciously and ask for news of Lancelot. Bors rejoices at seeing Galahad for the first time and is present at the procession of the Holy Grail. At Bors's insistence, Pelles agrees to let him sleep in the Palace of Adventures. Bors confesses his sins before entering the great hall, where he vanquishes a knight and witnesses a symbolic battle between a dragon and a leopard. Finally, an old man, playing a harp and being bitten by two snakes, tells Bors that he may leave, for he will do nothing more there. After this, Bors sees the avenging lance, and an old man tells him that he will know nothing about the lance until the Perilous Seat finds its master. Bors goes to the door of the Grail room, where he sees a man remove a piece of samite from the Grail. Bors is temporarily blinded by a bright light. The next day he sets out for Camelot.

170. Lancelot Rescues Kay, Unhorses Four Companions of the Round Table, and Meets King Brandegorre's Daughter.

Lancelot arrives at two pavilions, where a lady, fearful of her husband's reaction, refuses to give him lodging. Two armed knights arrive. One refuses to permit Lancelot to stay there; Lancelot kills him, then defeats the second knight, who takes him to a hermitage.

The following day, a maiden asks Lancelot for protection. A knight arrives and immediately kills her. Lancelot, furious that he failed to protect her, pursues the knight and beheads him.

Later, he sees a knight being attacked by two others. Hearing that the single knight is Kay, Lancelot defeats both attackers. The next morning, Lancelot accidentally takes Kay's armor and departs. He meets four knights, one of whom attacks him. Lancelot defeats that knight and the three others. He meets Gawain, Yvain, Hector, and Sagremor; Sagremor mistakes him for Kay and jousts with him, but he unhorses Sagremor and the three others. Learning who they are, Lancelot is grief-stricken to learn that he defeated those he loves. He flees and arrives at two pavilions. In one of them he finds the maiden who saved him from the poison at the spring. He fears that his four companions will find him there, but the maiden promises to hide him. A noble lady arrives at the pavilion with a large entourage; Lancelot learns that she is the daughter of King Brandegorre, and he meets her son, who was fathered by Bors.

171. Lancelot Returns to Camelot; Logres and Gaunes Prepare for War.

Hector tells his three companions that it was Lancelot who jousted against them and that he left in shame when he realized who they were. Arriving at Arthur's court, Gawain hangs Lancelot's shield in the great hall to honor him. Arthur finds that all the knights of the quest have returned except Kay and Lancelot.

Kay arrives but is mistaken for Lancelot. Then the knight Lancelot defeated at the bridge arrives and says he was beaten by Kay. The latter explains how Lancelot mistook his armor for his own and that it was Lancelot who defeated this knight.

In the morning, Arthur sees Lancelot approaching and goes to greet him. During Mass, Lancelot sees the dragon that the old man spoke to him about, and he realizes that Mordred will be the cause of Arthur's destruction. Later, the king rejoices at seeing all 150 knights seated at the Round Table. An inscription on the Perilous Seat foretells the death of Brumand. A knight arrives, hands Lancelot a letter, and sits in the Perilous Seat, where he is burned to death. The letter explains how Brumand declared himself bolder than Lancelot at the court of Claudas and attempted to prove it by sitting in the Perilous Seat. Arthur declares this an act of folly rather than bravery.

The knights begin jousting. Lancelot does not participate, but spends the day with Hector, Bors, Lionel, and the queen. The queen relates to Lancelot the shameful message Claudas sent to her. Lancelot and the others promise to avenge her. Two spies sent by Claudas return to inform him of the war to be waged against him. Claudas prepares for war, but many of his knights leave, and he has few men. He entrusts his people to his son Claudin and then receives news from the Romans, who agree to send them a great force of men in winter.

172. Pentecost Court at Camelot; Preparations for War Against Claudas.

The day after Pentecost, Arthur has the knights of the quest recount all their adventures. Later, Bors tells Lancelot that King Pelles's daughter invites him to come see his son, Galahad; Lancelot asks Bors to conceal this information from the queen. Guenevere asks Lancelot to tell her why he looked so often at Mordred, Arthur, and the dragon painted in the church. Lancelot explains that Mordred and Arthur will kill each other.

A messenger arrives to tell Arthur that Claudas is preparing for war. Huge forces of knights arrive in London to support Lancelot and the knights of the Round Table. Among them are knights brought by King Brandegorre, King Bademagu, Caradoc, King Cabarentin, and many others. At least ten thousand knights and men-at-arms set sail for Gaul. Lancelot remains with Arthur and the queen.

173. Beginnings of the War in Gaul.

The knights from Arthur's land arrive in Gaul and enter into battle against Count Aran, the lord of Flanders. Patrides is victorious in the first battle, and the companions of the Round Table thank God for giving them a fine beginning.

They then have to take Castle Pagon, held by Claudas. They do so, killing nearly everyone inside; Xerxes, the lord of the castle, manages to escape. Claudas and his lords plan an ambush at nightfall against the men of Logres. The ambush is a great success; Claudin and his men kill, injure, or imprison a great many men. Gawain, Hector, and the other knights grieve for the loss of their companions; however, Bors is the most distraught when he learns that Lionel was taken prisoner.

174. Claudas Organizes His Forces in Preparation for Battle Against the Men of Logres.

Claudin and his company escort their prisoners to Tower Castle. Claudas has the prisoners taken to the keep at Gaunes and prepares for battle against the men of Logres. He divides his men into twenty divisions, naming worthy knights to lead each one.

175. Prisoners Are Exchanged Following a First Battle; Roman Reinforcements Arrive to Help Claudas, and the War Continues.

Those of Logres ride to Tower Castle to fight Claudas and his men. The battle is long and fierce, the momentum shifting several times. Hector is wounded and Gawain and Gaheriet unhorsed, but finally, with Bors in the lead, they are able to push their enemy back to the city of Gaunes. The following day, Claudas decides not to attack again yet, but to remain in the city until help from Rome arrives. During a truce, the two sides agree on an exchange of prisoners. Soon Arthur's forces besiege the city of Gaunes.

Three days before St. Michael's Day, the Romans near the city of Gaunes. They are instructed to wait outside the city in order to attack the men of Logres from within the forest. The Lady of the Lake, who has come to visit Bors and Lionel and to seek news of Lancelot, sees the Romans and warns Bors of the impending attack. The battle begins the following morning, and at nightfall both sides withdraw. The battle continues for a week. Eventually, a truce is declared. Hector has been wounded, along with many others, but the men of Logres have taken Claudin prisoner, and they exchange him for Bademagu, who was captured earlier.

176. Lancelot and Arthur Go to Gaul; Claudas Abandons Gaunes; King Pelles's Daughter Deceives Lancelot; Guenevere Expels Lancelot.

Arthur, Lancelot, and more than twelve thousand men cross the sea and arrive in Gaul, where there is great discord over the choice of an overlord. Arthur announces that he will give them Lancelot as their overlord. All are overjoyed except a German count named Frollo, who wants the kingdom for himself. There is a battle between Arthur's men and Frollo's. At nightfall, Frollo sends a messenger to Arthur asking him to fight him in single combat. After Mass the next morning, Arthur enters into combat against Frollo and defeats him.

One of Claudas's spies overhears Arthur announce that he will arrive in the city of Gaunes in three days. The spy delivers this message to Claudas, who escapes at night and sends word back to Gaunes that he has gone to the emperor of Rome and will not be there to help defend his people. Claudin then greets Arthur and Lancelot and presents the keys to the city to Arthur. Lancelot refuses to become king of Gaul and proposes that Hector and Lionel become the kings of Benoic and Gaul, respectively. When Lancelot offers the kingdom of Gaunes to Bors, he refuses, not wanting to abandon knighthood.

Arthur returns to Camelot and announces that he will hold court at Pentecost. Pelles's daughter arrives in Camelot with Galahad, and Bors welcomes them. She is upset that Lancelot will not even look at her. Her governess, Brisane, goes to

Lancelot and asks him to follow her to his lady. Mistaking Brisane for one of the queen's attendants, he is thus tricked into bed with King Pelles's daughter. The queen, upset by Lancelot's absence, hears him moan in his sleep, as he and Pelles's daughter are in bed at the other end of the queen's room. She accuses him of being a traitor and forbids him ever to come near her. Once outside Camelot, Lancelot laments his fate and enters the forest, where he goes mad and attacks everyone he meets.

177. Lancelot Sought by Bors and Later by Perceval; Perceval and Hector Do Battle and Are Healed by the Holy Grail.

Bors, Hector, and Lionel go in quest of Lancelot, but have no success. When Arthur and the knights of the Round Table learn that Lancelot is missing, at least thirty-two more knights arm themselves and set out on the quest. For the next two years, none of the knights learns any news of Lancelot.

Eventually, Agloval arrives at his mother's house where he meets his brother, Perceval. Agloval asks Perceval if he wishes to leave with him to be knighted at King Arthur's court. Perceval deceives his mother by asking only if he may escort Agloval to the edge of the forest; later he sends a message to her, saying that he is going to Arthur's court with Agloval to be knighted. Receiving the message, she immediately dies.

Perceval and Agloval arrive at Carduel, where Arthur is holding court. Those at court are sorrowful because all the questing knights except for the three cousins returned to court with no news of Lancelot. Arthur knights Perceval. That night, a maiden instructs Perceval to sit in the seat at the Round Table next to the Perilous Seat; she explains that he and Bors will sit next to the Good Knight.

Mordred and Kay deride Perceval because he has stayed at court so long and has undertaken no adventures. As a result, Perceval leaves to seek Lancelot. He has many successful adventures, including freeing Patrides from captivity in a castle.

After a year, Perceval meets Hector. Not recognizing each other, they do battle. Both are wounded, and once they have exchanged names, each regrets having fought against another knight of the Round Table. The Holy Grail appears before them; they bow down before it, and all their wounds are healed. Hector explains the history and the meaning of the Holy Grail to Perceval. At daybreak, they depart together in search of Lancelot.

178. Lancelot's Madness and Subsequent Cure.

Lancelot loses all reason and changes so greatly in appearance that he becomes unrecognizable. He comes upon a pavilion where he sees a shield hanging and starts to attack the shield. The knight of the pavilion (Bliant) wants to keep Lancelot with him until he regains his senses. The man and his brother bind Lancelot to the bed and take him to Bliant's castle, where he stays for nearly a year without being healed. One day, after a battle in which he is injured, Bliant flees to his castle and enters the room where Lancelot is staying. His two assailants follow him, and Lancelot breaks his chains and helps Bliant drive them away.

Lancelot remains with Bliant for two years, but his memory does not return. Eventually, he wanders as far as Corbenic, where he is taunted and beaten until he enters the castle, at which time he is treated kindly. King Pelles's daughter recognizes him and takes her father to see him; Pelles has Lancelot bound and carried to the Palace of Adventures, where the Holy Grail heals him. Lancelot then asks Pelles to find him a place to stay where his identity will not be known. He is lodged at Bliant's Castle. He asks Pelles to have a shield made for him; it is black with a knight kneeling before a silver queen and begging for mercy. Lancelot sends a dwarf to a nearby tournament to challenge any knight in search of jousting to come to the Isle of Joy to fight against the Guilty Knight.

179. Hector and Perceval Find Lancelot, and They All Return to Camelot; Galahad's Arrival Is Announced.

Much later, Hector and Perceval approach Bliant's Castle. A maiden explains to them that the Guilty Knight has lived on the island for six years and has defeated every knight who has come to joust. Since only one knight is able to cross at a time, Hector grants Perceval the right to go first. Perceval and Lancelot fight until the latter learns that his adversary is one of Arthur's knights; then he declares himself defeated. When Hector arrives, he and Lancelot embrace, and a celebration begins.

Hector tells Lancelot that the queen summons him, and Lancelot states that he will gladly go. Pelles makes arrangements for Galahad to live with his sister, an abbess in Camelot Forest, so as to be near his father. Lancelot, Hector, and Perceval ride for many days before arriving at Carlion, where Lancelot is welcomed by all, and especially by the queen. Galahad stays at the abbey until the age of fifteen, when a hermit asks him if he will be knighted at Pentecost. Galahad responds affirmatively. The hermit meets Arthur and tells him that at Pentecost a new-made knight will sit in the Perilous Seat and will put an end to the adventures of the Holy Grail.

Volume VI

The Quest for the Holy Grail

1. Lancelot Dubs Galahad, and the Knights Discuss the Perilous Seat.

A young woman arrives at court and asks Lancelot to follow her. They ride to an abbey in the forest and find Bors and Lionel. A nun presents Galahad to Lancelot and asks the latter to knight the young man. After the knighting, Lancelot and his companions travel to Camelot, where the others speculate that the youth was Galahad. They examine the Perilous Seat at the Round Table and find words announcing that the seat will find its occupant on that very day. Arthur delays the meal, following the custom that prohibits eating until an adventure occurs.

2. Gawain and Lancelot Attempt to Remove the Sword in the Stone.

A youth announces that a stone is floating on the water, and they all find the stone, with a sword embedded in it. An inscription states that the sword can be borne only by the world's best knight. Arthur asks Lancelot to attempt to draw the sword, and the latter declines. Then the king asks Gawain, and when he fails at the test, Lancelot predicts that he will regret having tried. Perceval too fails.

3. Galahad Arrives at Arthur's Court.

When all the knights of the Round Table are seated, the doors and windows of the palace close by themselves. An old man enters, leading Galahad. The man announces to Arthur that the youth is the Desired Knight who will bring the Grail adventures to an end.

4. Galahad Sits in the Perilous Seat.

The old man leads Galahad to the Perilous Seat, which now bears the young man's name. Galahad assumes the seat; the knights rejoice, discuss the young man and his parentage, and inform the queen of these events. Arthur has Galahad attempt to draw the sword from the stone, and he succeeds easily.

5. A Stranger Announces the Arrival of the Grail, and King Arthur Holds a Tournament to Celebrate.

A woman arrives to proclaim that there is now a better knight than Lancelot and to announce that the Grail will appear in Arthur's court. Because Arthur understands that the Grail quest will soon disperse his knights, he announces a tournament. Galahad fights with great distinction.

That evening, the Grail enters the hall without being carried by anyone. As it passes each table, every person receives the food he most desires. Afterward, Gawain vows to set out to seek the Grail.

6. The Court Mourns the Knights' Departure, and the Queen Reveals Galahad's Identity to Him.

The other knights also swear to undertake the quest. Arthur grieves, because he knows that never again will all the knights gather at his court. When the queen hears of the impending departure, she is overcome by grief for Lancelot.

A wise man forbids the knights to take their ladies on the quest, and he predicts that God will reveal great secrets to his chosen knight, Galahad.

The queen sits with Galahad and elicits his confirmation that he is Lancelot's son. Arthur grieves again, because he knows that many of his knights will die during the quest.

7. The Knights Swear Solemn Devotion to the Quest.

Arthur asks Lancelot how the quest can be prevented; Lancelot replies that it is impossible. Galahad and then the other knights—one hundred fifty in all—swear to pursue the quest as long as necessary. They then bid farewell to the queen.

8. The Knights Depart and Journey Together to Vagan's Castle.

Guenevere laments bitterly but reluctantly gives Lancelot permission to depart. Galahad declines to take a shield with him, insisting that fate will provide one. The knights journey to Vagan's castle, where they spend the night. The next morning, they separate and set out through the forest.

9. King Bademagu Wrongly Takes the Shield from the Abbey.

At a Cistercian abbey, Galahad meets Bademagu and Yvain the Bastard. They tell Galahad that in the abbey there is a shield that no one can wear or carry away. The next day, Bademagu takes the shield and leaves. Soon he is attacked and defeated by a knight, who, telling him he was foolish to bear the shield, sends it back to Galahad. This knight agrees to explain the origin of the shield, but only if Galahad is brought back to hear it.

10. Galahad Wears the Shield, and "The White Knight" Recounts Its History.

Galahad accepts the shield and goes to meet the knight who sent it to him. The knight reveals the history of the shield, which was originally given to Evalach by

Josephus, son of Joseph of Arimathea. After bringing victory to Evalach, the shield was responsible for several miracles. Before dying, Josephus gave the shield to Evalach and revealed that it was intended for Galahad.

11.   Galahad Lifts the Tombstone, and a Good Man Explains Its Significance; Meliant Is Dubbed and Accompanies Galahad.

Galahad is told of a tomb from which a terrible voice comes. Approaching the tomb, he sees flames and a human figure come out of it; he understands that this is the devil. He finds a body in the tomb and is told that it is the body of a false Christian, who should be removed. Later, a man explains to Galahad the symbolic meaning of the adventure (the tombstone is the harshness of the world before Christ's coming; the body represents the people oppressed by their sins; the voice suggests the words they uttered before Pilate).

   The next morning, Galahad knights a young man, Meliant, who then asks to accompany him on his journey. Setting out, they come to a fork in the road and take separate paths.

12.   Meliant Is Wounded in a Battle with a Stranger in the Forest, and a Monk Explains Its Significance.

Meliant finds a throne and crown. He takes the crown and is soon challenged by another knight, who then wounds him and carries off the crown. Galahad defeats this knight and then takes Meliant to an abbey to have his wounds tended. A monk explains that Meliant's wounds resulted from the sin he committed by taking the wrong path when he first set out; he further explains that Meliant's taking the crown was also a sin (of pride and covetousness).

   Galahad leaves the abbey; he stops to pray in a ruined chapel, and a voice tells him to go to the Castle of Maidens and end the evil customs in force there.

13.   Galahad Battles Seven Knights at the Castle of the Maidens.

Galahad approaches the castle and ignores warnings to turn back. Seven knights, who are brothers, attack him, and after a long battle, he defeats them. He enters the castle and finds many maidens, who ask him to make all the knights and vavasors of the region swear never to observe that custom again. The maidens then explain that the seven knights had arrived ten years earlier, killing and plundering until they ruled the land; and because a young woman had angered them by predicting that all seven would be defeated by a single knight, they decided to detain every woman who came there until the arrival of a knight who could defeat them.

   The next day, Galahad learns that, after his battle with them, the seven brothers were killed by Gawain, Gaheriet, and Yvain. He leaves the castle.

14.   Gawain and His Companions Battle the Seven Brothers, and a Hermit Explains Its Significance.

Gawain meets Gaheriet, and the two of them join Yvain. The three of them defeat the seven brothers from the Castle of Maidens. They then separate, and Gawain comes to a hermitage. The hermit tells Gawain that he has abandoned God. He then explains that the Castle of Maidens represents Hell, and the maidens represent the souls who were in Hell before the passion of Christ; the knights are the seven deadly sins. God, he says, sent Galahad to liberate the maidens.

15. Galahad Battles Lancelot and Perceval; A Knight Is Healed by the Grail.

Galahad rides to the Waste Forest; he meets Lancelot and Perceval, who attack him because they do not recognize him. Galahad defeats them and leaves. Lancelot sets out after Galahad; he finds a ruined chapel, in which is a rich altar, but he cannot enter the locked gate.

A wounded knight arrives in a litter; he complains of his suffering and asking when the Holy Vessel will arrive. Soon the Grail approaches, and the wounded knight is healed. Taking Lancelot's arms, he mounts a horse and leaves, swearing to search until he learns the truth about the Grail.

16. The Hermit Tells Lancelot the Parable of the Gold Coins.

A voice describes Lancelot as harder than stone, more bitter than wood, and more naked than a fig tree; it also orders him to leave there. Departing on foot, he soon comes to a hermitage and enters the chapel. The hermit tells him the parable of the three men to whom gold coins were given. Lancelot is warned not to emulate one of the men, who kept his gift for himself and turned from God.

17. Lancelot Confesses His Infidelity to the Hermit.

At the hermit's urging, Lancelot confesses his sin, openly acknowledging for the first time his love affair with the queen. He describes how he was unable to approach the Grail and promises that he will never again sin with Guenevere or any other woman.

18. The Hermit Explains How Lancelot Is Like Stone, Wood, and a Fig Tree.

The hermit explains the words pronounced by the voice that spoke to Lancelot. The reference to stone identifies sinners whose hearts are hardened; Lancelot's bitterness, replacing the sweetness that should be in him, resembles that of a rotting tree trunk. The fig tree is the one Christ found on Palm Sunday: it had beautiful leaves and branches but bore no fruit.

19. Lancelot Converts.

A repentant Lancelot again promises to turn his back on sin, but he insists that he cannot abandon knighthood. The hermit preaches to him and makes him regret even more the waste of his life.

20. The Recluse Reveals Her Identity to Perceval.

Perceval asks the recluse about the knight who passed there and with whom he wishes to do battle. The woman reveals that the knight in question will be one of only three people who will win honor in the Grail quest. (Perceval himself and Bors are the other two.) She also tells Perceval that she is his aunt and that his mother died the day he left for Arthur's court.

21.   Perceval's Aunt Recounts the Story of the Three Tables.

The recluse tells about the establishment of three famous tables. The first was the table where Christ ate with his disciples. The second was the Grail Table, established at the time of Joseph of Arimathea; it had one vacant seat, reserved for Josephus, Joseph's son. The third is the Round Table.

22.   Perceval's Aunt Recalls Merlin's Prophecies.

The woman explains that Merlin established the Round Table, which, like the earlier table, had an empty seat; it was reserved for the chosen Grail Knight. And just as the Holy Spirit came to comfort the apostles on Pentecost, so did the Good Knight, Galahad, come to court to inaugurate the Quest.

23.   Perceval's Aunt Advises Perceval Before His Departure.

Perceval's aunt advises him to keep company with Galahad and to preserve his virginity. She then explains to him why she became a recluse: she feared King Libran, who waged war with her husband; when the latter was killed, she took her belongings and fled.

24.   Perceval Observes an Old Man at Mass.

Leaving his aunt, Perceval travels to an abbey, where he witnesses the Mass. He sees a bed on which there lies an old and seriously wounded man, wearing a crown. The man raises himself up only to take the Corpus Domini. Later, Perceval asks a monk to explain these events.

25.   Perceval Hears the Story of Mordrain.

The monk tells the story of Mordrain (formerly called Evalach), who had liberated Josephus, the son of Joseph of Arimathea, from prison. During a Mass, Mordrain came too close to the Grail and was blinded and wounded as a result. He prayed that God let him live until the Good Knight comes to him; God granted his wish. Since that time, Mordrain has lived in pain and blindness for four hundred years, but it is rumored that the Good Knight will soon come there.

26.   Perceval Attacked by Knights and Rescued by "The Red Knight."

Perceval is attacked by twenty men and is about to be killed when a knight in red armor comes to his rescue. Once Perceval is safe, the Red Knight rides away. Wishing to follow him, Perceval asks a squire for a horse he is leading, but the man refuses. In despair, Perceval asks the squire to kill him, but the request is denied.

27.   Left Without a Horse, Perceval Swears Allegiance to His Rescuer.

A knight steals the horse Perceval asked for, and the squire asks the latter to take his riding horse and pursue the thief; if he recovers the horse, he can take it. He finds the knight and they do battle; the enemy kills Perceval's horse and leaves. A woman (who is in fact the devil in human form) arrives and promises Perceval a fine horse if he will do as she asks. Perceval agrees, and the woman brings him a large black horse.

28.   Perceval Awakes on an Island and Befriends a Lion.

Preparing to cross a river, Perceval crosses himself, whereupon the devil flees from Perceval and throws himself into the water. Perceval prays until morning, when he finds himself on an island, surrounded by wild animals. He sees a serpent that has stolen a lion's cub. A fight occurs between the lion and the serpent, and Perceval intervenes to kill the latter. The grateful lion stays with its savior all day.

29.   Perceval Dreams of Women on a Lion and a Serpent.

With the lion nearby, Perceval falls asleep and dreams of two women: the younger one riding a lion, the older one a serpent. The former predicts a great battle for Perceval. The latter condemns him for killing her serpent. The following morning, he sees a ship approaching. In it is a man dressed as a priest and wearing a crown; he explains that God is testing Perceval.

30.   The Hermit Explains the Allegory of the Old and the New Laws.

Questioned by Perceval, the man explains that the two women in the dream represented the Old and the New Laws. The latter is the lady on the lion, which represents Christ. On the other hand, the serpent is the scripture poorly interpreted; it is hypocrisy and sin. The man also explains that Perceval had earlier been riding on the devil's back and that the devil had fled when Perceval crossed himself.

31.   Perceval Pledges His Love to a Lady Who Tempts Him.

The ship leaves with the man. Later, another ship approaches, and in it is a beautiful woman. She tells Perceval that she had seen the Good Knight almost drown while pursuing two knights. She then says that the man on the ship was a sorcerer who sought Perceval's death. She goes on to explain that she was a rich woman, that she was disinherited, and that she is raising an army to do battle with the king who banished her; she asks Perceval's assistance, and he agrees. Then, in a tent on her ship, she tempts him with rest, food, and drink; flushed with wine, he asks for her love. As he is about to sin with her, he sees the cross engraved on the pommel of his sword and comes to his senses.

32.   Perceval Repents His Weakness and Meets the Hermit Again.

Perceval, distraught and ridden with guilt, wishes to die. He wounds himself with his sword, and all through the night he prays for forgiveness. The following day, the ship returns with the wise man, and Perceval asks him to explain who the woman was.

33. The Hermit Explains the Temptation of Perceval.

The man explains that the woman was the devil. He offers an allegorical interpretation of the events (the tent representing the sinful world, nightfall signifying death, etc.). When the man leaves, a voice announces that Perceval has won and is healed. Perceval boards a ship and sets out, borne along by the wind.

34. A Squire Humiliates Lancelot for His Sinful Love of the Queen.

For three days, the hermit has instructed Lancelot in spiritual matters, predicting Galahad's entry into celestial chivalry. Leaving the hermit, Lancelot encounters a squire who berates him for his failure when he saw the Grail and condemns him for his sinful love. Lancelot leaves, praying that God will let his soul be saved.

35. The Devil Is Conjured To Explain the Death of the Religious.

Lancelot finds a hermit who is weeping for a dead man. The hermit conjures the devil and demands to know how the man died. The devil explains that the man assisted his nephew in battle against his enemy, whose own nephews then attacked this man. Unable to kill him with swords, they burned him to death, but the fire did not harm his skin or shirt.

36. The Hermit Condemns Lancelot's Sin with Guenevere.

The hermit praises Lancelot's former virginity, humility, patience, justice, and charity, but goes on to explain that the devil, wanting to deceive Lancelot, entered into Guenevere and made her lead Lancelot into sin. The hermit urges him to ask God to forgive him.

37. The Hermit Recounts the Parable of the Banquet.

The hermit recounts the biblical parable of the townspeople invited to a wedding feast; one man is excluded because he is improperly dressed. The wedding feast represents the Grail Table, and God will not accept those who are not clothed in confession.

38. The Hermit Guides Lancelot's Conduct.

Lancelot and the hermit speak together at length, and the hermit urges him to wear a hair shirt and to pray often. Leaving the hermit, he encounters a woman who tells him that he was once closer to what he is seeking than he now is, but that now he is also closer to it than ever. She does not explain the contradiction.

39. Lancelot Has a Vision and Prays for God's Help in His Effort to Remain Pure.

Lancelot sees a vision of a man wearing a crown and accompanied by seven kings and two knights. A man descends from heaven and blesses all but the elder knight; he then changes the younger knight into a lion with wings. Awakening, Lancelot thanks God and departs. He encounters the knight who took his armor the day before; the knight attacks Lancelot, who defeats him and leaves.

40. Lancelot Meets a Hospitable and Wise Hermit.

Lancelot takes lodging with a hermit. After confessing his sins, Lancelot tells of his vision and asks its meaning. The hermit explains that the vision contained the story of Lancelot's lineage.

41. The Hermit Explains Lancelot's Vision of the Man Surrounded by Kings.

The hermit tells of the past, beginning with Joseph of Arimathea, Evalach (baptized by Josephus), and Seraph, who took the baptismal name of Nascien. He recounts Evalach's vision of Celidoine, Nascien's son, from whom there sprang nine rivers. The rivers signify his nine male descendants: Narpus, Nascien, Alan the Fat, Isaiah, Jonah, Lancelot (the hero's ancestor), Ban, Lancelot, and finally Galahad, whom Lancelot fathered with the daughter of the Fisher King.

42. After Participating in a Tournament, Lancelot Is Captured and Released.

Lancelot is surprised to learn that the Good Knight is his son. He spends the night with the hermit. The following day, he rides until he comes upon a tournament. He helps the weaker side; he distinguishes himself initially but is eventually captured. His captors allow him to leave, provided he promises to do as they say.

43. Lancelot Reflects on His Moral Failings.

Lancelot attributes his unaccustomed loss in a tournament to his sin. When he falls asleep, he sees a vision of a man coming from heaven and warning him against his mortal enemy. The next day, he arrives at a chapel and attends Mass. Then a recluse asks him about himself; he tells of his vision and asks her advice.

44. The Recluse Explains the Meaning of the Tournament; Lancelot Gets Lost in the Wilderness.

The recluse explains to Lancelot that the two sides in the tourney represent heavenly knights (in white) and earthly knights (wearing black to symbolize sin). Both have embarked on the Grail quest. Lancelot, who is living in sin, chose the side of those like him. The woman warns him against further sin.

Leaving her, Lancelot meets a black knight, who kills his horse and then leaves. Lancelot, afoot, comes to a place where he has water before him, rocks on one side of him, and a forest on yet another. He prays for guidance and help.

45. Gawain and Hector Meet and Decide to Travel Together.

Gawain rides for a long time, puzzled and amazed that he has found no adventures.
He meets Hector, who has the same complaint, and they decide to ride together.
Eventually they come to a chapel, where they pray and keep vigil.

46. Gawain and Hector Are Puzzled by Strange Visions.

In his sleep, Gawain has a vision of a hayrack and one hundred fifty bulls. Most
are spotted, but one is only slightly spotted, and two others are completely white.
The bulls leave the pasture, and many of them fail to return. Of the three unspotted
ones, only one returns.

   In Hector's dream, he and Lancelot set out on a journey. Lancelot is unhorsed
and shamed by a stranger, and later he is unable to drink from a spring. Hector
wanders aimlessly; when he comes to a house and asks for shelter, the owner tells
him he is mounted too high.

   Discussing their dreams, they see a hand enter the chapel, holding a bridle and
a candle. A voice informs them that, because they lack the three things they have
seen, they cannot participate in the Grail adventures. They decide to find a hermit
who can explain their dreams and the voice.

47. Gawain Kills Yvain in Combat.

Gawain and Hector set out for a hermitage, and the former is challenged by a third
knight. They do battle, and Gawain mortally wounds the stranger, who asks to be
taken to an abbey for a proper burial. Once there, Gawain learns that the wounded
knight is Yvain the Bastard, son of Urien. At Yvain's request, Gawain pulls the
lance from his chest, and Yvain dies. He is properly buried.

48. Hector and Gawain Meet a Hermit.

Gawain and Hector ride on and come to a hermitage, where they find Nascien.
They tell him of their dreams and ask him to interpret them.

49. The Hermit Explains Gawain's and Hector's Visions.

The hermit explains that the hayrack represents the Round Table; the meadow
is humility and patience; the spotted bulls are sinful knights. The perfect bulls
are Galahad and Perceval, and the slightly spotted one is Bors. Their departure
represents the Grail quest, from which many will not return. Of the three chosen
knights, one (Bors) will return.

   He then explains Hector's vision. The horses on which they left court are pride
and arrogance. Christ unhorsed him (that is, delivered him from pride) and dressed
him in patience and humility. The spring is the Holy Grail, the grace of the Holy
Spirit. Hector, who continued to ride, will always live in mortal sin. The harness
and bit represent abstinence, and the candle is the truth of the Gospel.

50. Bors Meets the Religious, Who Explains the Importance of Confession to Him.

Bors meets a priest, who explains that the Grail quest can be accomplished only by the best and purest and that no one can expect to succeed in it or come to Christ who is not properly cleansed through confession.

51. Bors Vows to Eat the Food of the Spirit and Sees the Bird Sacrifice Itself to Its Young.

At the hermit's urging, Bors promises to consume only bread and water until he comes to the Grail Table. He then confesses all his sins and takes communion. After leaving, he sees a bird whose young are dead; the bird strikes its breast with its beak, and its blood revives the young. The large bird then dies. Bors wonders at the significance of this event.

52. Bors Hears the Story of King Amant and Volunteers to Combat Priadan the Black.

Bors meets a young woman who is at war with her older sister. The latter has threatened to take all the land if the younger sister cannot provide a champion to do battle the following day with Priadan the Black. Bors offers his services.

53. Bors Dreams a Series of Strange Visions.

In his sleep Bors sees a white bird and a black bird; each asks Bors to serve it. Then, in another vision, he sees a rotten tree and two lilies of the valley. A good man tends to the flowers and emphasizes to Bors that one should not let attention to the rotten tree allow the flowers to perish.

54. Bors Defeats Priadan the Black in Combat.

The following day, Bors defeats Priadan in battle, and the older sister flees. Bors then orders all those who have held land from that sister to return it to the younger one. Most do, and those who refuse are killed.

55. Bors Must Choose Between Saving Lionel and Rescuing a Captive Maiden.

The following day Bors sees two knights torturing his brother Lionel. Then he sees another knight abducting a maiden. He is torn between two duties but decides to rescue the maiden; he defeats the knight. He and the maiden then meet other knights who have been looking for her. Overjoyed, they ask Bors to return with them so they can honor him, but he refuses.

56. Bors Buries His Brother, and a Religious Chastises Him for Saving the Maiden.

Bors looks for Lionel, and a man in religious dress directs him to his brother's corpse. They take the body to a nearby chapel and place it on a marble tomb.

Bors then asks his companion, who has said that he is a priest, to explain his two recent visions. The man says that the white bird, a swan, represents a woman who loves Bors; the black bird represents his sin in rejecting her and causing her death. He also says that the rejection will cause Lancelot's death as well, and he berates Bors for saving the maiden rather than Lionel. He says that Lancelot's life depends on Bors.

57.   A Beautiful Maiden Tempts Bors.

A beautiful young woman asks Bors to sleep with her. He refuses, whereupon she informs him that he will be the cause of her death. She and twelve other young women climb to the top of the castle and throw themselves off. Shocked, Bors crosses himself, whereupon he finds himself alone; he understands that the devil arranged all this in an attempt to destroy him.

58.   Bors Arrives at an Abbey of White Monks and Asks for Guidance.

Coming to an abbey of white monks, Bors asks for the wisest of them and recounts his experience. He asks about the significance of it, but the abbot announces that he will explain it the next day.

59.   The Abbot Interprets Bors's Adventures.

The abbot explains the image of the birds (the principal one being the Creator, the others lost human beings) and of King Amant, who is Christ. The woman Bors defended represents Holy Church. The black bird and the white bird that resembles a swan represent the Church and the devil, respectively. The tree is Lionel, lacking in virtues; the rotten wood represents his sins. The two flowers represent two virgins—the knight Bors wounded and the maiden he rescued. The abbot also tells Bors that Lionel was freed and has resumed the quest.

60.   Bors Meets Lionel and Refuses to Fight Him.

Bors arrives at a castle where a tournament is to be held; he goes to a nearby hermitage, where he finds Lionel. Lionel accuses Bors of nearly causing his death and, refusing to accept his brother's apology, orders him to prepare for battle. Bors refuses and remains on his knees, whereupon Lionel knocks him to the ground and prepares to cut off his head. A hermit throws himself on Bors's body and says that it would be better to kill him than Bors. Lionel strikes the hermit and breaks his neck.

61.   Lionel Kills Calogrenant in the Battle Against Bors.

As Lionel is preparing to behead Bors, Calogrenant arrives and defends the latter. Lionel challenges him to battle. As Bors is preparing to join the battle, Lionel kills Calogrenant.

62. God Intervenes and Commands Bors to Meet Perceval at the Sea.

Lionel attacks Bors; Bors prays for assistance, and a voice tells him not to strike his brother. A lightning bolt knocks both of them to the ground, and a voice directs Bors to go to the sea to meet Perceval.

At the shore, Bors enters a ship, which sails away. The following morning, he sees that Perceval is also on board. They greet each other and tell each other of their adventures; the ship drifts wherever the wind carries it.

63. After a Tournament, Galahad Rides to the Magic Ship and Meets Bors and Perceval.

Galahad comes to a tournament and helps the side in deepest trouble. He attacks and unhorses Gawain, and after the tournament he quickly leaves. Gawain, seriously injured, is taken to a castle to have his wounds cared for. Galahad is met at a castle by a lady who asks him to accompany her. She leads him to the coast, where he finds Bors and Perceval on their ship. The wind carries them out to sea, and they tell one another of their adventures.

64. Perceval Meets His Sister on a Second Magic Ship.

The ship drifts for a long time and finally comes to a bay. There they see a second ship, in which, they are told, lies the adventure for which the Lord brought them together. An inscription on the ship invites only those who are full of faith to enter. The young woman reveals to Perceval that she is his sister, and he decides to board the ship.

65. The Knights Discover the Magic Sword.

They all board the ship and find a rich bed. At its head is a gold crown; at the foot is a beautiful sword. The cloth covering it contains letters saying that only one man can ever grip the sword. Perceval and Bors try and fail. Galahad sees an inscription on the sword itself; it forbids anyone to draw the sword unless he can fight better than anyone else.

66. Perceval's Sister Recounts the Story of the Sword.

Perceval's sister explains that the sword dates to the time of King Lambor (father of the Maimed King) and King Varlan. During a battle between the two, Varlan came to the ship, took the sword, and killed Lambor. As a result of that blow, their two kingdoms became a Waste Land. Varlan died when he went back to claim the scabbard.

The knights examine the scabbard and see that its belt is poor and weak. They find an inscription announcing that the man who wields the sword will never be defeated as long as he does not remove the belt: it will be removed only by a woman who will replace it with a new belt made from what she values most.

Perceval's sister tells them that, forty years after the Passion, Nascien (Mordrain's brother-in-law) found this same ship, bed, and sword. Later, in a battle, he drew the sword, but it broke at the first blow. Mordrain later rejoined the pieces. Nascien was wounded by a sword, and a voice rebuked him for drawing this one.

She then tells them about Parian, who later found the same ship. When he started to draw the sword, a lance struck him between the thighs. His wound has never healed, and he is known as the Maimed King. When she completes her story, they all notice that the bed was constructed with two vertical spindles (one white, the other red) joined by a green crossbar.

67.   The Legend of the Tree of Life.

The story explains these colors. When Eve gave the apple to Adam, she held in her hand part of the tree branch. Once they were expelled from Eden, she stuck the branch in the ground, and it grew. This Tree of Life was entirely white, signifying the virginal state of the first couple. (The text explains the difference between virginity and maidenhood.) All the twigs from this tree that were put into the ground also grew into white trees. Then God commanded Adam and Eve to have carnal relations, in order to establish the human race. Afterward, the tree became green, symbolizing the seed that had been sown and the loss of virginity. Cain eventually came to resent Abel and to plot his murder.

68.   The Story of the Death of Abel.

Cain treacherously killed Abel, and the death prefigures the death of Christ on the Cross. After the murder, God cursed Cain. At that time, the Tree of Life turned completely red, like the blood spilled beneath it. The tree flourished and grew, but henceforth shoots taken from it always died.

69.   The Tree of Life Throughout Time.

The Tree of Life and the others that had grown from it survived the great flood and lived into the time of Solomon. Solomon was very wise, but his wife was a scheming and deceitful woman.

70.   Solomon's Wife Suggests How to Signal that Galahad Is Anticipated.

As Solomon was lamenting the perfidy of women, a voice assured him that a woman of his lineage (that is, the Virgin) would eventually bring great joy to men. The voice further told him that the last of his line would be a superior knight who was also a virgin. Solomon then sought a way to let that knight know that his ancestor had known of his coming. Solomon's wife suggested that he build a ship that would not rot and that he fit King David's sword with a pommel of precious stones; she would make the sword belt.

71.   Solomon Constructs the Ship and Dreams of Its Consecration.

The ship was constructed, and a fine bed was put into it. Solomon placed his crown and the sword on the bed. His wife had made a belt of rough hemp but assured him that a virgin would eventually provide a proper belt. Then she had pieces cut from the red tree and from a white and a green one. She had two of them placed as spindles at the sides of the bed, with the third a crossbar that connected them. The next day there appeared on the side of the ship an inscription forbidding anyone to enter the ship who was lacking in faith.

72.   A Belt Is Fashioned from the Hair of Perceval's Sister.

Under the crown, the three companions (Galahad, Perceval, and Bors) find a purse in which there is a letter that presents the history of the ship. They decide that they should look for a proper belt, but Perceval's sister produces one woven from gold and silk and her hair. She reveals that the sword is called the Sword of the Strange Straps, and the scabbard is called Memory of Blood (a reminder of Abel's blood).

At the urging of the others, Galahad grips and draws the sword, proving that it was meant for him; then Perceval's sister girds it on him and informs him that only now is he properly a knight.

73.   The Companions Liberate Carcelois Castle and Witness the Death of Count Ernol.

The wind drives the ship to a castle called Carcelois. When the inhabitants learn that the companions are from Arthur's court, they attack them. The companions defeat the others and liberate the palace. Then they see a priest carrying the Corpus Domini in a chalice. He explains to them that the people they had killed were evil, and he tells how the three sons of Count Ernoul had imprisoned and mistreated their father, but the count announced that three servants of Christ would avenge the wrong.

They free Ernoul from prison; he is at the point of death, but before dying he says that God has directed Galahad to go to the castle of the Maimed King and restore him to health.

74.   A White Stag Changes into a Man, and a Priest Explains Its Significance.

The companions set out from the castle. They see a white stag protected by four lions. They follow it and come to a hermitage where a wise man is ready to sing Mass. Entering the chapel, they see that the stag has become a man. The lions, transformed into forms representing the four evangelists, lift the chair in which the man is sitting and depart through a window without breaking it. A voice explains that this is the way Christ entered the Virgin without destroying her virginity. The wise man then explains that the stag represents Christ, who was himself transformed on the Cross.

75.   The Leper Woman Is Cured with Blood from Perceval's Sister, Who Dies.

Leaving the hermitage, the companions come to a castle. A knight asks them if the young woman with them (Perceval's sister) is a virgin. They are then told that custom requires any virgin who comes there to fill a dish with her blood. The companions fight against heavy opposition all day to prevent this outrage. That night, their opponents give them lodging and explain the custom: their lady suffers from leprosy and can be cured only by the blood of a virgin, preferably a princess who is Perceval's sister. For fear that they may not recognize the person in question, they have decided to take the blood of any woman who passes that way.

Perceval's sister volunteers to give her blood. The act costs her life but heals the lady. Before dying, the sister asks Perceval to place her body in a ship, assuring him that chance will take it to Sarras, where Perceval and Galahad will eventually find her and they will all be buried together. They do as she asks, placing in the ship a letter explaining who she was.

As they leave the castle, a great storm partially destroys it. Later, they see a wounded knight being pursued by another knight and a dwarf. Bors follows them in order to help the wounded man. The companions agree that if Bors does not return, they will meet at the house of the Maimed King.

76. Perceval and Galahad Witness Divine Punishment and Decide to Separate.

Perceval and Galahad return to the castle and find all the inhabitants dead. A voice informs them that the destruction is revenge for the blood that was spilled there. They then find a cemetery holding the bodies of the virgins whose lives were lost to satisfy the evil custom of the castle. The two companions separate and set out from the ruined castle.

77. Lancelot Happens upon a Ship and Meets Galahad, Who Explains the Strange Straps.

As Lancelot is sleeping, a voice commands him to board the first ship he sees. He does so, and the following morning he notices a beautiful bed on which is the body of a maiden. A letter with the body explains that this was Perceval's sister.

The ship comes to shore near a chapel. An old man boards the ship, reads the letter and learns of the Sword of the Strange Straps, and urges Lancelot to remain chaste. After he leaves the ship, Lancelot drifts for a month, his life sustained by God.

Eventually he comes to shore and meets Galahad, who explains and shows the Sword of the Strange Straps. They remain on the ship for six months. After Easter, they come to the shore, where a knight meets them and orders Galahad to mount a white horse and fulfill the adventures of the kingdom of Logres. A voice tells Lancelot and Galahad that they will not see each other again until Judgment Day. Lancelot remains on the ship and drifts for another month.

78. Lancelot Arrives at the Castle of the Grail, Where He Is Injured in His Attempts to Approach the Holy Grail.

Lancelot comes to Corbenic Castle, which is guarded by two lions. A voice commands him to enter the castle, where he will see part of what he has sought. When he draws his sword to fight the lions, a fiery hand strikes his arm; a voice rebukes him for not trusting God. He enters the castle and finds a door he cannot open. Believing the Grail to be beyond the door, he prays and then finds the door open before him. The room is filled with light. Lancelot wants to enter, but a voice forbids it. Through the door he sees the Grail, angels, and an old man performing the Mass. Three figures are above the priest, and two of them place the youngest in the priest's hands. Thinking the weight of the man too great for the priest to bear, Lancelot enters the room to assist him. He is struck and burned by great heat, and he feels hands remove him from the room.

The following day, others find him, apparently dead. They care for him for twenty-four days; when he awakens, he tells them that he has had beautiful spiritual visions. He understands that he had lived in sin for twenty-four years and that these twenty-four days were penance for his sin. He is informed that his quest is ended.

King Pelles greets him and informs him of the death of his (Pelles's) daughter, Galahad's mother. Lancelot stays with him for four days, after which Hector arrives at the castle. Learning that Lancelot is there, Hector flees because he has been shamed by his failures.

79.   Lancelot Finds Bademagu's Tomb and Returns to Court.

Lancelot leaves Corbenic to return to Logres. On the way, he finds the tomb of Bademagu, then other tombs surrounded by upright swords. When he arrives at Arthur's court, he is greeted warmly. Many knights have not returned from the quest, and those who have come back are the ones who had accomplished nothing.

80.   Galahad Witnesses Mordrain's Death, Hears Simeon's Voice, and Rides to the Castle of the Maimed King.

Galahad comes to the abbey where King Mordrain lies ill; his arrival permits Mordrain to meet the death he has been awaiting. Upon his death, his wounds are healed. Galahad leaves two days later and rides to the Perilous Forest. Coming to the boiling fountain, he plunges his hand into the water, and the boiling ceases. Later, he comes to the land of Gorre and to the abbey where Lancelot had found the tomb of Galahad, son of Joseph of Arimathea. In a crypt, Galahad sees a burning tomb and is told that it is an adventure that can be undertaken only by the best of all knights. As he descends the steps, the flames subside. Inside the tomb he finds the body of Simeon, and a voice informs Galahad that he has saved the soul of Simeon, who had sinned against Joseph of Arimathea.

Galahad, accompanied by Perceval, leaves and wanders for five years before coming to the house of the Maimed King. They meet Bors and decide not to separate again.

81.   The Three Companions Witness the Wonders of Corbenic Castle.

The companions come to Corbenic Castle. There they are presented with the broken sword with which Joseph of Arimathea was wounded. Bors and Perceval are unable to rejoin its pieces; Galahad succeeds.

The skies darken and a hot wind blows; a voice announces that all who are not worthy must leave the room. Pelles, his son, a maiden, and the companions remain. Nine knights enter. A bed is brought into the room, and its occupant welcomes Galahad; he says that he has awaited Galahad, whose arrival would finally let him die. A voice commands those who are not companions on the quest to leave; Pelles, his son, and the maiden leave. From the sky there descends a man dressed as a bishop; four angels are carrying him on a throne. An inscription on the figure's forehead identifies him as Josephus, the first Christian bishop.

82.   Josephus Performs the Grail Liturgy, and the Knights Witness the Mysteries of the Grail.

The lance is bleeding, and an angel has the blood fall into the Grail. Josephus begins to celebrate the Mass, and the figure of a child enters the bread. Then Josephus disappears. The figure of a man issues forth from the Grail, his hands, feet, and body bleeding. He presents the Grail to Galahad and the others, and they drink. Then he explains that what he holds in his hand—the Grail—is the platter from which Christ and his disciples ate the Paschal lamb. He informs them that the Grail will no longer be seen there and that they must journey with it to Sarras. Before they leave, Galahad is to use the blood from the lance to heal the Maimed King. He does so, and the king joins a community of white monks.

83.   The Ship Departs with the Three Companions and the Holy Grail.

Galahad, Perceval, and Bors ride to the sea, where they find the ship that holds the Sword with the Strange Straps. They discover that the Holy Grail is already on the ship. A wind comes up and drives the ship from shore.

84.   The Companions Come to Sarras, Where Galahad Performs a Miracle and Perceval's Sister Is Buried.

On the ship, Galahad regularly asks God to allow him to die whenever he requests it; a voice says that God will grant it. His companions tell Galahad that he should lie on the bed that, according to the inscription, was prepared for him. He does so, and when he awakens, the ship has come to Sarras. A voice commands them to take the Grail to the place where Josephus was consecrated as bishop. They then see that the ship carrying the body of Perceval's sister has arrived also.

   The companions take the Grail Table and set out for the palace. Along the way, Galahad tells a beggar on crutches to help them; when the beggar rises, he is healed. After they place the table in the palace, they return and bury Perceval's sister. They explain the Grail to the treacherous king of the city, Escorant, who has them imprisoned for a year. God sustains them during that time.

85.   Galahad Dies.

Escorant dies, and a reluctant Galahad is chosen king. One year later, they see the figure of a bishop before the Grail. He celebrates Mass and invites Galahad to come forward and see what he has wanted to see. In the Grail Galahad sees great spiritual mysteries and then asks God to let him die. The bishop identifies himself as Josephus. Galahad takes leave of Perceval and Bors and falls dead before the Grail Table. At that moment, a hand comes down from heaven, takes away the Grail and the lance, and disappears.

   Perceval retires to a hermitage; Bors accompanies him but does not join the order because he intends to return to Arthur's court. A year and three days later, Perceval dies and is buried alongside his sister and Galahad. Bors then returns to Arthur's court, where he receives a joyous welcome. At Arthur's request, Bors then recounts the adventures of the Holy Grail, which the king's clerks put into writing.

Volume VII

The Death of Arthur

1. Aftermath of Grail Quest; The Tournament at Winchester.

Bors has returned to court and has recounted the conclusion of the quest. Arthur then asks for an accounting of the number of knights lost in the quest; Gawain acknowledges that he himself killed eighteen, including Bademagu. Because the adventures of Logres are completed, and because Arthur does not want his knights to give up bearing arms, he announces a tournament at Winchester.

Lancelot and Guenevere soon lapse again into their sin and conduct themselves so indiscreetly that Agravain is persuaded that they love each other. When Lancelot announces that he will not go to the tournament, Agravain speaks with Arthur and proposes to surprise Lancelot and the queen together.

Lancelot leaves to go incognito to the tourney. On his way, he meets a young woman who asks him for a promise and, receiving his assurance, informs him that she wishes him to wear her sleeve on his helmet and be her champion. Lancelot distinguishes himself as the best knight in the tournament, but he and Bors wound each other.

2. Suspicion that Lancelot Loves a Woman Other Than Guenevere.

The king announces another tournament, at Taneburgh, for the following month. Arthur and his knights, on the way to Camelot, stop at the castle of Escalot, where they meet the young woman whose champion Lancelot had been. Gawain asks her for her love, and she refuses, pointing out that she loves a knight whose name she does not know. She shows Lancelot's arms to Gawain, who recognizes them. Gawain and Arthur later talk of this situation, and Lancelot's apparent love for the maiden confirms the king's conviction that Lancelot and Guenevere are innocent of wrongdoing.

3. Return to Camelot; The Queen Convinced of Lancelot's Infidelity.

Learning that Lancelot wore the emblem of another woman, Guenevere thinks he has betrayed her. She then learns from Bors that Lancelot was seriously injured. Not long afterward, Gawain again reveals to Arthur his belief that Lancelot loves the maiden of Escalot, and Guenevere, overhearing the conversation, is persuaded that she has been betrayed.

Bors and his entourage leave Camelot and unsuccessfully seek Lancelot at Escalot.

4.   Maiden of Escalot Rebuffed by Lancelot; Lancelot Found by Bors.

Lancelot lies near death for a month but eventually begins to recover. The maiden whose sleeve he wore asks him for his love, but he explains that his heart belongs to another. She declares that her unrequited love will kill her.

Distraught that he cannot attend the tournament at Taneburgh, where the queen will be, Lancelot falls ill anew and nearly dies. He commissions a squire to go to Taneburgh and greet Gawain and the queen for him. The squire informs Gawain that Lancelot is seriously wounded.

Sorry not to see Lancelot at this tournament, the king announces another one, at Camelot, for the following month. Gawain tells Guenevere that Lancelot's absence was due to his injury, but, thinking her lover is staying away to remain with the maiden whose champion he had been, she hates him.

Gawain, Bors, and the latter's companions seek Lancelot and find him largely recovered. Bors reveals that it was he who wounded Lancelot, but he conceals from the latter all news of the queen's jealousy and ire.

5.   Arthur's Discovery of Paintings Depicting Lancelot's Love for the Queen.

Returning from Taneburgh, Arthur takes lodging at the castle of his sister Morgan. He goes to sleep in the room in which Lancelot had once been imprisoned and where he had painted on the walls images of his love with the queen. The following morning, Arthur notices the paintings. At his urging, Morgan, jealous that Lancelot loves the queen, reveals the truth about the adulterous relationship and the circumstances of Lancelot's stay there. Arthur and Mordred discuss ways to catch the lovers in the act.

6.   Lancelot Rebuffed by Guenevere; Bors's Reflections on the Perfidy of Women.

Once Lancelot is well enough to leave, the maiden whose champion he was comes to speak with him. She tells him that she will soon die of unrequited love. She goes to bed to await her death.

Lancelot and his retinue leave and travel to Camelot. Guenevere refuses to receive Lancelot. That night Bors asks her for an explanation, and she replies that she hates Lancelot. Bors defends Lancelot and then launches into a diatribe against female perfidy, citing women who have been the ruin of men such as David, Solomon, Samson, Hector, Achilles, and Tristan.

Lancelot and Bors leave court, and the latter explains that the queen is angry because Lancelot championed another woman. On the advice of Bors, Lancelot decides to stay away from court and to frequent tourneys until such time as the queen seeks him. Then he agrees to attend the Camelot tournament if possible, saying that he will bear white armor without any emblem.

7.   A Knight Poisoned by the Queen; Lancelot Wounded by a Hunter.

Returning to court and learning that Lancelot departed quickly, Arthur concludes that his knight was innocent of any wrongdoing with the queen.

At dinner, a knight named Avarlan tries to poison Gawain, whom he hates, by giving poisoned fruit to the queen, who he thought would give it to Gawain. Instead, she gives it to Gaheris of Carahew, who eats it and dies.

Returning for the Camelot tournament, Lancelot sends a squire to bring him plain white armor. While waiting, Lancelot is hit in the thigh by an arrow shot at a stag. In pain, he returns to the hermitage where he has been staying, and he reluctantly concludes that he cannot attend the tournament.

8.   The Queen Accused of Murder; The Body of the Maiden of Escalot Discovered at Camelot.

Bors proves himself the best knight at the Camelot tournament. He refuses to keep company with Arthur, because Lancelot is not there. Bors and Hector (and then Gawain and Arthur) speculate that Lancelot is ill or wounded.

Mador of the Gate arrives at court and finds his brother's tomb. He asks for the right to seek justice by doing battle with the queen's champion. Distressed, the king agrees. Mador publicly accuses Guenevere, and she is given forty days to find a defender.

The next day, a boat reaches Camelot. Gawain and Arthur find on the boat the body of the Maiden of Escalot and a letter stating that she died because of her unrequited love for Lancelot. Guenevere learns of the letter and is more distraught than before, because she falsely suspected Lancelot and because she now fears that he will not save her from death.

9.   Lancelot's Plans to Defend the Queen.

Lancelot learns of the accusations against the queen and determines to defend her. He meets Hector, who has the same plan, and they start for Camelot together. On the way, they meet Bors. Lancelot asserts his intention to defend Guenevere but laments that he will be fighting on the side of wrong. He directs Bors and Hector to proceed to Camelot and ask the queen if she will be reconciled with Lancelot.

10.   Lancelot Comes to Court and Defeats Mador.

At Camelot, Bors feigns ignorance of the accusation against the queen, and she explains it to him. He accuses her of betraying Lancelot and says that he has not seen him.

Arthur asks Gawain to defend the queen, but Gawain refuses to do anything contrary to his honor. The queen asks Hector and Bors for assistance, and the latter agrees to defend her if she does not find a better champion. The following day, both Mador and Lancelot (the latter bearing unfamiliar arms) come to court, and after the accusation is repeated, the two knights engage in battle. Lancelot is victorious. Arthur, Gawain, and others rejoice when they learn that the unknown knight is Lancelot; Guenevere is declared innocent of the charge against her.

11. Entrapment of Lancelot and the Queen by Agravain.

Reconciled, Lancelot and Guenevere conduct themselves indiscreetly; as a result, Gawain and his brothers are aware of their love. One day, Arthur hears the brothers talking and insists on knowing the subject of their conversation. Threatened by Arthur, Agravain informs him of the adultery. Arthur orders them to catch the lovers in the act.

At Agravain's suggestion, Arthur invites his knights to go hunting with him, but he refuses to allow Lancelot to go along. Bors explains to Lancelot that Arthur has been told about him and the queen. Nonetheless, as soon as the hunting party leaves, the queen sends for Lancelot. Unable to dissuade him from meeting the queen, Bors tells him of a secret path to her chambers.

Yet Agravain has set spies everywhere and knows that Lancelot is with the queen. He orders his men to break down the door; before they do, Lancelot opens it and kills the first man (Tanaguin) to enter. He then escapes and later rejoins Bors and Hector. Bors predicts war with Arthur. The three of them agree that, if the queen is sentenced to death, they will rescue her. Lancelot sends a squire to Camelot to await news of her fate.

12. The Queen Condemned to Death but Rescued by Lancelot.

Arthur sends knights to arrest Lancelot, but he cannot be found. The queen is condemned to death. Agravain, Gaheriet, and their men are ordered to watch for Lancelot at the field where she is to be put to death. Lancelot is lying in wait and, with his men, attacks Arthur's soldiers; he kills Agravain and Gaheriet, and Bors kills Guerrehet. Of eighty knights, only Mordred and two other opponents of Lancelot survive. Lancelot takes the queen into the forest. Bors informs Lancelot that the latter killed Gaheriet, and Lancelot predicts a great war with Arthur's forces.

It is decided that, for her safety, they will take the queen to the castle of Joyous Guard. Arriving there, they are received with great joy.

13. Grief for Gawain's Brothers; Arthur's Declaration of War on Lancelot.

Arthur orders that no one be allowed to leave the country. Arriving at the battlefield, he finds the bodies of Agravain, Guerrehet, and Gaheriet. Gawain soon comes there and, seeing the bodies, grieves bitterly. The three brothers are buried. The king asks advice concerning the way to avenge their deaths. Several men advise against undertaking a war against Lancelot, but when Arthur learns from Mador that Lancelot and Guenevere are at Joyous Guard, he resolves to fight. He requires that all his men swear to follow him. News of his plan reaches Joyous Guard, and Lancelot orders all his barons to stock their castles and prepare for war.

14. Battle Between Arthur's Forces and Lancelot's.

Arthur selects new members of the Round Table. The next day, he sets out for Joyous Guard with one thousand men. They camp at some distance from the castle.

Lancelot's forces have sent knights to wait in the forest, so that they are prepared to attack on two fronts, from the woods and from the castle. Lancelot sends a messenger to Arthur to try to preserve the peace. Arthur rejects the offer.

The war begins but is indecisive on the first day. The following day, Lancelot's forces begin to get the upper hand. Gawain, Bors, and many others are wounded. Eventually, Arthur himself attacks Lancelot, but the latter, recognizing the king, refuses to fight. Hector attacks Arthur, but when he is in a position to kill the king, Lancelot intervenes to save Arthur and to help him remount. Arthur later expresses his admiration for Lancelot. However, the war continues unabated for two months and more.

15.   The Pope's Intervention; Lancelot's Decision to Leave Logres.

The pope, learning that Arthur had threatened the queen's life, announces that the king's lands will be placed under interdict unless he takes her back. Guenevere is informed of the pope's decision and urged to return to Arthur. Lancelot determines to return her to her husband, and she agrees on the condition that Arthur will guarantee Lancelot's safety. Arthur agrees.

The next day, Lancelot delivers her to Arthur. Gawain says that the king wants Lancelot to leave the land; he also threatens Lancelot with war, and Arthur must intervene to prevent an immediate fight between the two knights. After speaking of the kindnesses he has done for Gawain in the past, Lancelot agrees to leave.

16.   Lancelot's Departure from Logres; Arthur's Attack on Lancelot.

Lancelot leaves Joyous Guard and, with his company, makes his way to the sea. He boards a ship and, looking back, speaks of the glory of Logres and of his happiness there. Then they return to his land. Lancelot invests Bors with Benoic and Lionel with Gaunes. The same day, he hears that Arthur, at Gawain's urging, intends to march against him at winter's end.

When Arthur is ready to set out, he leaves the queen in Mordred's keeping, and she is angry about that because she expects the worst. With forty thousand men, Arthur travels to Benoic and, at Gawain's suggestion, decides to attack the city of Gaunes. An old woman meets the army, berates Arthur and Gawain, and predicts that the latter will never return safely to Logres.

Lancelot decides to attack Arthur's army. In the first battle, Arthur's men would have been defeated except for the king's valor. The armies fight four battles in a week's time; many men are lost on both sides, but Arthur loses more.

17.   Mordred's Plan; The Queen's Retreat to a Tower.

Mordred undertakes to win the allegiance of the barons of the land. He also falls in love with Guenevere. Then he writes a letter, with a counterfeit seal identical to Arthur's, saying that he has been mortally wounded and his army destroyed; it asks that Mordred be accepted as king of Logres and that the queen be married to him. The barons agree, but Guenevere asks for time to consider the marriage. The delay gives her the opportunity to take refuge in a tower. Mordred besieges it and suffers heavy losses.

Eventually the queen sends a servant to try to learn whether Arthur is really dead. If he is alive, the man is to ask him to come to the queen's aid; if he is dead, the servant must find Lancelot and ask instead for his assistance. It is learned that the king is alive and has besieged Gaunes.

18. Lancelot's Decision to Meet Gawain in Battle.

Gawain sends a messenger to Lancelot to suggest that the two meet in single combat. With the challenge accepted (on the condition that if Lancelot wins, Arthur will return to his own land), Gawain asks Arthur's permission to accept the challenge. Arthur is displeased; he and Gawain ask Lancelot to come and speak with them. When they meet, Lancelot, denying that he killed Gaheriet intentionally, offers to go into exile for ten years and to become thereafter Arthur's and Gawain's companion. The king is moved, but Gawain rejects the offer, and his companions lament the tragedy that may now occur.

19. The Battle Between Lancelot and Gawain; Explanation of Gawain's Strength.

Lancelot and Gawain do battle. The combat is even at first, but Gawain's strength increases near noon, and that phenomenon is explained. After noon, his power decreases again, and Lancelot has the upper hand. The latter offers to stop the battle, and Gawain haughtily refuses. Thereupon, Lancelot asks Arthur's permission to leave the battlefield without being thought a coward. The king agrees, and Lancelot leaves to have his wounds tended in the city.

20. Arthur's Battle Against the Romans.

A physician announces that all of Gawain's wounds can be healed except a serious head injury. Arthur decides to return to Gaul and stay until he knows whether Gawain will survive. Gawain is transported in a litter and soon appears to be on the way to recovery.

A messenger announces that the Romans have invaded, have destroyed Burgundy, and will soon attack Arthur. The king inquires after Gawain's health, and Gawain says that he will be able to bear arms. The Roman emperor insists that the land is not Arthur's and that the Romans have come to avenge the death of Frollo. The battle begins, and Gawain is seriously injured, his head wound reopened. The emperor kills Kay and is killed by Arthur. The Romans are routed, and Arthur sends the emperor's body back to Rome.

21. Arthur's March on Mordred; The Queen's Flight to a Convent.

The queen's messenger informs Arthur of Mordred's treason, and the king swears to avenge it; in so doing, he reveals for the first time that Mordred is his son. Arthur's army sets out the following day for Logres, transporting Gawain in a litter. The latter announces that he is nearing death and expresses regret for his treatment of Lancelot.

Mordred pursues the siege of the tower and continues to use his generosity to win the allegiance of nobles. He learns that Arthur has landed in the country, and his advisors urge him to confront the king. He sets out with his army.

Learning that Arthur has come, the queen fears for him but also fears that she will be killed either by Mordred or by Arthur (the latter because he may believe she betrayed him with Mordred). She flees from the tower and takes refuge in a convent. If Mordred should defeat Arthur, she will join the order.

22.   Deaths of Gawain and of the Lady of Beloe.

Arthur and his army arrive at Dover. Gawain dies from the wound inflicted by Lancelot. His body is taken back to Camelot to be buried beside his brothers. Those transporting the body stop at the castle of Beloe. The lady of the castle laments Gawain's death and declares her love for him; her husband, hearing these words, kills her and is then killed by Arthur's knights, who then take the woman's body to Camelot along with Gawain's.

23.   The Battle of Salisbury Plain.

Arthur dreams that Gawain comes to him to warn him not to fight Mordred. The following night, he dreams that he is on the Wheel of Fortune and is warned of impending disaster. The next day the archbishop warns him again, but in vain: Arthur rides on to Salisbury Plain, where he sees an inscription that announces the tragedy to come.

A great and terrible battle takes place between Arthur's forces and Mordred's, and many valiant men die on both sides. When most are dead, Arthur strikes Mordred a mortal blow, but the latter, before dying, wounds his father. By the end of the day, only Arthur, Lucan, and Girflet remain.

24.   The Death of King Arthur.

Arthur, Lucan, and Girflet ride to the Black Chapel, where the king spends the night in prayer. The next morning, Lucan speaks to Arthur, who in his grief embraces and crushes him.

Arthur and Girflet ride to the shore, and the king orders his companion to throw Excalibur into the water. Twice Girflet cannot bring himself to do so; the third time, he follows Arthur's order, and a hand emerges from the water to take the sword. Arthur then orders Girflet to leave. When the latter is some distance away, he looks back and sees a ship arrive. Morgan and other ladies take Arthur aboard the ship, which then departs and disappears from view.

After several days, Girflet returns to the Black Chapel, where he finds tombs bearing the names of Lucan and Arthur. He is informed that some ladies brought Arthur's body to the chapel. Girflet dies eighteen days after Arthur.

25. Battle with Mordred's Sons; Deaths of the Queen and of Lancelot.

Mordred's sons begin to overrun the land, and the queen takes the habit of a nun. Hearing of Arthur's death, Lancelot and his men decide to ride against Mordred's sons. Guenevere dies, and news of her death reaches Lancelot on the day when the battle is to take place. Nevertheless, Lancelot's forces are victorious, but his cousin Lionel is killed.

Lancelot wanders until he comes to a hermitage, where the archbishop of Canterbury and Blioberis took refuge after the battle of Salisbury Plain. Lancelot decides to remain there with them.

After the same battle, Bors returns to his country, and Hector wanders until he finds the hermitage where Lancelot is staying. He remains there for four years and then dies. Soon Lancelot realizes that he too is about to die, and he asks that his body be taken to Joyous Guard after his death. The archbishop and Blioberis follow his instructions, and Bors arrives at Joyous Guard at the same time as they. Lancelot's body is placed in the tomb that holds the body of his friend Galehaut.

Bors, Blioberis, and the archbishop remain together until death.

Volume VIII

The Post-Vulgate, part I. The Merlin Continuation

1. The Conception of Mordred; The Bizarre Beast.

Soon after his coronation, Arthur convenes a great court at Carduel. The wife of King Lot of Orkney attends; Arthur falls in love with her, not knowing that she is his sister. He keeps her at court for two months and lies with her; Mordred is conceived. Later, Arthur has a dream in which a dragon destroys the kingdom of Logres and Arthur's army. Arthur kills the dragon but is mortally wounded in the struggle.

During a hunt, Arthur hears and sees a beast that makes the sound of thirty barking hounds. Soon a knight appears and explains his quest for the beast. Arthur wants to take up the quest himself, and the two promise to fight one day to see who is the better knight.

2. Merlin Demonstrates Remarkable Knowledge and Eventually Reveals His Identity to Arthur.

Merlin, disguised as a child, comes to tell Arthur that his dream will come true; he also reproaches Arthur for the incest he committed with Lot's wife. Arthur promises the child anything he might want, provided he can tell who the king's parents were. Merlin reveals that his parents were Uther Pendragon and Igerne.

Merlin leaves but then returns as a very old man. He repeats that Arthur's dream will come true. Then Arthur asks him where and when Mordred will be born, so that the child maybe killed. Merlin reveals the time and place. Arthur learns that the beast is an adventure of the Grail and that the knight is the father of Perceval the Welshman, who will kill the beast. Merlin then explains that Uther lay with Igerne by deception when she was married to another man. The magician instructs the king to hold court and send for Igerne and her daughter Morgan.

3. Court at Carduel; The Revelation of Arthur's Parentage.

Igerne, fearing that Arthur is plotting to take away her land, asks Lot for protection. Merlin sends for Urfin and Ector, who approve of his plan to reveal Arthur's parentage to all the barons of the kingdom. Upon Igerne's arrival, Arthur greets her with kindness. Morgan arrives with her.

At dinner, Urfin loudly reproaches Arthur for having seated a false woman. Arthur pretends to be angry and demands that Urfin name the woman. Urfin accuses Igerne of murder and treason. Stunned, Igerne demands that he fight to prove his case. Urfin offers his gage and accuses Igerne of murdering the first child she had with Uther. Arthur feigns surprise. Igerne shifts the blame to Merlin, who says that he gave the child to Ector; the latter's neighbor, testifies that he raised Arthur. The assembled barons recognize Arthur as the rightful heir to Uther's kingdom.

4. The First Adventure; Pellinor and Girflet.

A squire arrives, bearing on his horse a mortally wounded knight. The squire seeks redress for the wrong done his lord. Arthur broods without responding, and Merlin reproaches him for this inadequate response to his first adventure. The squire informs them where the offending knight is. Girflet asks that Arthur make him a knight so that he may undertake this adventure. Arthur reluctantly agrees. The wounded knight dies.

Merlin warns Arthur not to send Girflet, for he will have to fight an experienced knight, the one who chases the Bizarre Beast. Merlin tells Arthur not to worry about his own death, for he will die with honor, whereas Merlin will die shamefully, buried alive. Arthur agrees to make Girflet promise to return after his joust. A message from Rome informs them that the emperor demands truage from Arthur, and they warn of dire consequences if Arthur fails to comply. Arthur responds with defiance.

Girflet challenges the knight at the edge of the forest. The two joust, and Giflet is speared through. Nonetheless, he returns as promised.

5. Arthur Meets Pellinor and Learns about Excalibur.

Bloodied, Girflet returns from his joust and expresses admiration for the knight who has wounded him. Arthur sneaks out of the castle to meet the knight. He first encounters Merlin, who is being pursued by three peasants. Arthur frightens off the peasants, and Merlin explains that they were enraged when he predicted their imminent deaths. He also warns the king not to fight the knight. Arthur finds the knight, and they joust. In two encounters, both knights shatter their lances. On the third joust, Arthur's horse falls, then runs off. Arthur insists on a sword fight, and the knight dismounts to do battle. Arthur's opponent regains the advantage and is about to behead the king when Merlin appears and casts a spell. The knight falls asleep. Then Merlin tells Arthur of a good sword in a lake where fairies live. Arthur demands to be taken there.

6. Arthur Receives the Sword Excalibur.

Merlin and Arthur go to a deep lake by the sea. An arm dressed in white silk rises out of the lake, sword in hand. A maiden approaches them on horseback and offers to bring Arthur the sword if he promises to give her the first gift she asks of him.

Arthur agrees. Merlin tells him that the value of the scabbard is ten times that of the sword, for it will protect him from mortal wounds.

Arthur asks how the young lady walked over the lake; Merlin explains that the water is an illusion. Everyone at Carduel is happy to see Arthur's safe return. King Urien asks Arthur's permission to marry Morgan. On their wedding night, Urien and Morgan conceive Yvain.

Arthur leaves for Carlion, where a knight brings him a message from King Rion of North Wales. Rion demands that Arthur pay him homage and forfeit his beard. Arthur responds defiantly.

7.   Arthur Sets the Children of Logres Adrift at Sea.

To avoid the destruction of Logres, Arthur has all newborn infants imprisoned. Lot and his wife agree to send their child, Mordred, to Arthur. The ship on which Mordred travels is caught in a storm and destroyed. All on board perish, except Mordred. A fisherman and his wife take the baby to Nabur the Unruly, who raises him with his own son, Sagremor. A note in Mordred's cradle tells Nabur the foundling's name.

Arthur wants to have all the children killed, but he has a dream in which a man warns him that God would avenge such an evil deed. The man suggests that Arthur instead set the children adrift on a ship. Arthur complies; the ship arrives at Amalvi, where King Orians and his entourage discover the children. They decide to hide them on an island in the Castle of Boys. The barons in Logres consult Merlin, who explains Arthur's actions and assures them that the children are safe.

8.   Balin Claims an Ill-Fated Sword.

A wounded knight arrives to tell Arthur that Rion is laying waste his kingdom, and the king summons all his barons. A maiden arrives and asks for Arthur's help: she wears a sword that she cannot draw; only the best knight in the kingdom can relieve her of the burden. Arthur and all his barons try but fail to remove the sword. Then a poor knight from Northumberland frees the sword and decides to keep it. The maiden protests; she warns that the first one he kills with the sword will be the one he loves most, and that he and another will die from it.

The lady who gave Excalibur to Arthur arrives to claim her gift: the head of the maiden or of the knight who freed the sword. The knight beheads the lady, then plans to bring Arthur the head of Rion.

Merlin explains that the maiden sought vengeance on her brother, who killed her lover. The Lady of Avalon told her that whoever freed the sword would avenge her, but this man would also kill the two best knights in Logres. Merlin asks that Arthur forgive Balin the Wild, who beheaded the lady. Merlin assures Arthur that he will triumph over Rion.

9.   The Tragic Tale of Launceor and Lione; Merlin Prophesies the Dolorous Stroke.

Launceor, under orders from Arthur, challenges Balin and is run through. A maiden arrives; seeing her lover dead, she commits suicide with his sword. Balin sees his brother, Balan, and explains his adventures at Arthur's court. A dwarf tells Balin that harm will come to him because he has killed the son of a king. King Mark happens by on his way to Arthur's court. On hearing the story of Launceor and Lione, Mark sends for a rich tombstone to be put on their grave. Merlin writes on the tombstone that Lancelot and Tristan will meet in battle but neither will die; Balin learns that he will deliver the Dolorous Stroke from which three kingdoms will suffer. Merlin offers to help Blaise finish his book.

10. Balin and Balan Defeat King Rion.

Mark asks Balin's name, and Balan identifies him as the Knight with Two Swords. Merlin tells Balin and Balan how they may intercept Rion. He guides them to a mountain pass, where Balin unhorses Rion and the brothers overcome the king's escort. Wounded, Rion begs for mercy. Merlin instructs the brothers to take their prisoners to Tarabel, where Arthur waits to fight Rion's army. Merlin arrives first and tells Arthur the good news.

11. Arthur Receives Rion Prisoner, Learns of Lot's Enmity.

The prisoners arrive at Tarabel, and Rion puts himself at Arthur's mercy. Merlin tells Arthur that the knight who bested Rion is the one who beheaded the maiden but that this knight will not return to his court. He tells Arthur that Rion's brother Nero will lead his army against Arthur. Merlin also warns Arthur that Lot, who blames Arthur for the murder of his son, intends to fight the king. The magician reassures Arthur and urges him to confess his sins to God.

12. The Battle with King Rion's Brother Nero.

Arthur readies his army for battle. A boy brings word of the impending battle to Balin and Balan. They plan to join the battle, concentrating their efforts on Nero himself. While preparing his army for battle, Nero conceals Rion's absence. Though Arthur's men are outnumbered, the battle turns in their favor. Arthur, with Excalibur, distinguishes himself in battle, as do others, but all marvel at Balin's prowess in particular.

13. The Death of King Lot.

Merlin reproaches Lot for his intention to commit treason; he also says that Mordred is alive, but Lot refuses to believe it. Undeterred by the prediction of the harm that will come to him and to his men, Lot spoils for a fight, but Merlin slows his advance by enchantment. Although Lot learns of Rion's defeat, he is convinced that he has no choice but to attack Arthur. A battle ensues, and the men of Orkney soon go down to defeat.

14. The Aftermath of Battle; Merlin Predicts the Beginning of the Grail Quest.

Arthur has the dead knights and twelve kings buried with great honor. Gawain determines to take revenge on Pellinor, his father's killer. Arthur has statues made of the dead kings and of himself. Each of the kings holds a candle, and

Arthur's likeness holds a sword. Merlin enchants the candles so that they will not be extinguished until the day he dies; he predicts that on that day the Knight with Two Swords will strike the Dolorous Blow and initiate the adventures of the Holy Grail; for twenty-two years thereafter, storms and troubles will plague Great Britain. Merlin warns Arthur to guard his scabbard well. Rion does homage to Arthur. Morgan determines to learn enchantments from Merlin.

15. Merlin's Infatuation; Morgan's Counterfeit Scabbard.

Merlin, in love with Morgan, agrees to teach her his enchantments. Their union produces an infant named Yvain. Once she learns enough of Merlin's necromancy, she drives him away, threatening him with torture and death if he approaches her.

Arthur gives Morgan his sword and scabbard for safekeeping. When she tells her lover of the protective quality of the scabbard, he asks for it. She has a counterfeit made, but then confuses the counterfeit with the real, and the knight carries away the former. He believes himself protected from serious harm, but, when fighting another knight, he is badly wounded. Thinking that Morgan has intentionally deceived him, he seeks revenge. He tells Arthur that Morgan wants him dead; she gave the knight the scabbard to ensure Arthur's assassination. Morgan begs Merlin to lie for her, and he tells Arthur that the knight stole the scabbard from Morgan. Arthur kills the knight and returns the false scabbard to Morgan, telling her to guard it more carefully.

Merlin tells Urien's cousin, Bademagu, that his friend Gawain will kill him. Merlin also tells Sagremor's father that his adopted son will kill him and Sagremor, and on that day will occur the battle of Salisbury Plain, which will destroy the kingdom of Logres.

16. Balin's First Unknown Knight.

Arthur sends the Knight with Two Swords after a knight who has refused to explain why he is sad. Balin finds the knight talking to a maiden. The knight agrees to return to Arthur when Balin offers to continue his quest. As they approach Arthur, the knight is struck by a lance. Before dying, he instructs Balin to return to the maiden. Merlin tells Arthur that the adventures are only beginning and that when he learns the dead knight's name, great joy will come to his court.

17. Balin Starts His Quest; The Second Unknown Knight.

A knight sees Balin lamenting and asks him the source of his sorrows. When Balin refuses to answer, the knight threatens him. Balin knocks him off his horse. The knight then joins Balin in his quest. Merlin tells Balin that the one he seeks is Garlon, brother of Pellehan; he also warns Balin to abandon the quest, for, if he continues, he will strike a blow that will bring great sorrow. Balin rejects Merlin's advice. His companion is killed by a lance through the body. When he is buried, they see writing on the knight's headstone predicting that Gawain will kill Pellinor. A squire tells them that Merlin has written these words. Balin meets the maiden, and they ride together to a castle, where the portcullis falls behind Balin, trapping him inside.

18.   The Castle of the Basin of Blood.

Balin sees two knights threatening the maiden; they make her promise to follow the custom of the castle. She consents, and is told that she must fill a large silver basin with her blood, which the lady of the castle needs to fight her leprosy. Balin is eager to pursue the one who killed the knights under his protection, but he agrees to stay until the maiden is ready to leave. The next day, Balin and the maiden leave. The lady of the castle has not been cured and will not be until she receives blood from Perceval's sister.

19.   The Knight with Two Swords and the Father of a Wounded Man Go to Pellehan's Court to Seek Vengeance.

Balin and the maiden lodge with a valiant vavasor. Their host's son has been wounded by the unseen knight. Balin tells the vavasor that this knight, Garlon, can conceal himself only when riding. The vavasor offers to help Balin find Garlon at Pellehan's court at the castle of the Perilous Palace; only Garlon's blood can heal the wounds of the vavasor's son. The three arrive at the castle, but the vavasor cannot enter, for each knight must be accompanied by a woman.

20.   The Dolorous Stroke.

At Pellehan's feast, Balin learns which knight is Garlon. Deep in thought, Balin neglects his food, and Garlon slaps him; Balin splits Garlon's head with his sword. Pellehan, demanding that he be allowed to avenge his brother's murder, breaks Balin's sword. Balin runs through the palace looking for a weapon. He enters a room and sees a lance upright in a vessel of silver and gold. A voice warns him not to touch the lance, but he seizes it and thrusts it through Pellehan's thighs. The palace begins to shake and crumble. A voice announces that the adventures of the Kingdom of Adventures have begun; because unworthy hands have touched the Holy Lance, many innocent people will suffer.

   Hundreds of people in the palace are wounded or killed. Merlin sends a monk into the room of the Holy Grail to retrieve Pellehan and Balin; he leads Balin out of the castle. Balin sees that the maiden and the host have been killed and that the whole kingdom of Listinois has been laid waste.

21.   Balin's Third Unknown Knight and His Lady.

Balin comes upon a knight lamenting his lady's failure to keep their rendezvous. Intervening to prevent the knight's suicide, he promises not to sleep until he has found the knight's lady. The latter leads Balin to the fortress where the lady lives and shows Balin the way in. Balin finds the lady sleeping with a hideous knight. The knight who loves her sees the sleeping couple and collapses. When he awakens, he kills the couple, then himself. Balin leaves.

22.   Balin is Forced to Meet a Stranger in Battle.

Coming upon a well-protected castle, Balin sees a stone cross that warns knights errant not to approach the castle. Balin refuses to turn back. Joyous maidens and knights welcome him to the castle. Balin learns that, according to custom, he must fight with the knight of the island tower. The seneschal gives Balin a new shield. A maiden tells Balin that the change of shields will bring his death and that God is sending him this misfortune in retribution for his deeds at Pellehan's castle.

23.   Balin and Balan Kill Each Other; Merlin Sets the Sword in the Stone.

The knight who emerges from the tower is so elegant that he reminds Balin of his brother. The battle is long and bloody, and finally both of the knights proclaim that they are killed but not defeated. When Balan identifies himself, Balin is aghast at having fought his brother. He asks the lady of the tower to have him and his brother buried together.

Merlin indicates on their tomb that it contains Balin, who struck the Dolorous Stroke. Then Merlin enchants a bed, so that all who sleep on it will lose their memory. In addition, he replaces the pommel on Balin's sword: no one will be able to grip the sword until Lancelot tries, and with that very sword he will kill Gawain. Merlin fixes the sword into a great stone of marble, which he casts adrift on the sea; then he returns to Arthur, who has just knighted Bademagu.

24.   Arthur Betrothed to Guenevere; The Round Table Transferred to Arthur's Court.

Arthur asks for advice on choosing a wife. He loves Guenevere, daughter of King Leodegan of Carmelide. Merlin tells Arthur that her beauty could be a hindrance but that one day it will help him. Leodegan happily agrees to the marriage. He sends Arthur the Round Table and its one hundred knights, and the king asks Merlin to choose knights to fill the table's remaining places. Merlin chooses forty-eight knights. He tells Arthur that the Perilous Seat will be taken by a knight who is not yet two years old. The archbishop of Canterbury blesses the seats of the table, and the names of the knights miraculously appear on the seats. Arthur swears to maintain the knights in great honor.

25.   Arthur's Marriage; The Knighting of Gawain and Tor; Pellinor Completes the Round Table.

Arthur agrees to grant Gawain a favor; Gawain asks that Arthur make him a knight on the day the king marries Guenevere. A peasant then requests that Arthur knight his son, Tor. Arthur is married, and Tor and Gawain become knights. Merlin tries to make the peasant confess that Tor is not his son, for Tor's true father is a king. Tor asks Merlin to desist. Pellinor arrives, and Merlin shows him to the last place (except the Perilous Seat) at the Round Table. Gawain and Gahariet discuss ways to take vengeance on Pellinor.

26.   The Three Adventures Assigned to the Three New Knights.

Merlin announces the coming of three great adventures. All assembled see a white stag bounding through the garden. Close behind the stag are a brachet, a maiden on horseback, and thirty dogs. As the stag enters the great hall, it is bitten by

the brachet, which is then seized and taken away by a knight. The maiden asks
Arthur for redress, and Merlin assures her that she will lose nothing. Merlin sends
Gawain to find the stag and dispatches Tor to catch the knight with the brachet. A
mounted knight enters the hall and kidnaps the maiden. Merlin assigns her rescue
to Pellinor.

27.   Gawain and the Stag.

Gawain and Gaheriet see the stag enter a fortress. The dogs kill the stag, and a knight
begins killing the dogs. Gawain does battle with him until the knight's mistress
puts herself between the two. Gawain cuts off her head and sends the surviving
knight to Camelot. Four knights attack Gawain; an archer shoots a poisoned arrow
into his arm, and Gaheriet kills the archer. Gawain loses the struggle, but a maiden
prevents the four from killing him. Gawain and Gaheriet are imprisoned, but the
lady of the palace sets them free. She forces Gawain to return to Camelot with the
dead maiden's head around his neck and to tell the truth of his adventures.

   When Gawain returns, Merlin has Arthur make a custom of having knights
recount all their adventures. The ladies of the court make Gawain swear that he
will harm no more maidens and will help those in distress, and Merlin adds that
Gawain must give mercy to those who ask for it.

28.   Tor Does Battle to Regain the Brachet; Merlin Reveals to Arthur That Tor Is
Pellinor's Son.

A dwarf provokes Tor into fighting two knights. He defeats both of them, then
accepts the dwarf as his squire. The dwarf leads Tor to the knight who stole the
brachet. Tor finds a maiden asleep with the brachet; when he takes the dog, the
maiden protests, and her knight charges Tor. Victorious, Tor offers mercy, but the
knight refuses. Yet when a maiden approaches and asks for the knight's head, he
pleads for mercy. The maiden refuses, for he killed her brother, and so Tor obliges
her. Tor then returns to Camelot, where he swears to tell the whole truth. Merlin
reveals that Tor is Pellinor's son.

29.   Pellinor Rescues the Maiden and Returns to Court, Bearing the Head of
Another Maiden.

A maiden, with her wounded lover, asks Pellinor for assistance and then reproaches
him for not helping her. When her lover dies, she kills herself.

   The knight who abducted the maiden is fighting with her first cousin over her.
Pellinor asks to take the maiden back to Camelot. The knights refuse and decide
to attack Pellinor together. When Pellinor kills one of the knights, the other grants
Pellinor's request.

   On the return to Camelot, the woman and Pellinor are resting when they overhear
two knights talking about plans to have Arthur poisoned. Resuming their journey,
she and Pellinor come upon the woman who asked Pellinor for help: wild beasts
have eaten her body. Pellinor has the lover buried and carries the maiden's head
to Camelot, where he tells of his adventure. When Pellinor asks about the identity
of the dead maiden, Merlin reminds him that a fool once told him that the son of

a king who was killed would remove his crown, and that lions would eat his flesh the year he became another man's vassal. Merlin also reminds him that the dead maiden prayed that he would suffer the same fate as she.

30.   Tor Revealed as Pellinor's Son; Merlin Predicts Details of Pellinor's Death.

Merlin has Tor's mother summoned and asks her to tell who begat Tor. She says that she was raped by a knight whom she cannot identify, but Merlin adds details and identifies Pellinor as Tor's father.

   The huntress maiden, Ninianne, thanks Arthur for righting the wrongs done her, and Arthur and Guenevere convince her to stay at Camelot. Merlin tells Arthur that the dead maiden was Pellinor's daughter and the dead knight her first cousin. He also tells Arthur how, after twelve years, Pellinor will die when Tor ignores his cries for help. Arthur agrees to keep the prediction a secret; he also learns that his own son Mordred is not dead.

31.   Merlin, Infatuated with Ninianne, Goes with Her to Brittany, Where He Predicts Greatness for Lancelot and Failure for Claudas.

Blaise records the adventures that Merlin recounts to him. Having fallen in love with Ninianne, Merlin promises to teach her magic and pledges not to use this magic against her. When her father, the king of Northumberland, asks Arthur to send her home, Merlin accompanies her to Brittany, where they cross the land of King Ban of Benoic. Ban's wife, Elaine, shows them her infant son, Lancelot. Merlin predicts that Lancelot will be the greatest knight ever, and he further predicts the defeat of Ban's enemy, Claudas.

32.   The Lake of Diana; Ninianne Increasingly Ensnares Merlin.

Merlin shows Ninianne the Lake of Diana and the tomb of Faunus. He tells Ninianne the story of Faunus, in love with Diana. She fell in love with Felix and therefore killed Faunus; Felix then cut off her head and threw her body in the lake. Merlin agrees to help Ninianne build a house by the lake; once the house is finished, Merlin conceals it through magic, so that it appears to be part of the lake.

   Ninianne hates Merlin but uses enchantments to keep him from knowing her thoughts. She urges him to return to Britain, and although he fears that someone will kill him there, Ninianne convinces him to return to Camelot to save Arthur from Morgan's plot to switch his sword and scabbard.

33.   Merlin and Ninianne Return to Great Britain; Merlin Breaks an Enchantment.

Merlin, Ninianne, and their escort pass through the Perilous Forest. They come upon a plain, where they find two thrones; a man playing a harp sits on each throne. Merlin tells the others that the music of these harps casts a spell that saps listeners' strength. He blocks his ears, but those who are with him fall to the ground. Casting a spell on the harpists, he throws them into ditches, which he fills with sulfur and sets on fire. Merlin revives his companions and tells them that the fires will last as long as Arthur reigns.

34. The Invasion of the Five Kings; New Knights Chosen for the Round Table.

Kings of Denmark, Ireland, the Valley, Sorelois, and Far Isle have invaded Arthur's land. When they attack, they take Arthur's army by surprise. Arthur and Guenevere are advised to seek refuge on the other side of the River Humber. Kay, Girflet, Gawain, and Arthur stay to joust, and they kill the five kings. Guenevere shows them a ford, but the enemy army charges into deep water, and many drown. Arthur names the crossing the Queen's Ford. Arthur, Girflet, Gawain, and Kay prepare to attack, but the knights of Logres arrive first and slay the enemy. Arthur has an abbey built and names it Good Adventure.

When Arthur and his men return to Camelot, he asks Pellinor to name eight knights to the Round Table to replace those who were killed. Pellinor names Gawain, Girflet, Kay, Tor, Urien, Lach, Hervieu of Rivel, and Galligar the Red.

35. Bademagu's Pique; His Departure from Court and His Oath.

Bademagu is jealous and angry when he sees Tor take a seat at the Round Table. He leaves court, accompanied by a squire, and he swears that he will not return to Camelot until he has defeated a knight of the Round Table and performed other feats that will prove his worth to everyone. Through his prowess, he eventually becomes King of Gorre.

36. Morgan and the Counterfeit Sword; Arthur Against Accalon.

Arthur and Pellinor regret Bademagu's departure. During a hunt for a stag, Arthur, Urien, and Accalon (Morgan's lover) come to a river, where they find the stag, as Urien predicted. A ship covered in red silk approaches; twelve maidens invite Arthur, Urien, and Accalon to be their guests for the night. The next morning, Urien finds himself at Camelot sleeping in Morgan's arms. Arthur awakes in a dark room with twenty knights in iron fetters. Accalon finds himself in a meadow near a tower. He swears never to help ladies in the future, but rather to dishonor them when possible.

A dwarf brings Accalon word from Morgan: tomorrow he will fight the knight of whom she spoke. The dwarf gives him Excalibur and the scabbard, and the people of the tower thank Accalon for coming to their aid. Arthur learns that he is in the Tower of Ambush; the lord of the tower, Domas, imprisons knights of Arthur's court in the hope of finding one who will fight his brother, with whom he is feuding. Asked if he is willing to fight in exchange for his freedom and for that of the other prisoners, Arthur agrees.

37. The Death of Merlin.

Merlin, Ninianne, and her companions come upon a valley full of stones. In the valley is a room chiseled in the rocks. Merlin tells how the room was created by the son of a king, who sought to hide the woman he loved from his angry father. They enter the room to see the tomb of these lovers, and Ninianne has Merlin remove the cover of the tomb. The two of them decide to stay the night; she enchants Merlin so that he falls asleep. Her companions put him in the tomb, and she seals the lid with spells.

38.   Battle of Arthur and Accalon Continued; The Lady of the Lake Intervenes to Save Arthur's Life.

As Arthur and Accalon prepare to do battle, Morgan gives Arthur the counterfeit sword. Eventually, Accalon, using Excalibur, has the upper hand, and the king's sword breaks, leaving him defenseless. In vain Accalon urges Arthur to surrender. When Arthur is near defeat, the Lady of the Lake casts a spell and stops Accalon long enough for the king to take Excalibur and its scabbard. The tide of battle turns immediately. Accalon refuses to yield, and Arthur, preparing to kill him, asks his name. They both identify themselves, and Accalon reveals Morgan's treachery and her hatred for Arthur; the latter swears to take vengeance on her.

The two brothers whose battle Arthur and Accalon were fighting are forced by their people to reconcile. The two wounded men are cared for by nuns, but Accalon dies nonetheless. Arthur commands that the body be placed in a litter and taken to Camelot, where it is to be presented to Morgan. Arthur's threat is also to be conveyed to Morgan.

39.   Yvain Stops Morgan from Killing Urien.

By enchantment, Urien has been placed in a bed beside his wife Morgan. Discovering him there, she wishes to kill him and sends a servant for a sword. Their son Yvain, who has been sleeping nearby, overhears her plan and prevents the murder. Protesting that she was under the devil's power, she asks Yvain's forgiveness.

When Urien awakens, Morgan asks about Arthur and feigns concern. She sends Urien and his men to seek Arthur, but they find no trace of the ship in which Urien last saw him.

40.   Morgan, Fleeing from Arthur, Steals Excalibur's Scabbard and Throws It into a Lake.

Accalon's body arrives at Camelot; Morgan flees, on the way stopping at the abbey where Arthur is recovering. There she steals his scabbard and throws it into a deep lake. She escapes Arthur's pursuit by turning herself and her followers to stone. Morgan rescues Manasses of Gaul and sends word to Arthur that Ninianne has protected him against her magic. Morgan settles in Garlot, with a tomb inside which is written the account of how Arthur and Gawain are to die.

41.   In His Anger at Morgan, Arthur Banishes Yvain; Yvain and Gawain Join Morholt; Each Takes on an Adventure.

Arthur returns to Camelot and banishes Yvain; Gawain goes with him. They witness maidens defiling Morholt's shield. Morholt fights Yvain and unhorses him.

Then he does battle with Gawain. The battle lasts all day, and the text comments that Gawain's strength always increases at noon (so that he never fought a knight without defeating him, except for six: Lancelot, Hector, Bors, Gaheriet, Tristan, and Morholt). This battle ends in a truce. Yvain, Gawain, and Morholt go to Morholt's for the night and then ride out together in the morning. In the forest of Aroie, at the Spring of Adventures, they meet three maidens with three adventures: Yvain takes the oldest, Gawain the youngest, Morholt the other one; they agree to meet back at the spring in a year.

42.   Arthur Is Saved from a Poisoned Mantle by Ninianne, Who Promises to Protect Him Because He Honors Chivalry.

Arthur mourns the departure of Gawain. Manasses arrives and tells Arthur of his encounters with Morgan. The next day, Ninianne, the Lady of the Lake, arrives in disguise and warns Arthur that Morgan is sending him a maiden to offer him a rich mantle that causes the immediate death of the person who puts it on. On Ninianne's advice, Arthur asks the maiden herself to put on the mantle; not knowing its power, she does so, and she dies instantly. Ninianne says she will protect him because he honors the flower of chivalry; she then leaves court. The narrator comments that he will speak no more of Merlin but will turn to the story of the Grail, which is "the beginning of this book."

43.   Gawain at the Plain of Adventures: Pellias and Arcade.

At the Plain of Adventures, Gawain and the maiden see a knight (Pellias) who defeats ten opponents in succession. Then the defeated knights capture him and lead him away. Gawain witnesses an encounter between a knight and a dwarf. They argue about which of them has the right to a maiden, and she chooses the dwarf. Two knights appear and challenge Gawain; as one of them is fighting with Gawain, the other lures away his maiden, squire, and host. After the battle, the knight who was fighting Gawain tells him how the Plain of Adventures got its name.

Later, the knight tells Gawain about a tournament in which Pellias once judged Arcade the most beautiful woman at court. She treated him with disdain, and it is she who has required him to fight against ten knights. Gawain leaves and, meeting Pellias, tells him that he knows how to make the woman do Pellias's will.

Gawain goes to Arcade's castle and tells her that he has killed Pellias. She is delighted, and moreover she quickly falls in love with Gawain. Gawain returns her love. They remain together until Pellias decides that Gawain has failed; he goes to Arcade's dwelling and finds her in bed with Gawain.

44.   Gawain's Adventure with Pellias and Arcade Continued.

Finding Gawain in bed with Arcade, Pellias leaves his sword next to them to indicate that he has discovered them but has magnanimously chosen not to kill them. He leaves them asleep, returns, and prepares to die of grief. He asks that, after his death, his companions take his heart in a silver basin and present it to Arcade.

45. Gawain's Adventure with Pellias and Arcade Continued.

Gawain and Arcade awaken and find the sword; recognizing it as Pellias's, she knows that Gawain lied when he said he killed Pellias. Gawain explains and repents his treachery. He persuades Arcade to agree to be reconciled with Pellias, and he then makes amends by bringing the grateful Pellias to her.

46. Gawain and the Maiden Who Chose the Dwarf.

Pellias and Arcade marry, and when they first lie together they conceive Guivret the Younger. Gawain meets the knight who took away his damsel; he defeats the man but refuses to take the woman back. He then finds the maiden who chose to leave a handsome knight for a dwarf; she is now being mistreated by the dwarf and six knights, and Gawain saves her. He then conducts her to her castle.

47. Morholt at King Pellinor's Celebration; The Lady and Dwarf Threatened with Death by Burning.

Morholt comes upon a great celebration, which is for the anniversary of King Pellinor's coronation. Invited to participate, he declines and is then challenged by a knight, whom he defeats. Pellinor sends his son to learn Morholt's identity. Thereafter, Morholt and his companions enter the Wood of Plessis and hear a voice calling for help. He finds knights about to burn a lady and a dwarf, having accused them falsely of adultery. He prepares to defend them.

48. Morholt Saves the Lady and the Dwarf; The Stone of the Stag; The Old Lady's Spell.

Morholt drives off the knights, rescues the lady and dwarf, and takes them to an abbey. The dwarf explains that a knight who loved the lady led her husband (the king) to believe she was betraying him with the dwarf; as a result, the king wanted the two of them to die.

The next day, Morholt leaves with the maiden and squire; in the forest they come to a cross and a block of marble known as the Stone of the Stag. On the stone are inscriptions announcing many of the marvels of the Grail and threatening any knight who stays there to see them. They see two knights fight, kiss each other, and depart without speaking. Then they see a stag killed by four beagles, which are in turn devoured by a dragon. The dragon revives the stag and vomits up the live dogs; all the animals leave.

During the night, the maiden and squire are killed mysteriously, and Morholt is wounded through the thighs. A knight agrees to take Morholt and the bodies to an abbey. They set out, but when the knight learns Morholt's name, he says that Morholt killed his father; he attacks Morholt and leaves him for dead. Gawain arrives, takes Morholt to a place where he can be healed, and buries the two bodies. (On a tomb is written the story of Gaheriet's great deeds and his self-imposed ten-year exile from Arthur's court.)

After Morholt is healed, he and Gawain ride out together and soon come to a tent, in which they fall asleep. An old woman arrives, recognizes them, and asks both of them to be her lovers. Both refuse, and they leave. Suddenly, they begin to hate and berate each other, and they begin to fight.

49.   Gawain and Morholt Freed of the Spell.

As they do battle, a young woman arrives; she serves the Lady of the Lake. Recognizing them, she breaks the enchantment that made them hate each other. She explains that the spell was cast by the old woman, who was in fact a beautiful young woman in changed form. Morholt and Gawain go to a Cistercian abbey to be healed.

50.   Morholt and Gawain at the Rock of the Maidens.

Morholt and Gawain come to a large rock on which are twelve maidens who are speaking of future events. Morholt understands that the oldest of them tried to kill Merlin and, with her sisters, was punished by banishment to this rock.

The women make prophecies about the deaths of Gawain and Morholt. At the knights' request, the women bring them magically up to the top of the rock. There they fall in love with two of the maidens and stay there, living in idyllic happiness while believing—because of the spell they are under—that they are doing great deeds of chivalry in other lands.

51.   Yvain at the Rock of the Stag; Gawain and Morholt Miss the Rendezvous; Yvain at the Rock of the Maidens.

With his squire and the lady, Yvain comes to the Rock of the Stag; reading the inscription on it, he decides to spend the night there in order to see the Grail adventures. Kay and Girflet pass by and say that they have looked for him, and they ask about Gawain. Yvain explains that in fifteen days, he, Gawain, and Morholt are to meet. Two ladies arrive and take Kay and Girflet away.

During the night, Yvain is wounded by a sword, and the woman and squire are killed; Yvain is unable to find any trace of the attacker. Kay and Girflet return and comfort him, but he vows to wander until he finds out how the two were killed. On the appointed day, he comes to the spring where he is to meet Gawain and Morholt. A maiden tells him that Gawain and Morholt are on the Rock of the Maidens, where they are so happy that they no longer remember Yvain. The maiden talks to Yvain of the Grail marvels at the Rock of the Stag and says that they will eventually be accomplished by the Good Knight who will sit in the Perilous Seat on Pentecost. Yvain goes to the Rock of the Maidens, where he meets a knight who hates everyone from Arthur's household.

52.   Yvain Fails to Free Gawain and Morholt from the Rock of the Maidens; He Returns to Court.

Yvain defeats the knight, who then explains that he loves one of the maidens on the Rock; she formerly loved him but left him for Gawain. He takes Yvain to the Rock, where a woman predicts Yvain's death in battle. Yvain speaks to Gawain and Morholt, but they do not recognize him.

Later, Yvain is asleep beside a spring in a forest near Camelot; the queen finds him. He tells her of his adventures, and she then takes him back to Camelot, where he again recounts his adventures.

53. Merlin's Death Becomes Known; Gaheriet Is Knighted in Order to Free Gawain and Morholt.

Yvain tells Arthur about Gawain and Morholt; Arthur sends men to search for Merlin. Tor and Aglant meet and fight Bademagu, who tells them that Merlin is dead but that before his death he said that only Gaheriet, once he is knighted, can free Gawain and Morholt from the Rock. When Arthur prepares to knight Gaheriet, Agravain jealously demands to be knighted first. Arthur agrees to do so, but then a madman (Marins), who has been mute for years, speaks and urges Arthur to knight Gaheriet first. Arthur does so; then Gaheriet knights his brother Guerrehet and other young men, but Agravain insists that he be knighted by Arthur instead.

54. Gaheriet Sets out, Followed by Agravain.

Marins, the madman, foretells Gaheriet's greatness and his sin, and then he dies. Arthur and his men are out riding when they encounter a Red Knight (Baudon, son of the Duke of Avarlan) who does not return their greetings. Another knight (Gallin) arrives and explains that he was to fight with Baudon, who imprisoned his brother. Gallin is wounded, however, and so Gaheriet agrees to fight in his place. In honor of Gaheriet's adventure, the maidens at court write the Ballad of the Rose, later set to music by Tristan.

Agravain, furious that Gaheriet is undertaking this adventure, leaves court soon after his brother. He changes his armor so as not to be recognized and then lies in wait for Gaheriet. When the latter arrives, Agravain challenges him to a joust and is defeated.

55. Gaheriet Rescues Bademagu.

Agravain decides to follow Gaheriet in order to take revenge; his squire, shocked by his hatred of his brother, deserts him. Gaheriet finds Bademagu naked and bound; Bademagu says this was done to him by King Pellinor, with whose wife he has slept. Bademagu, dressed and equipped with armor, sets out with Gaheriet. They agree to meet at the Rock after each has fought a battle the following week.

56. Gaheriet Defeats Baudon and Agravain.

Gaheriet arrives at the castle of Avarlan. He meets Gallinor, the man for whom he is to fight, and Gallinor explains the enmity between him and Baudon. (A woman loved by Baudon betrayed him with his cousin and then, because Gallinor discovered her perfidy, tried to discredit him by accusing him of attempted rape.)

Gaheriet, on the verge of defeating Baudon, agrees to stop the battle on condition that Baudon will make peace with Gallinor. Gaheriet leaves and is soon attacked by Agravain, who has been following him; Gaheriet defeats Agravain.

Later, Gaheriet meets a maiden to whom he owes a boon. She demands the head of a lady who has stolen her lover. Gaheriet does not wish to kill a woman but is told that if he does not keep his promise, he will never free Gawain and Morholt. He then goes to the woman and knight and announces his intention to take the woman's head. Her lover prepares to defend her.

57. Gaheriet Satisfies the Wronged Maiden, Who Promises to Help Him Free Gawain and Morholt; They Are Imprisoned, the Maiden to Be Given to a Giant.

Gaheriet defeats the knight, but the jilted maiden intervenes and asks Gaheriet to spare him. Gaheriet then prepares to cut off the other maiden's head, and the knight, in turn, prepares to kill the woman who has just saved his life, offering to spare her only if she will ask Gaheriet to spare the other one. She does so, and then she and Gaheriet leave for the Rock of the Maidens.

On the third day of their travels, they encounter an old knight and a dwarf. The knight warns Gaheriet not to take the maiden into a nearby castle (Tarquin), but they enter nonetheless, and Gaheriet is soon captured by a group of knights. A woman explains to him that each year the inhabitants have to give twelve maidens to a giant; Gaheriet has been taken prisoner so that he can be required to swear to hold the people guiltless. So swearing, Gaheriet is released. He lies in wait for the giant (who is Aupatris, the father of Caradoc the Huge, lord of Dolorous Guard) and challenges him to battle.

58. Gaheriet Defeats the Giant, Rescues the Maiden, and Frees Gawain and Morholt.

Gaheriet kills the giant and puts an end to the custom of Tarquin; the people make a copper statue of him killing the giant. (Later the statue will be destroyed by Mordred's sons.) Gaheriet goes to the Rock of Maidens. There he asks the maidens to tell him how he will die, and he is informed that the foreign knight whom he will love best will kill him, though without knowing it.

Gaheriet cannot climb the rock to rescue Gawain and Morholt, but the maiden with him advises him to do battle with the maidens' brother and, having defeated him, to threaten to behead him if he does not arrange to have Gawain and Morholt freed. He follows her advice and so rescues the captives.

59. Gawain and Morholt Freed from Enchantment; Gawain Returns to Court; Morholt, After Many Adventures, Is Killed by Tristan.

Gawain and Morholt awaken with no memory of being on the Rock; Gaheriet explains the situation to them. Gaheriet and Gawain return to court, and the former sets out to visit Morholt in Ireland. Morholt, on his way there, defeats Agravain, Guerrehet, Mador of the Gate, Dodinel the Wild, and Sagremor the Unruly. Going on to Ireland, he receives Gaheriet. The text refers to his eventual return to Cornwall, where he will fight Tristan and will be killed.

60. Gaheriet Kills His Mother; Arthur Defeats Claudas and Frollo; Lancelot Comes to Logres; Elaine Brings Galahad to Court; Start of Lancelot's Madness.

Gaheriet hates Lamorat, one of Pellinor's sons, because Lamorat loves Gaheriet's mother, the queen of Orkney. Gaheriet goes to the castle where the queen is in bed with Lamorat. He kills the queen but spares Lamorat. Courtiers take the queen's body to Camelot so that Arthur and everyone will know who killed her. Gawain, Agravain, and Mordred swear vengeance on Gaheriet; Guerrehet demurs, finds Gaheriet, and comforts him. Gaheriet and Hector, heading for a tournament, encounter and fight Gawain, Agravain, and Mordred. Gaheriet and Hector are losing when Lamorat rescues them and makes peace. Recognizing Lamorat, Gawain quarrels with him because Pellinor killed Lot. They separate, and Gawain, Agravain, and Mordred return to court. Arthur sends them back to bring Gaheriet to court.

Arthur sends Gawain, Bors, Hector, and others to Gaul to dispossess Claudas. Arthur follows them and finishes the task; he kills Frollo, prince of Germany, and brings Lancelot back to Logres. At Pentecost, Pelles's daughter Elaine brings Galahad to court. Guenevere finds Lancelot in bed with Elaine; he believes he is lying with the queen instead. Guenevere banishes him from court.

61. The Quest for Lancelot Begins; Eric's Adventures.

Bors, Hector, and Lionel leave to seek Lancelot. Then Gawain and his brothers leave as well, as does Eric. In all, thirty-two knights go on the quest. Then some return to Camelot and twenty stay on; Eric, chosen to return, instead continues on the quest alone.

62. Eric at the Castle of the Ten Knights.

Eric meets a maiden with a knight who was wounded at the Spring of Marvels. Eric comes to the Castle of the Ten Knights, where he learns that he must fight ten knights. He defeats all ten with one lance. He promises a maiden a boon and then is defeated by the eleventh knight, who is Hector. Eric must therefore remain as lord of the castle. The origin of this custom is explained.

63. Lancelot, Running Mad, Is Helped by Bliant, Wounded by a Boar, and Fed by Herdsmen.

Lancelot, wandering in madness, meets Bliant, who binds him, takes him to Bliant Castle, and tries to cure him. Lancelot breaks his bonds and rescues Bliant from two enemies. Bliant does not replace his chains, but Lancelot remains there two years. Once he follows a wild boar and is wounded by it; he is healed by a hermit who recognizes him. Leaving there, Lancelot wanders for three months through the forest; he then stays six months at Lancelot's Spring. Herdsmen come there and give him bread; he sleeps in front of a hermit's house.

64. Eric Leaves Gawain Lord of the Castle; Eric at the Spring of Marvels; Eric and Hector Find Lancelot; Eric Makes the Fatal Promise.

Eric stays at the Castle of the Ten Knights for three months. Gawain arrives and defeats the ten knights, only to be defeated by Eric, who then leaves; Gawain is made lord of the castle. Eric comes to the Spring of Marvels, where local knights test themselves against knights errant; if they defeat a knight of Arthur's household, they hang his shield from a tree. The place is called the Spring of Marvels, because everyone who comes there is made angry or sad (over a friend's misfortune) and glad (at finding his mortal enemy there). This is a marvel that will be ended by Galahad. Eric finds his father's shield hanging there. He fights and defeats Mordred.

A maiden agrees to tell Eric about his father; he promises her a boon and swears that he will never break a promise or tell a lie. (This will eventually lead him to kill his own sister.) The maiden tells him that Lancelot is nearby; she then informs him where his father lies wounded and explains that Hector avenged his defeat.

The maiden leads Eric to Lancelot. Hector arrives and recognizes Lancelot, but Lancelot, failing to recognize them, flees. Hector has Eric and the maiden swear that they will never reveal Lancelot's plight. They unsuccessfully seek Lancelot. Hector then lies ill from grief for four years, with Eric keeping him company. Arthur mourns for Lancelot and Hector but knows they are alive, because their names remain on their seats at the Round Table.

65. Lancelot Is Cured of His Madness, Stays on the Isle of Joy.

In the fifth year of his madness, Lancelot comes to Corbenic but is unable to remain in the presence of the Grail. Lamorat recognizes him and tells Pelles who he is; they bind Lancelot and leave him in the Palace of Adventures with the Grail. A demon is driven out of him; overcome with shame, Lancelot wants to withdraw from the world, and Pelles lets him have the Tower of Giants (Island of Joy). He lives there for ten years, calling himself the Wicked Knight and jousting with all comers.

66. Lamorat's Last Adventures and Death at the Hands of Gawain, Agravain, and Mordred.

Gawain stays six years in the Castle of Ten Knights. Lamorat arrives and defeats the ten and Gawain; he is then made lord of the castle. He marries the maiden, and the custom ends. Agloval, Drian, and Tor come to help Lamorat celebrate, and they take him away with them; he never returns.

Drian is mortally wounded by Agravain, Mordred, and Gawain together, and they then kill Lamorat. A hermit takes Lamorat's head to Arthur; it changes color in Arthur's hands, indicating that Arthur's kin killed him.

67. Perceval's Youth, Knighting, and Seating at the Round Table; Perceval and Gaheriet Fight on Perceval's Sister's Island.

Agloval, searching for Lancelot, comes to the tower where Perceval lives. Seeing Agloval, Perceval wants to become a knight; he runs away but is brought back by

Agloval. Perceval's mother dies; then Perceval and Agloval ride away together and find Arthur at Carduel.

Everyone has returned from the quest except Bors, Hector, Lionel, and Eric. Hector has just been healed, and he and Eric have left the hermit's dwelling. Arthur knights Perceval. The Mute Maiden moves Perceval to a seat at the Round Table, next to the Perilous Seat. He soon rides out to find adventures; he meets a maiden who seeks the rescue of a knight, and he promises her a boon.

Perceval's sister imprisons Gaheriet on an island, where he is obliged to fight all comers. Perceval and Gaheriet do battle, recognize each other, and leave the island together. Perceval's sister has words carved on a cross to indicate that the best knight in the world can be seen on the island; she knows that if Gawain passes, he will cross over to the island, where she can have him killed and thus avenge her father's death.

68.   Further Adventures of Eric and Hector.

Eric stays with the ill Hector for four years. One day he meets a rude knight, Montenart of the Isle Reposte; he follows him, gets lost, and meets the Ugly Hero, with a maiden who asks his help. Eric fights the Ugly Hero until they recognize each other. They then free the maiden.

The Ugly Hero tells Eric that Montenart is to fight Sagremor in two days. Eric goes to find Montenart; the Ugly Hero is to keep Hector company. Eric enters the castle of Nabon the Enchanter. He fights and defeats a prisoner, who turns out to be Bors. Bors explains that Eric is protected against enchantment. Bors goes to the hermitage to see Hector, while Eric goes to High Rock Castle, meets Sagremor, and asks to have the battle with Montenart. Sagremor refuses, whereupon Eric, joined by Brandeliz, goes out to waylay Montenart. Eric kills Montenart and has Brandeliz take his adversary's head to Sagremor.

Returning to Hector, Erec meets a maiden who gives him a message from the Lady of the Lake: Lancelot is cured. Eric tells Hector, who is then healed and rides out with Eric to seek Lancelot. They come to a castle where each time a knight errant arrives, an inhabitant dies. They meet the Ugly Hero and then Lionel; the latter knocks Eric down. The four of them separate.

69.   Hector and Gawain on Perceval's Sister's Island.

Hector arrives on Perceval's sister's island, thinking that Lancelot is there. He is imprisoned and forced to swear to kill Lamorat's killer. Gawain arrives; they fight and then, recognizing each other, make peace. They make common cause against the islanders and kill them. Perceval's sister reveals all, and Hector and Gawain leave together.

70.   Eric Rescues Bors; Gaheriet Saves Perceval from a Dilemma, Fights Lancelot on the Isle of Joy.

Eric arrives at the Castle of August, where he finds Bors about to be beheaded for having killed the son of the castle's lord. He rescues him. They meet Blioberis and Sagremor and stay four days with Blioberis's brother. An ugly maiden arrives and berates Eric for not entering the castle (in chapter 68): he could have ended the adventure but did not.

Perceval and Gaheriet, leaving Perceval's sister's island, meet the maiden who brought Perceval there. She demands that Gaheriet become her captive or that his head be taken; he becomes her prisoner. She heals his wounds and wants him to fight the knight (Lancelot) who killed her lover. Gaheriet fights Lancelot, loses decisively, and later sets out to find Bors and fight the mystery knight.

71.   Perceval and the Impoverished Maiden.

Perceval, after leaving Gaheriet, seeks shelter in a ruined castle called Beautiful Home. There a maiden says she has only poverty to offer him, because Clamadam stole her inheritance when she refused to marry him. Perceval defeats him and makes him promise to restore everything to her.

72.   Perceval Meets the Fisher King.

Perceval leaves the maiden. He rescues another maiden from the Ugly Hero and Sagremor, who have kidnapped her and are fighting over her. She promises to reward her rescuer. Perceval then rides off alone and meets Pellehan (the Rich Fisherman/Maimed King). He rides on and meets Hector.

VOLUME IX

THE POST-VULGATE, PART II. THE QUEST FOR THE HOLY GRAIL

73.   Galahad Is Knighted.

During Pentecost, at Camelot, one of Elaine's maidens summons Lancelot to an abbey in the Forest of Camelot; he knights Galahad. Lancelot rides back with Bors and Lionel.

74.   The Adventure of the Burning Knight; The Sword in the Stone; Eric and Helain Seated at the Round Table.

Finally, four hundred fifty-three years after Christ's death, the Perilous Seat is to have a lord. A knight from Ireland falls, burning, from a window, a letter in his hand. A block of marble, floating in the river with a sword imbedded in it, arrives at Camelot. Lancelot refuses to try to draw the sword; Gawain tries and fails. Eric and Helain the White henceforth belong to the Round Table, for their names appear on the seats of two knights who are now dead.

75.   The Perilous Seat; Galahad Achieves the Adventure of the Stone; Tournament at Camelot.

As the knights are seated at the table, the doors and windows of the hall close by themselves. A hermit leads in the young Galahad, who sits in the Perilous Seat. He is to deliver the land from the marvels and adventures that have been occurring. Galahad then draws the sword from the marble block. A maiden arrives and tells Lancelot that he is no longer the best knight in the world. Arthur decides to hold a tournament, because this is the last time all his knights will be together.

76.   Tristan Arrives; The Round Table Is Complete; The Holy Grail Appears; The Knights Vow to Seek It.

Tristan arrives, and the Round Table is complete for the first and last time. As the knights are seated, there is a great storm, and the Holy Grail appears before them, moving around the room. Gawain vows to leave on the quest, and others follow his lead. Arthur, as a result, is filled with sorrow.

77. The Test of the Bloody Sword; The Ugly Maiden Prophesies that Gawain Will Kill Many Knights on the Quest.

A maiden arrives, bearing a sword that becomes bloody when drawn by Gawain, because he is to kill so many knights during the quest. Arthur urges him not to go.

78. Preparations for the Quest.

Arthur tells the maiden that he will forbid Gawain to go. Everyone learns that Galahad is Lancelot's son. Arthur reads the letter that was taken from the Irish knight who burned. An old monk forbids the knights to take their ladies with them on the quest; he exhorts them concerning the importance of confession, penance, and communion. Arthur mourns all night. All one hundred fifty of the knights (that is, all except Gawain) swear to follow the quest; the knights are named.

79. Departure; Gawain's Slaughters Foretold; The Suicide.

The queen grieves at Lancelot's departure. Arthur rides with them part of the way and then turns back. The knights ride to the Castle of Vagan, where they spend the night. An ugly maiden again tells Gawain to turn back, predicting that he will kill nineteen of his companions. A knight arrives and asks Galahad to kill him; he then kills himself. The next morning, the knights separate and ride off.

80. Galahad Wins His Shield; Meleagant Asks to Become a Knight.

Three days later, Galahad meets Bademagu and Yvain the Bastard at a Cistercian abbey. There is a shield that no one can bear without being killed or wounded; Bademagu tries to do so and is wounded by a knight in white armor, who tells the squire (who is Meleagant, though not yet named in the story) to take the shield to Galahad. The knight will tell Meleagant and Galahad together the truth about the shield. Galahad rides out with it, with Meleagant and a hermit (who accompanies him everywhere, instructing him about the Holy Grail). The knight tells them about Joseph of Arimathea, Evelac king of Sarras, his enemy Tolomer, Josephet, and the shield with a red cross on it. Galahad is the last of Nascien's line, and the abbey where the shield was found is Where Nascien is buried. The knight disappears, and Meleagant asks Galahad to make him a knight.

81. Galahad Returns to the Abbey and Drives a Demon out of a Grave.

Galahad and Meleagant return to the abbey. Galahad visits a grave from which a terrible voice issues; he drives out the demon, and a good man explains the significance of this adventure, pointing out that Galahad figures Christ in semblance though not in nobility. The text comments that Robert de Boron did not translate everything about the Holy Grail from Latin into French.

82. Galahad Knights Meleagant, Who Is Wounded.

Galahad knights Meleagant, who then asks to ride with him until chance separates them. They find a wooden cross with an inscription announcing that the road to the left is reserved for an exceptional knight. Meleagant wishes to take that road, and they part. Meleagant comes upon a sleeping old man wearing a crown. He takes the crown and also takes the lady from Amador (wounded by Bors), who follows, wounds Meleagant, and kills himself and the woman. Galahad finds them, witnesses Amador's death, and defends Meleagant against two knights. He takes Meleagant to an abbey to be healed; Amador is to be buried.

83.   Galahad and Yvain the Bastard Are Guests of Dalides's Father; Dalides and His Father Kill Themselves.

Galahad and Yvain the Bastard come to the castle of Dalides's father. Dalides arrives with Dodinel, his captive for having boasted about Galahad. Galahad and Yvain leave; Dalides follows, challenges Galahad, and is defeated. Dalides kills himself in pique, and his grieving father kills himself.

84.   Adventures of Galahad, Gawain, Dodinel, Bors, and Kay; The Bizarre Beast; The White Stag.

Galahad, Yvain, and Dodinel come to a place where three roads divide. Yvain follows the Bizarre Beast; Dodinel follows Tristan, carrying the wounded Asgares; Galahad follows a white stag and lions. Gawain, trying to avenge Dalides, attacks Galahad and is wounded. Bors, in an effort to avenge Gawain, attacks Galahad, who kills his horse but then recognizes him. Kay kills a knight whom Bors and Galahad are trying to shield and who was trying to kill Lucan. Kay returns to Gawain and accompanies him to a monastery for healing.

85.   Yvain the Bastard and Girflet Wounded by the Knight of the Questing Beast; Dodinel and Asgares the Sad Wounded by Tristan.

Yvain, following the Bizarre Beast, stops with a hermit who has lost five sons to the beast; Yvain continues his pursuit of the beast. He is wounded by a knight (a pagan later identified as Palamedes) who then wounds Girflet, also pursuing the beast. Dodinel follows Tristan, challenges him, and is wounded. Tristan recognizes both Dodinel and Asgares; mortified to have wounded them, he rides off in grief. Dodinel takes Asgares to a place where he can be healed.

86.   Galahad and Bors in the House of King Brutus, Whose Daughter Kills Herself for Love of Galahad.

Bors and Galahad come to Castle Brut and spend the night. The king's daughter, fifteen years old, falls in love with Galahad. She gets into bed with him, but when he awakens and rejects her, she kills herself. Bors awakens; then two ladies come and raise the alarm. When others arrive, Bors holds off the attackers while Galahad arms himself. The king, impressed that two men will take on fifty, stops the fight and challenges Bors to single combat. Bors defeats him, and peace is made.

87.   Galahad and Bors Chase the Questing Beast and Meet Palamedes and His Father, Esclabor the Unknown.

Bors and Galahad leave Castle Brut. They see the Questing Beast; then they are joined by another knight, and all three follow the beast. They spend the night with Esclabor the Unknown, who tells them how he marr ed a giant's daughter and had twelve sons, eleven of whom were killed following the Questing Beast. He says that he himself became a Christian but that his remaining son, still chasing the beast, remains pagan.

88.   Yvain of Cenel Dies; Gawain Escapes, Is Blamed by Yvain's Sister.

Yvain of Cenel and Gawain meet and arrive at the castle where Gawain killed Lamorat. They are warned not to enter; Gawain turns away, but Yvain enters and is captured and burned in vengeance for Lamorat. Arthur will eventually destroy the castle. Gawain rides away and meets Yvain 's sister; she goes on to the castle, learns of Yvain 's death, and blames Gawain bitterly

89.   Gawain Kills Patrides.

Yvain's sister incites Patrides (the nephew of Bademagu) to avenge Yvain 's death. He fights Gawain and is killed by him. The sister sets out for Arthur's court.

90.   Further Aventures of Hector of the Fens, Helain the White, Gawain, King Bademagu, Yvain's Sister, and the Knight of the Questing Beast.

Gawain meets Hector, and together they meet Helain the White, who has been wounded (by Palamedes). Hector goes on to avenge him and is defeated. Gawain and Helain meet Bademagu and Yvain's sister. The woman incites Bademagu to do combat with Gawain in revenge for Patrides, but once Bademagu learns who Gawain is, he stops the battle.

91.   Helain, Hector, and Gawain see Visions in the Ancient Chapel.

Helain, Hector, and Gawain spend the night at an ancient chapel. As the others sleep, Helain experiences a marvelous scene: the church shakes violently, and amid wondrous smells the figure of a bishop appears. A woman emerges from a tomb, and the bishop feeds her with a mass wafer. Helain and Hector find that they are healed of their wounds.

Hector and Gawain ride to the Perilous Chapel, after getting news that Gaheriet has been wounded. There, while sleeping, they see visions: Gawain has a vision of a corral with one hundred fifty bulls, while Hector dreams of himself and Lancelot on high chairs, on tall horses, in receding water. Then they see a hand with a candle and bridle. The following morning, a maiden directs them to Nascien.

92.   Gawain Kills Yvain the Bastard; Gawain's and Hector's Visions Explained.

Gawain and Hector meet Yvain the Bastard but do not recognize him; Gawain jousts with him and kills him. Gawain and Hector go to Nascien's hermitage, where

Nascien explains their visions: he tells Gawain he is in mortal sin, that "adventures are things that show to good men the meaning of other things." Gawain says that if he had time, he would talk with Nascien; he and Hector then leave.

93. Bors Cleanses Himself Spiritually and Chooses to Save a Strange Maiden Rather than His Brother Lionel.

Galahad and Bors leave Castle Brut and meet a knight (the pagan, Palamedes) who knocks Bors down. Galahad follows to avenge Bors. Bors spends the night with a hermit, who recommends confession; Bors takes the advice and begins a diet of bread and water. Leaving the hermit, he meets two knights carrying off Lionel in one direction and another knight carrying off a maiden in the other. Bors prays that God will help Lionel while he helps the maiden. He has the knight promise to marry her, and the text says that they will be the parents of Licanor, who will kill Meraugis. Bors leaves to help Lionel.

94. The Lady of the Tent; Lionel Saved by Bors's Prayer.

Coming to a tent, Lionel speaks with a lady. Her father and husband return and assume that Lionel has lain with her. They kill her and wish to kill Lionel as well, but the father is instead killed by him. The husband and his two brothers pursue and capture Lionel but, because Bors has prayed that God might save Lionel, the captors fall dead. Lionel is furious with Bors.

95. Lionel's Revenge; Calogrenant's Death; Bors Rides to the Sea.

Lionel and Bors meet at a tournament, and the former attacks and wounds the latter. A hermit tries to intervene in order to save Bors's life, and Lionel kills him. Then Calogrenant intervenes, and he too is killed. God sends fire between Lionel and Bors to stop the fight; He tells Bors to ride to the sea, where Perceval awaits him. Bors goes directly to a seaside abbey. During the night, he is awakened by a voice, and he leaves secretly.

96. Perceval Saves the Good Man from Suicide, Learns More About the Quest.

Perceval, although he appears bent on pleasure, fasts and prays as he rides along on the quest. He arrives at a hermitage and hears a voice predict that he will eventually see the Holy Grail. He then finds an old hermit, who is about to hang himself. At Perceval's coming, the demon that has been tormenting the old man leaves him, and he tells of the events that brought him to this pass.

Perceval asks the hermit what the quest is. During Mass, a letter appears on the altar; it says that Perceval will make his way to the Fisher King's house and that he will be one of twelve companions who are good in the sight of God. It further says that God will guide Perceval, Galahad, and Bors to another land, Sarras, where the first two will die. It announces that the Round Table company will never again be assembled as at Pentecost, and it predicts that Agloval will be killed. Perceval leaves.

97.   Perceval and the Knight of the Questing Beast.

Perceval sees the Questing Beast. He follows it and meets the pagan knight (Palamedes). The latter urges Perceval to seek the Grail instead of the beast, both because Perceval is a great knight and because he, the pagan, wishes to pursue the beast as he has previously done. Perceval responds that he will not be intimidated by the other knight. They do battle, and both are wounded.

98.   Gaheriet Takes Perceval to Be Healed; Perceval Finds Lancelot Dreaming.

Perceval meets Gaheriet, who is also following the Questing Beast. Like Perceval, he has been defeated by the pagan knight. Gaheriet takes Perceval to a place where he can be healed. Once his wounds are cared for, Perceval leaves and happens upon Lancelot, who, sleeping and dreaming, is sighing, weeping, and moaning.

99.   Lancelot's Dream.

Lancelot dreams first of a poisoned river from which a number of figures emerge. First come seven crowned figures, then a wretched one, then a ninth, who is more worthy and finer than any of the others. Angels arrive, bearing a crown for the ninth figure; they take all the crowned ones to heaven but leave behind the one who is wretched. In a second dream, Lancelot sees Morgan accompanied by devils. Morgan delivers Lancelot to them, and they take him to a dark valley, where he sees a chair in a fiery pit: Guenevere is in the chair. Then he goes into a beautiful garden and sees his parents, Ban and Elaine. In turn they rebuke and condemn him for his sin with Guenevere.

100. Perceval and Lancelot at the Hermitage of the Red Olive Tree; Lancelot Confesses.

Lancelot awakens, deeply grieved by his dreams. Perceval tells him that they are a warning. They ride to the hermitage of the Red Olive Tree. There Lancelot has another dream, in which Iseut, enveloped in flame, condemns him for his sin with Guenevere. In the dream, she strikes him in the thigh; he awakens with a painful burn on his thigh. Perceval awakens to find a letter in his hand. When he touches Lancelot's thigh, the wound is healed, though it is still black the following day. The letter explains that God is rebuking Lancelot because of his sin. Lancelot then confesses and promises to change his ways.

101. Perceval and Lancelot Seek to Learn Why the Olive Tree Has Red Leaves; The Adventure of the Man in the Chair.

After eight days, Perceval and Lancelot prepare to leave the hermitage. They ask the hermit about the Red Olive Tree, but he does not know why its leaves are red. He tells them about the dead man seated in the rich chair and holding a letter in his hand. The three go together to see the man. Lancelot tells Perceval that many years ago he saw Pellinor dead, on an island, where he will stay until Gawain is dead. Neither Lancelot nor Perceval can take the letter from the man's hand.

102. Perceval and Lancelot Meet Galahad at Perceval's Aunt's Cell.

Perceval and Lancelot come to the cell of Perceval's aunt. A knight arrives and asks their help against another knight pursuing him to kill him. Galahad arrives, but they do not recognize one another. Galahad defeats Perceval and Lancelot. Then the knight pursued by Galahad asks and receives mercy. Galahad departs. Lancelot follows him, while Perceval remains at the cell.

103. Lancelot Follows Galahad and Stays with Two Hermits.

Following Galahad, Lancelot comes to a hermitage. The text explains why there are so many monks and hermits in Logres. Hermits tell him that the knight he is following is the best knight in the world and that he is of King Arthur's house; Lancelot suspects that it is Galahad. Lancelot discusses his spiritual condition with the hermits, who condemn his sin with Guenevere and give him a hair shirt to wear. He rides off, in constant prayer.

104. Lancelot Gives His Only Food to a Maiden and Has His Horse Killed by a Black Knight.

Lancelot rides through the Waste Forest. After four days without food or drink, he kills a roebuck. A maiden arrives and asks him for the roebuck; then she refuses to give him even a little to eat. Lancelot rides to the Marcoisa river, where a knight in black armor kills his horse, leaving him alone and starving on the river bank. He prays.

105. Perceval at His Aunt's Cell.

Perceval and his cloistered aunt learn each other's identity. She tells him he may not avenge his father's and Lamorat's deaths on a companion of the Round Table. She says that the knight Lancelot is following is Galahad and that Perceval should not seek to avenge his defeat at Galahad's hands. She adds that God will keep Galahad from killing his father or committing another such sin. The aunt lives more than ten years, eating nothing but raw greens. The very day she dies, Arthur, who once sought her love, has a vision of her, rebuking him for his sensuality. He goes to the Waste Forest and takes her body back to Camelot for proper burial.

106. Galahad Rescues Perceval and a Maiden; Perceval Refuses to Knight an Unknown Boy Who Later Turns out to Be Arthur the Less.

Leaving his aunt, Perceval meets Gansonais and a maiden he is trying to escort to the castle where her brother lies ill. They explain that her cousin, who wants her castle, killed the rest of the party and wounded him; the cousin is part of a group of knights who will return to attack her. Because Gansonais is wounded, Perceval undertakes to escort her. On their way, they meet Galahad, and the maiden asks him to take over the task from Perceval. Galahad objects that it would be ignoble to assume a task already accepted by another knight; however, he follows them at a distance. The cousin attacks with many knights; Perceval fights well but is unhorsed; then Galahad rides up and defeats them all. After the battle, Perceval escorts her to her brother.

Perceval then stays with a widow who heals his wounds. She asks him to knight an unknown boy (who will later be revealed to be Arthur the Less). Perceval refuses because the youth's lineage is not known.

107. Perceval and Gawain, Defeated by the Unknown Knight (Who Is Arthur the Less).

Perceval meets Gawain and asks the latter if he killed Perceval's father and brothers. Gawain says he did not. An unknown knight—it is Arthur the Less—arrives, challenges Perceval, and knocks him down. Gawain tries to avenge Perceval and is himself knocked down. Gawain forces the young man to undertake a sword fight. Finally, Perceval makes peace, and the knight reveals that he is the youth whom Perceval earlier refused to knight. He was instead knighted by Tristan.

108. Perceval, Gawain, and Claudin.

Perceval and Gawain meet Claudin. They fight, reveal their identities, and make peace. Claudin says that Tristan defeated him and made him promise not to follow the quest until he was a companion of the Round Table. Gawain and Perceval ride together until they reach a crossroad; they separate, and Perceval rides to the sea.

109. The Temptation of Perceval.

Perceval sees a tent and finds in it a beautiful lady. She asks him for help, and, seized by desire, he agrees to help her if she will grant him her love. She accepts, but then there is thunder, followed by a voice that rebukes Perceval. He realizes that the woman is a demon whose purpose is to tempt him. She then assumes her true form, and she and the tent disappear. A ship arrives, and a voice commands him to enter it; a wind takes the ship away from shore.

110. Bors and Perceval on the Mysterious Bark; Galahad at a Tournament.

A voice tells Bors to go the sea, where Perceval awaits him. He does so; finding a ship, he boards it, and the next morning he finds Perceval there.

After leaving Perceval, Galahad has many adventures. One day he comes to a castle where a tournament is in progress. Tristan and those within the castle are losing; Tristan has distinguished himself but is wounded. Galahad helps them; he knocks down Girflet, Hector, Lucan, and Gawain. The last is wounded with the sword that Galahad drew from the marble block. Hector and Sagremor realize who Galahad is, but as soon as the tide of battle is turned, the latter leaves, followed by Tristan. Gawain stays in the castle until he is healed.

111. Gawain and His Brothers in Morgan's House Learn Lancelot's Secret.

Gawain meets a knight (Mordred, though unrecognized) who is being pursued by another (Gaheriet); Gawain tries to defend Mordred, and several battles ensue. Eventually, all identities are revealed; Gaheriet is happy to see Gawain but describes

Mordred as one of the falsest knights alive, saying that, the day before, Mordred badly mistreated a maiden, dragging her behind his horse.

Morgan passes by and finds the brothers wounded. She takes them to her lodging and heals them. While there, they find the room where Lancelot was imprisoned and see the pictures he painted on the wall. Morgan tells them about Lancelot and Guenevere and urges them to tell Arthur. Gawain and Gaheriet refuse; Mordred agrees. They leave Morgan and go their separate ways.

112. Mordred Brutally Kills a Maiden; Bademagu Wounds Mordred; Gawain Wounds Bademagu Mortally.

Mordred encounters a knight riding with a squire and a maiden (his brother and sister). He kills the squire and maims the knight. He is about to rape the maiden when Bademagu arrives and asks him to stop; Mordred then beheads the woman. Bademagu wounds Mordred and leaves him for dead. Yvain and Gawain arrive; the former takes Mordred to an abbey to be healed, while the latter follows Bademagu to seek revenge.

He wounds Bademagu mortally before he recognizes him.

113. The Death of King Bademagu; Meraugis Fights Gawain; Eric Makes Peace.

Bademagu forgives Gawain and then dies. Gawain takes the body to a hermitage for burial. A knight (Meraugis) challenges Gawain in order to avenge Bademagu's death. Gawain is losing the battle when Eric arrives and puts a stop to it. After their names are revealed, they bury Bademagu.

Meraugis, who does not know he is the illegitimate son of King Mark of Cornwall, has been told that he will learn his identity at King Arthur's court.

114. Eric and Meraugis with a Maiden Free Castle Celis and Eric's Sister.

Eric and Meraugis ride off together. They meet the maiden who took Eric to Perceval's sister's island; she is seeking Eric to claim the boon he promised her. At Castle Celis, where Eric's father was killed by his nephews, the maiden tells Eric that he must give her the head of a woman in the castle. Eric and Meraugis enter the castle, kill the evil nephews, free Eric's sister, and receive the homage of the castle inhabitants. That night, Eric has a dream in which a wolf bitch brings him a lamb and requires him to kill it, after which another wolf tears him apart.

115. Eric Kills His Sister.

The maiden asks Eric for his sister's head. He is horrified but also determined to keep his promise; unmoved by pleas from his sister and from others, he kills her and gives her head to the maiden, who then condemns him for doing such a terrible deed only to keep a silly promise. She then leaves with the head but is consumed by flame; Eric's sister's head is not burned. Eric and Meraugis ride away, the latter predicting retribution for Eric's scandalous act.

116. Eric Mourns His Sister.

Eric leaves Meraugis quietly in order to mourn alone. He wanders five days without food and then comes to the lodging of a recluse. He tells her how he killed his sister; then he recounts the dream he had before killing her. and the recluse tells him that it means that his death is approaching. Preferring tc spend the rest of his days in the service of God, he accepts some bread from the woman and then resumes the quest for the Grail.

117. Meraugis and Hector Look for Eric.

Meraugis awakens to find himself alone; he grieves for Eric. A knight approaches, and the two learn that both are seeking Eric. They set out together to find him.

118. Eric Incurs the Enmity of Gawain and Agravain.

Gawain, at a castle, is jousting in order to win a crown and a maiden. Eric arrives, defeats him, takes his horse, but refuses the maiden, citing his bitterness at having been betrayed by a woman. He leaves. Gawain soon follows him and meets Agravain, whom Eric has knocked down. Agravain says that Gawain is fated to die at the hands of either Lancelot or Eric.

119. Eric Is Paralyzed by the Spring of the Virgin.

Eric dismounts at a spring to rest; there he is paralyzed by an enchantment. Three maidens and an old lady arrive, and the story of the spring is told. It once happened that the devil persuaded Nabor, son of King Nascor, that the king's daughter Aglinde was not really his sister. Thinking them unrelated, Nabor tried to rape Aglinde but fell dead. As a result of this adventure, any knight who comes to the spring is enchanted and paralyzed unless he is a virgin. The old lady says that Eric will soon die; the maidens carry him away from the spring, and the paralysis leaves him. He rides away.

120. Eric Defeats Sagremor, Kills Yvain of the White Hands, and Is Attacked by Gawain.

Eric, dreading death, weeps and prays for forgiveness. He meets Sagremor, who challenges him and is defeated. Eric rides on and overtakes Yvain of the White Hands, who challenges him in order to avenge Gawain's fall; Yvain is killed. Gawain arrives, finds Yvain's body, and follows Eric. The latter admits that he killed Yvain, and Gawain then attacks him, killing his horse.

121. Eric's Death; Hector and Meraugis Take His Body to Camelot.

After wounding Eric, Gawain rides off. Hector and Meraugis arrive; Eric tells them what has happened and asks them to take his body to King Arthur's house, place it in his seat at the Round Table, and tell everyone what happened to him. They promise, and Eric dies. Hector and Meraugis take his body to Camelot, where everyone is mourning the number of knights already dead, their deaths being known because their names have disappeared from their chairs. They place Eric in his seat and recount events to Arthur. Then they bury Eric.

122. Hector and Meraugis at Court with Claudin and Arthur the Less.

Arthur welcomes Hector and Meraugis, giving to the latter Eric's seat at the Round Table. Claudin and another knight (who is actually Arthur the Less) arrive with the letter from the recluse to Meraugis. Claudin gets Bademagu's seat at the Round Table, and Arthur the Less gets that of Yvain of the White Hands.

123. Arthur the Less and Meraugis Learn Who They Are and Return to the Quest with Hector.

About the time Galahad was conceived, King Arthur took a maiden by force and conceived a son, later naming him Arthur the Less. Morgan sends word confirming that the unknown knight who has now come to court is Arthur the Less. The king tells him how he was conceived and adjures him to avoid battle with King Ban's line, but the text notes that Arthur the Less will later attack Blioberis and will be killed by him. Meraugis learns his lineage from the letter given to him. It is learned that twenty-one knights of the Round Table are dead. Guenevere gives Hector a ring to give to Lancelot, and Hector, Meraugis, and Arthur the Less return to the quest.

124. Galahad and Tristan Ride Together.

Tristan follows Galahad away from the tournament. He overtakes him, and they introduce themselves. They ride together, talking about the Questing Beast. They stop for the night at a ruined house in the mountains; in the dark, another knight (Palamedes) arrives, stopping on the other side of the house.

125. Galahad and Tristan Overhear Palamedes's Confession of Love for Iseut; Tristan, Furious, Follows Him.

Palamedes laments his love for Iseut. Galahad and Tristan overhear him, and Tristan is furious. In the morning, Palamedes awakens and rides off, seen only by Galahad, and meets Hebes the Famous; he knocks him down and, because of what he said about Iseut, exchanges shields with him in order to conceal his identity. Galahad awakens Tristan, who asks what shield the other knight bore. Galahad has to tell him. They set out, and soon Tristan overtakes Hebes, assumes that he is the knight he is seeking, and challenges him.

126. Tristan Wounds Hebes and Fights Palamedes; Blioberis Makes Peace.

Hebes recognizes Tristan and asks him to stop, but Tristan charges, seriously wounding Hebes, who explains about the switched shields. Gaheriet arrives and stays with Hebes. Tristan pursues Palamedes, and they fight until Blioberis arrives and stops the battle. Once names are revealed, they make temporary peace, but Tristan swears future vengeance. They separate, and Tristan meets Lambeguez, who tells him of a gathering, with much jousting, before a nearby castle.

127. Palamedes Rescues Tristan at the Castle Lespar; Galahad Rescues Them Both.

Tristan arrives at the castle. The coronation of the king's son is being celebrated, and as part of the festivities, knights are challenging any Round Table knights who come there. Two knights attack Tristan, and he kills them. The king sends his brother to ask Tristan his name; when Tristan will not reveal his identity, the brother detains him and is promptly killed. The king sends one hundred knights to capture Tristan, who is losing when Palamedes arrives and helps him. Together they are again losing when Galahad arrives. His assistance turns the tide, and the king calls off his men. The knights leave, Palamedes riding off alone, Tristan and Galahad riding together for three days. At that time, Tristan stops at an abbey to have his wounds healed.

128. Galahad at King Pelles's Castle.

Galahad rides on, seeking adventure. He comes to Corbenic during the April celebration of the day Pelles was crowned. A magician who has been entertaining the court is unable to do any of his tricks in Galahad's presence. The magician explains that he served a demon and for that reason was able to perform enchantments and tricks; when Galahad came there, the demon left, unable to remain where such a holy man was. He insists that a great marvel will occur if Galahad leaves the tent. When Galahad leaves, the magician burns and is taken away by demons. When Galahad leaves, Pelles's son Eliezer follows him to find out who he is. Galahad refuses to divulge his identity to Eliezer, and the latter attacks him in anger and is wounded.

129. A Maiden Takes Galahad to Cure a Madwoman.

Galahad spends the night with a hermit. During the night, a maiden (Perceval's sister, though unidentified at present) comes and tells him to get up and ride. She takes him to the castle where her cousin has gone mad and is in chains. The cousin is cured at Galahad's coming. They ride on and meet Blioberis.

130. Galahad Repels Attacks by Envious Knights and Cures a Woman of Leprosy; His Companion Is Identified as Perceval's Sister.

As Galahad and Blioberis are talking, five sons of Desert, who hate King Ban's line, arrive and attack them. They are killed, after which Galahad and Blioberis ride to the house of a knight who lives on a mountain. There they find Amatin, Agamenor, and Arpian, Round Table knights who are envious of Ban's line and of anyone reputed to be an excellent knight; they therefore plot to kill Galahad.

The host's daughter, a leper, tells Perceval's sister that she will be cured if she can put on Galahad's hair shirt; she is healed. The next morning, Blioberis rides off one way, Galahad and Perceval's sister another, with the three envious knights after them. The three challenge Galahad; he defeats them and rides off. The three then meet Acorant and Danubre, who belong to King Ban's line; they challenge them, and the five knights all kill one another.

131. Galahad and Perceval's Sister Join Perceval and Bors on the Bark; The Ship of Faith; Solomon's Bed; The Sword of the Strange Straps.

Galahad and the maiden ride to the sea, where they find Bors and Perceval in a bark. They go on board and discuss their adventures, agreeing that Tristan and Palamedes are the best knights. Reaching a harbor, they see another ship with an inscription forbidding anyone to board who is lacking in faith. They go on board the ship and find Solomon's bed and the sword, crown, and letter. Perceval's sister tells Galahad to draw the sword, and he does so. The sword belt is poor, but the letter says that it is to be replaced by a king's virgin daughter, who will make a fine belt from what she loves most about herself. Perceval's sister produces a belt and straps made from her hair; she girds it on Galahad and, only then, reveals her identity.

132. Galahad, Perceval, and Bors Encounter Caiaphas.

The ship sails away. It comes to land, and they find a very old man who explains to them that he is Caiaphas, once bishop of Jerusalem. Deposed, he was set to sea in a boat, and he drifted for more than two hundred years without food or water. Galahad determines that they cannot take him aboard their ship (the ship of faith, symbolizing Holy Church) because he sinned in consenting to the death of Christ. They leave him there, return to their ship, and sail off again.

133. Galahad, Perceval, and Bors Free the Castle of the Count Arnault.

They land near a castle and find Galahad's shield at an ancient church. Armed knights attack them and try to take Perceval's sister. They kill sixty of the enemy. They then encounter Count Arnault, father of the knights, who is dying from a wound inflicted by his sons when he wanted to punish them for their incest with their sister. A hermit arrives and reassures Galahad about the virtue of killing all the evil knights. Arnault urges the hermit to tell Arthur about Guenevere and Lancelot; he then dies in Galahad's arms.

134. The Adventure of the White Stag; The Death of Perceval's Sister; Galahad, Perceval, and Bors Part.

The companions see a white stag guarded by four lions; they follow it to a hermitage, where they witness the transformation of the stag into a man seated at an altar and of the lions into an angel, an eagle, a more beautiful lion, and an ox. Then the creatures take the man and pass through a window without breaking it. A voice announces that this represents the way Christ entered into the Virgin without her virginity being lost. The hermit further interprets what they saw. Perceval takes the sword that Galahad drew from the marble block (and that he has now replaced with the one from the ship).

They ride on and are overtaken by knights who demand that Perceval's sister give them a basin of her blood. They fight all day, until Perceval's sister says that she will give her blood voluntarily. She does so, telling them to put her body in a bark and let it go, promising that she will reach Sarras before them. She asks them to bury her in the Spiritual Palace there; then, telling Galahad to return to Camelot to help Arthur, she dies. The leper is cured. They put the maiden's body in the bark, along with a letter telling the whole story. As they leave the castle, a great storm destroys it.

A wounded knight arrives, pursued by another knight and a dwarf. Bors follows to help him; Perceval and Galahad inspect the aftermath of the storm and a cemetery where maidens are buried; then they separate.

135. King Mark of Cornwall Invades Logres, Besieges Arthur in Camelot.

Mark hates Arthur for having helped Tristan when he eloped with Iseut; having heard that most of the Round Table knights have died in the quest, Mark summons Saxons to help him invade Logres. They take Joyous Guard by surprise, send Iseut back to Cornwall, and advance on Camelot. Arthur summons all the help he can. He is wounded in the first day's fighting, and Mark besieges Camelot.

136. Galahad, on His Way to Help King Arthur, Is Followed by Palamedes and Arthur the Less.

Galahad comes upon Arthur the Less fighting Palamedes. The latter says that Galahad is the best knight alive; Arthur the Less, doubting it, follows Galahad to challenge him. Arthur the Less attacks Galahad twice and is knocked down twice.

Palamedes has heard of Mark's attack and wants to go help. Arthur the Less joins forces with Palamedes and Esclabor; they follow Galahad and observe him at a bridge guarded by Guinglain. Galahad is sleeping and is knocked into the river; Guinglain explains that he will not permit anyone to cross the bridge, and Galahad therefore crosses in the water. Arthur the Less belittles Galahad and crosses the bridge, knocking Guinglain down.

Galahad and the other three come to an abbey where Simeon, father of Moses, has been tormented by flames since the time of Joseph of Arimathea. It is predicted that the torment will end with the arrival of the Good Knight, and indeed the flames die down in Galahad's presence. The voice of Simeon explains his story; they then look into his tomb and find his charred body.

137. Defeat of King Mark.

The companions defeat five enemy knights, from whom they learn that King Caradoc Shortarm has come to Camelot's aid and will ride out to attack Cornish and Saxons the next day. They plan to join the battle but spurn Palamedes's help because he is not Christian; insulted, he then leaves them and goes to help Mark, but turns against him when Mark knocks down his father, Esclabor. Mark's men wound Palamedes, but Galahad rescues him and, by his prowess, greatly impresses Arthur the Less. Galahad and the others rout the enemy. After the battle, Galahad rides away after revealing his name. Caradoc and the others go to Arthur, who welcomes them; he asks Palamedes to be baptized, but Palamedes declines.

138. King Mark Tries to Kill Galahad.

After leaving Camelot, Galahad stops for the night at a Cistercian abbey, where he finds Faram the Black. Mark and ten knights arrive, recognize Galahad's shield, and try to poison him and Faram. The latter is killed, but Galahad, warned in a dream, is miraculously saved, after which he forces Mark to admit his treachery.

139. Galahad Confounds Envious Knights.

The abbey is renamed "Galahad's Marvel." Galahad rides on and meets a squire (Samaliel), who is the son of Frollo. Together they meet Guerrehet, Agravain, and Mordred. Galahad refuses to fight them, and Samaliel, disgusted by the refusal, declines to serve him any longer. They all ride on together to a castle, where they are challenged by four knights. Galahad dissuades his opponent from fighting, and as a result, everyone thinks Galahad a coward.

They leave the castle to go to the Kingdom of the Strange Land, where the Maimed King is. Galahad leaves the others. They meet Gawain, Kay, and Brandeliz and tell them about Galahad the Bad. When they overtake Galahad again, Kay challenges him and is defeated, as are Brandeliz, Mordred, Agravain, and Gawain. They realize that this is Galahad and beg his pardon. Then Hector and Meraugis arrive and challenge Gawain because of Eric's death. Gawain says he will answer in Arthur's house: if he is challenged there, he will defend himself. Galahad, Hector, and Meraugis ride off together, seeking the Kingdom of the Strange Land.

140. Galahad, Hector, and Meraugis in the Castle of Treachery.

Galahad, Hector, and Meraugis come to the Castle of Treachery, where a maiden warns them that nobody who enters ever comes out. The castle is inhabited by pagans, skilled knights who hate Arthur. They enter and are trapped in a prison cell, but a storm arises, and the tower splits in half, freeing them. They kill everyone except the captive maidens, whom they free.

Arthur, told of the castle, goes there with an army and tries to rebuild the towers, but they keep falling; moreover, everyone who tries to live there dies. A voice advises Arthur not to try again to construct the towers, saying that only a king named Charles, a lesser knight but a better Christian than Arthur, will ever make them stand. The text notes that when Charlemagne eventually conquers England, he rebuilds the castle and erects a fine statue of Galahad, which will remain there more than two hundred years.

141. Lancelot, on the Bark with Perceval's Sister's Body, Meets His Grandfather Galegantin; They Are Joined by Galahad.

Lancelot is on the ship with Perceval's sister's body; the ship lands near a chapel, where he meets his maternal grandfather Galegantin, who admonishes him to continue in virtue. On the ship a long time, Lancelot is fed with the grace of the Holy Spirit. Finally, the ship lands near a forest.

Galahad leaves the Castle of Treachery and rides until he finds the wounded Tristan. When Tristan hears that Mark has sent Iseut back to Cornwall, his wounds open, and he remains ill for months. A voice directs Galahad to the sea, where he finds the bark with Lancelot and Perceval's sister. They are on the ship together a long time, and they accomplish many adventures. When they finally land, a knight in white armor brings Galahad a horse. Galahad and Lancelot separate tearfully, expecting never to see each other again.

142. Galahad, Bors, and Perceval Defeat Count Bedoin.

Bors and Perceval find Galahad besieging the Castle of the March (because Count Bedoin has disinherited his sister). Samaliel, King Frollo's son, arrives and asks Galahad to knight him. Three knights come out of the castle; Bors defeats two of them, and the third flees. Samaliel asks and receives permission to claim the armor and horse of one of the dead knights. The count goes with two cousins to kill Galahad while he sleeps. Galahad, however, is awake, praying; he arms himself, defeats all three, and spares Bedoin's life on the condition that he will become his sister's prisoner and restore all her lands.

143. Adventures of Samaliel.

Bors and Perceval take the count to his sister. Galahad goes to the hermitage and knights Samaliel. They separate, and when they meet again later, Samaliel has been badly wounded by Yvain, son of Urien. Samaliel rides after a maiden who has taken his sword. Galahad goes to find Yvain and asks him for assistance. Samaliel recovers his sword and thus bears two of them; Kay explains that the man who does so must fight two men if challenged. Samaliel declares his enmity for all of Arthur's men because Arthur killed his father Frollo. Samaliel then defeats Kay, Gaheriet, and Girflet.

144. Lancelot, Hector, Gaheriet, and Gawain at Corbenic.

Lancelot is on the ship many days, but it finally brings him to land at Corbenic. The text explains that a knight can find Corbenic only by chance and not by effort; this is the result of an enchantment, which will be broken only much later, when Charlemagne will destroy Corbenic. In the castle, Lancelot enters the room containing the Holy Grail; he immediately falls unconscious and remains so for twenty-five days. Three days after that, he is at the table with King Pelles when all the doors begin to shake and close. Pelles explains that this is a sign God sends when an unconfessed knight arrives on the quest. That knight is Hector, who is refused admission. Later, Gawain and Gaheriet are also denied admission.

145. Galahad Defeats Palamedes, Who Is Then Baptized and Seated at the Round Table.

Lancelot, Gaheriet, and Hector see the Questing Beast; they meet Palamedes, who defeats and wounds Gaheriet and Hector; then he and Lancelot wound and knock down each other. Palamedes rides away; he overtakes Gawain, who is following the Questing Beast, and knocks him down.

Galahad finds Gawain, who tells him that Palamedes defeated him and killed Lionel; Galahad then challenges Palamedes. The wounded Palamedes, asking for twenty days' truce, then rides back to his father and promises that if he comes out of the fight alive and with honor, he will be baptized.

On his way to meet Galahad, Palamedes encounters Gawain, knocks him down, and promises a later sword fight. Galahad defeats Palamedes but spares him on the condition that he will be baptized. The two go to Esclabor's house; there Palamedes is baptized and instantly healed of all wounds. Galahad tells him to go to Arthur and to become a knight of the Round Table, so that he can enter the quest for the Holy Grail. Palamedes follows the instructions and is made a knight of the Round Table.

146. Galahad and Palamedes at the Spring of Healing, Where They Free Gawain, Gaheriet, Blioberis, and Sagremor from the Giant's Tower.

A year later, Palamedes rejoins Galahad; they go to the Giant's Tower, and Palamedes fights Atamas, who is repeatedly healed by drinking from a spring that restores strength and health. (The Maimed King will later tell Galahad about the Spring of Healing and other marvels.) Palamedes eventually prevails and forces his adversary to free Gawain, Gaheriet, Blioberis, and Sagremor from the tower.

147. Galahad Accomplishes the Adventures of the Burning Tomb and the Hot Spring; Palamedes Kills the Questing Beast.

Galahad rides alone to the abbey where Moses, Simeon's son, burns in his tomb. Moses is freed at Galahad's coming. Later, Galahad meets a knight, traveling with a squire and maiden. They seek water and find a spring, but when the maiden tries to drink, she falls in and is killed, because the water is boiling. The squire and knight are unable to reach into the hot spring, but Galahad prays that the water will become cold, and it does.

Galahad then sees the Questing Beast; he meets Perceval and Palamedes, and together they follow the beast. They find it in a lake. Palamedes kills it; in its death agony it releases flames that make the lake boil. The lake becomes known as "the Lake of the Beast."

148. Galahad at Corbenic; The Quest Is Accomplished.

Galahad, Perceval, and Palamedes arrive at Corbenic. The doors open to them, and they meet nine other knights. Galahad is summoned to enter the presence of the Holy Grail and of the lance. Galahad heals Pellehan, and the lance and basin ascend to heaven. Pellehan leaves, vowing to spend the rest of his life in a hermitage. A voice summons the knights into the chamber of the Holy Grail. There a figure in white appears and offers them the Host. They then ride out and separate. Galahad, Perceval, and Bors are reunited.

149. The Death of Palamedes.

Palamedes meets Lancelot and Hector but does not recognize them. Lancelot challenges him; they do battle, and both are badly wounded, but they make peace and then part. Palamedes meets Gawain and Agravain, who fight him. Gawain wounds him fatally; Lancelot and Hector find him and remain with him until he dies. Esclabor arrives, and they take Palamedes to be buried. Esclabor kills himself, and his blood is used to make an inscription on the tomb.

150. Pellehan Explains the Questing Beast, the Spring of Healing, and the Lady of the Chapel.

Reunited, Galahad, Perceval, and Bors arrive at a hermitage where Pellehan explains to them about the Spring of Healing, the Questing Beast, and the old lady of the chapel.

151. Galahad, Perceval, and Bors Take the Holy Grail to Sarras on Solomon's Ship; Burial of Perceval's Sister.

They ride to the coast and find the ship with the Holy Grail. They board it and sail across the sea. Galahad prays that his life will be ended when he asks, and a voice promises that his wishes will be realized. The Holy Grail has left England forever, and three years of famine will follow. The companions arrive in Sarras, where they are met by a boat containing the body of Perceval's sister. They carry the table and Holy Grail to the Spiritual Palace; then they bury Perceval's sister. Excorante, king of Sarras, imprisons them for a year, but they are nourished by the Holy Grail.

152. Death of Galahad and Perceval; Bors Returns to the Kingdom of Logres.

After a year, Galahad prays to be allowed to die, but instead King Escorante dies, and the people choose Galahad king. A year later, Galahad asks again to die, and this time his prayer is granted. A hand comes down from the sky and takes away the Holy Grail. Perceval becomes a hermit near the city, and a year and two months later he dies. Bors returns to Camelot and tells all that has happened. Hector refuses to forgive Gawain for killing Eric; King Ban's kin lament Lancelot's sin with the queen.

THE POST-VULGATE, PART III. THE DEATH OF ARTHUR

153. Lancelot's Disloyalty Revealed to King Arthur.

Gawain and his brothers argue about whether or not to tell Arthur about Lancelot and Guenevere; finally Agravain tells him. Arthur goes out to hunt, ordering Lancelot not to accompany him. During the king's absence, the brothers surprise

Lancelot with Guenevere. Lancelot kills Einaguis and escapes; he and Bors and the others ride to the outskirts of the forest and then send a squire to learn the queen's fate. King Iom sentences the queen to death by burning. Gawain renounces his feudal oath to Arthur, and Guenevere is brought out to be burned.

154. Lancelot Rescues the Queen, Takes Her to Joyous Guard; Death of Agravain, Guerrehet, and Gaheriet; King Arthur's Grief.

A squire brings the news to Lancelot. Lancelot and his men ride in and rescue the queen; in the process, they kill Agravain, Guerrehet, and Gaheriet. They then ride to Joyous Guard. Arthur and Lancelot both summon all the support they can.

155. War between King Arthur and Lancelot in Britain and Gaul; Gawain Receives His Death Wound; Arthur Defeats the Romans.

King Arthur chooses knights to take the seats at the Round Table formerly occupied by King Ban's kin and by those killed during the queen's rescue. Lancelot sends a maiden to try to make peace, but she is unsuccessful. The archbishop of Canterbury orders peace and requires Arthur to take Guenevere back. Lancelot crosses to Gaunes; on Gawain's advice, Arthur follows him. Gawain challenges Lancelot to single combat, during which he receives a wound that eventually proves fatal. After the battle, Arthur calls an end to his quarrel with Lancelot.

The emperor of Rome attempts to take Gaul and Logres. Arthur fights and kills him and then sends his body back to Rome as the tribute the emperor says he owes.

156. Mordred's Rising; Death of the Knights of Logres; King Arthur in the Ancient Chapel.

Arthur hears that Mordred has assumed power in the kingdom. Kay dies before embarking, and Gawain dies as soon as they land. Arthur kills Mordred, who deals him a mortal wound in return. Only the archbishop of Canterbury, Blioberis, Girflet, Lucan, and Arthur are left alive. The archbishop and Blioberis construct a tower on Salisbury Plain; in it they put the heads of all the dead, hanging Mordred's at the top. The text announces that it will stay there until it is eventually removed by Ganelon, when Charlemagne comes to the land.

Arthur, Lucan, and Girflet go to the Ancient Chapel. There Arthur accidentally crushes Lucan. Arthur and Girflet ride to the sea.

157. Blioberis Goes to Look for Lancelot; Death of Arthur the Less.

After building the tower, the archbishop leaves to become a hermit; Blioberis sets out to look for Lancelot. Arthur the Less is killed when he attacks Blioberis to avenge Lancelot's betrayal of Arthur. Blioberis has him buried.

158. The Death of King Arthur.

Arthur and Girflet ride to the sea. The king sends Girflet to throw Excalibur into the lake. Then he sends him away, and Girflet, watching from a distance, sees Morgan and other ladies coming across the sea in a bark. They take Arthur on board and sail away. Girflet rides to the Ancient Chapel, where he finds a tomb with an inscription announcing that it is Arthur's; inside it, however, is nothing except Arthur's helmet. Girflet stays on in the chapel, spending the rest of his life as a hermit.

159. Guenevere's Death; Lancelot's Last Deeds and Death.

Mordred's sons fortify Winchester, and Guenevere becomes a nun. Lancelot, Bors, and Lionel gather an army and sail for Logres. Lancelot hears news of Guenevere's death and then attacks Mordred's sons at Winchester. One of the sons (Melian) kills Lionel and is killed by Bors. Lancelot pursues the duke of Gorre and kills him. Separated from his army, Lancelot comes to the hermitage where the archbishop and Blioberis are; he vows to stay there for the rest of his life. The army returns to Gaunes with Bors, but Hector stays and joins Lancelot.

Hector dies four years later. A year later, Lancelot dies; the archbishop and Blioberis take his body to Joyous Guard, where Bors joins them. They bury Lancelot alongside his friend Galehaut. Bors returns with the archbishop and Blioberis; Meraugis meets and joins them.

160. The Final Destruction of Logres.

Iseut and Tristan are both dead. Mark learns of Lancelot's death, assembles an army, goes to Britain, and destroys every trace of King Arthur's reign: all the churches and monasteries, Joyous Guard, and Camelot itself. He then disinters Lancelot's body (still uncorrupted) and Galehaut's and burns them. Out of hatred for Galahad, he destroys the Round Table. Then he decides to kill Bors, Blioberis, the archbishop, and Meraugis. He goes to the hermitage and kills the archbishop, but he is then killed by an armed knight, Paulas, and his body is buried nearby, though outside of sacred ground.

Index of Proper Names

by Samuel N. Rosenberg

with

Daniel Golembeski

Index of Proper Names

This index covers all sections of the present work, which are identified as follows:

The index includes all proper nouns except the names of the days and months, the various words and phrases used for the deity, and the names of sacred beings and objects occurring in exclamations, salutations, and the like.

Names of places and things, as well as other entries of a non-personal type, are accompanied by an identifying word in parentheses, e.g., Corbenic (castle), Excalibur (sword), unless their reference is obvious, e.g., Perilous Bridge, Feast of Our Lady, Auvergne.

Names of persons are not normally accompanied by an identifying word. However, if a character's name occurs in the text with an immediately preposed title, the entry is followed by that title, capitalized and in parentheses, e.g., Bademagu (King), Guinas (Count).

In addition, if a character is known in the text by the name of a place, the entry is followed by his or her title printed with a lower-case initial and in parentheses, e.g., Roestoc (lady), Tannings (duke); such an entry should be read: "the lady of Roestoc," "the duke of Tannings."

The text includes numerous designations composed of a common noun followed by a prepositional phrase (generally with the preposition "of"); such nouns may be of personal or non-personal reference, e.g., knight, lady; chronicle, feast, isle, rock, spring, tale, wood, and they may not always occur in the text with capitalization. In some instances, we have judged it appropriate or useful to list phrasal names of this type under the common noun; in others, we have preferred to enter them under the object of the preposition; numerous cross-references facilitate the location of such names.

If a name sometimes occurs in the text with a preceding or following adjective or noun complement, the entry shows that word or phrase in brackets, e.g., [Great] Britain, Bertelay [the Old].

In most cases, the names in this index have a corresponding entry in G.D. West, *An Index of Proper Names in French Arthurian Prose Romances* (Toronto: University of Toronto Press, 1978). Such names are followed by the West equivalents in bracketed italics.

Cross-references are indicated by the word *see* following an empty entry or by the words *see also* following a reference-bearing entry. In addition, the equal sign (=) is occasionally used in cases where the text itself explicitly designates particular names as equivalent.

In numerical references, the number to the left of the colon is that of the *chapter* in the *English* text; the number to the right of the colon is that of the original *Old French* (or Portuguese or Spanish) *page* number indicated in brackets in the body of the English translation. There are no references to pages of the English text.

References are complete for any given chapter unless the page numbers are followed by "etc." The meaning or purpose of other features of the index will be obvious to readers.

Aacena (forest)
        Post2• 124: 99
Aban
        Post2• 78: 49
Abbey of the Cross
        Hist• 39: 279
Abel [the Just] [*Abel*]
        Hist• 21: 460, 461,462, etc.
        Quest• 67: 215, 216; 68: 217, 218, 219; 69: 219; 71: 224; 72: 227
Abelin [*Abelin*]
        Post1• 28: 104
Abilas [*Abilas*] *see also* Ausile
        Lan5• 143: 101
Abraham [*Abraham*]
        Hist• 4: 128
Absalom [*Absalon*]
        Hist• 26: 41
        Quest• 36: 125
Acadoes [*Escadés*]
        Lan3• 76: 86
Acanor [*Acanor*] *see also* Ugly Hero
        Post1• 7: 209
Acantan the Agile
        Post2• 78: 49
Accalon [*Accalon*]

Agravain [the Proud] [*Agravain*]
    Hist• 37: 270
    Merl• 4: 73; 5:96; 10:128,130; 12:134,136,137; 13:139; 18:160; 23:182,184, etc.; 25:192,193,194; 26:196,197; 27:204; 32: 252; 33:262,266,267; 34:275; 37: 302,305; 39: 323; 41: 342,343,344, etc.; 43: 351, 352,353, etc.; 44:357, 358,363; 45:368,369,370, etc.; 48:400; 51: 415; 57: 453
    Lan1•41:424, 425
    Lan2• 51: 39; 60: 230, 231, 233, etc.; 63: 33C; 64: 369, 379, 392; 70: 431, 432
    Lan4• 112: 97; 118: 182; 140: 410, 419
    Lan5• 141: 1, 2, 3, etc.; 142: 61; 143: 86, 91, 99, etc.; 147: 162; 155: 394, 399
    Lan6• 162: 96; 171: 5, 15; 172: 58, 63; 175: 148
    Death• 1: 3, 4, 5, etc.; 2: 29, 30; 5: 64; 11: 107, 109, 111, etc.; 12: 121, 122, 123, etc.; 13: 128, 129, 132
    Post1• 1: 147
    Post2• 48: 56; 53: 90, 91, 92; 54: 98, 99, 100, etc.; 55: 101, 102,105; 56: 113; 58: 125; 59: 131,132; 60: 5, 6, 9, etc.; 61: 22; 64: 51; 66: 76, 77; 78: 49; 118: 44, 45; 120: 65; 123: 97; 139: 262, 263, 265, etc.; 149: 387, 388, 389, etc.; 152: 417; 153: 418, 419, 423, etc.; 154: 430, 431, 436, etc.
Agravain's Hill [*Tertris*[4]] *see also* Hill of Wretches
    Lan5• 143: 91
Agraveil [*Agraveil*]
    Merl• 15: 148
Agregam the Angry
    Post2• 78: 51
Agrestes (King) [*Agrestés*]
    Hist• 34: 195, 196
    Lan4•131:321,322, 323, etc.
Agricol the Well-Spoken [*Agrocol*]
    Lan4• 119: 192
Agrippa [*Agripe*[1]]
    Hist• 3: 122
Agrippes (King) [*Agrippe*[1]]
    Lan4• 118: 172
Aguig(n)eron the Seneschal [*Aguig(n)eron*]
    Merl• 45: 374; 47: 384; 48: 395, 400
    Post2• 71: 142, 143, 144, etc.
Aguinier [*Aguinier*]
    Lan2• 70: 436
Aguisant [of Scotland] (King) [*Aguisant*]
    Merl• 5: 88, 95, 96; 7: 115, 117, 118; 11: 132; 18: 164; 19: 164, 165, 166, etc.; 29: 212; 36: 293, 294, 297; 45: 372; 48: 400; 53: 427; 54: 437
    Lan1• 8: 60; 10: 96
    Lan2•51:39;52:56

Ambush *see* Tower of Ambush, Wood of the Ambush
Amide
  Lan4•115: 139
Aminadap [*Aminadap*]
  Hist• 40: 290, 292
Aminaduc/Minaduc (King) [*Aminaduc*]
  Merl• 7: 113; 21: 175,176
Amint (castle) [*Amint*]
  Post1• 30: 134
Amite (=Helizabel) [*Amite*] *see also* Elaine[1]
  Lan1•8:59, 60
Ammaduc (King) [*Ammadus*]
  Merl• 21: 174
Amores the Swarthy [*Amores*]
  Merl• 15: 148
Amustan (Brother/Sir) [*Amustant*]
  Merl• 37: 302; 38: 314
  Lan3• 80: 159, 164, 165, etc.
Anarom the Fat
  Post2• 78: 51
Anascor [*Nascor*[2]]
  Hist• 12: 295
Anasteu [*Anasteu*]
  Post1• 37: 192
Anathites (bishop)
  Hist• 13: 305
Anbe (castle) [*Anbe*]
  Post1• 27: 81
Ancient Chapel
  Post2• 156: 459; 158: 465, 469, 472
Aneblayse (city) [*Daneblaise*]
  Merl• 14:141; 16:156; 29:213; 30: 226,236; 31: 238; 37:300
Angale of Raguidel [*Orvale de Guindoel*]
  Lan4• 138: 397
Angelica
  Post2• 119:49
Angelis of the Vaaos
  Post2• 78: 51
Anguin [*Anguins•*]
  Lan1• 18: 232
Anguingeron *see* Aguig(n)eron
Animal [*Beste*[1] *Diverse*]
  Hist• 1:25, 26, 28, etc.
Anseliam the Poor
  Post2• 123: 99
Anselm *see* Alelme

Arfusat the Fat [*Alpharsar*]
    Lan4•119: 190
Argant (King) [*Agans*]
    Merl• 50: 409, 411
Argistes [*Agristes*]
    Hist• 37: 270
Argodras [the Red] [*Argondras*] *see also* Red Knight
    Lan4• 120: 223; 121: 244, 245, 246
Argon [*Argon*[1]]
    Hist• 35: 216, 218
    Lan4• 132: 337, 338
Arguel (King)
    Lan3• 82: 182
Arguste [*Argustes*]
    Quest• 44: 143
Aride [of Galore] (King) [*Aride*] *see also* Agravadain[1]
    Merl• 50: 409
Arimathea (city) [*Arimachie*] *see also* Joseph of Arimathea
    Hist• 2: 47; 4: 141, 152; 25: 12, 23; 27: 100, 102; 28: 103; 35: 210, 215;
    37: 271
    Lan4• 132: 330
Arion
    Post2• 65: 70
Aristobokis [*Aristobokis*]
    Merl• 48: 398
Arnal the Handsome
    Post2• 78: 51
Arnantes (forest)
    Post2• 136: 229; 147: 365
Arnauld (Count)
    Post2• 133: 183, 187
Aroans [of Betinia] (King) [*Aroans*]
    Merl• 30: 223, 224
Arodian of Cologne [*Arodions*]
    Lan2• 71: 488
Aroel (duke) [*Aroel*]
    Death• 14: 149
Arpian[1] of the Narrow Mountain
    Post2• 130: 155, 163
Arpian[2] of the Strange Mountain
    Post2• 78: 51
Arpian[3] of the Treacherous Castle
    Post2• 140: 280
Arramant the Fat [*Atramant*]
    Lan4• 121: 229

Arrant [*Arrant*]
     Merl• 21: 175; 41: 340
Arroux (river) [*Aroaise*]
     Merl• 33: 261
Arrow (castle) [*Fleche*]
     Lan4• 121: 240
Arsie (river) [*Arsie*]
     Lan1• 2: 21
Arsonne (river) [*Aisurne, Saverne*] *see also* Severn
     Merl• 28: 208
Artel
     Post2• 78: 51
Arthur[1] [the Adventurous/of Britain] (King) [*Artu*]
     Hist• 7: 184; 32: 160; 34: 199; 35: 224; 36: 241; 37: 270, 271; 38: 275;
     40: 292, 296
     Merl• 4: 68, 76, 77, etc.; 5: 83, 84, 85, etc.; 6: 101,102, 104, etc.; 7: 109, 110,
     111, etc.; 8: 121, 122, 123, etc.; 9: 125, 126, 127, etc.; 10: 128, 129, 130, etc.;
     11: 132, 133; 12: 133, 134, 135; 13: 138, 141; 14: 141, 143, 145; 15: 145, 146,
     147, etc.; 16: 151, 153, 154, etc.; 17: 157, 158, 159; 18: 159,161; 19: 165,
     167; 20: 171,172; 21: 177, 178; 22: 178, 179; 23: 180, 181, 183, etc.; 25: 193,
     195; 26: 196, 199, 200, etc.; 27: 205; 28: 207, 208; 29: 213, 214, 215, etc.; 30:
     222, 225, 226, etc.; 31: 236, 237, 238, etc.; 32: 243, 244, 246, etc.; 33: 256,
     259, 260, etc.; 34: 268, 269, 270, etc.; 35: 279, 281, 291; 36: 292, 293, 298;
     37: 299, 300, 301, etc.; 38: 312, 313, 314, etc.; 39: 315, 316, 317, etc.; 40:
     335, 336, 337, etc.; 41: 340, 341; 42: 346, 347; 43: 352, 353; 44: 359, 364; 45:
     371, 373, 374; 46: 374, 375, 377, etc.; 47: 384, 385, 386, etc.; 48: 393, 394,
     395, etc.; 49: 401, 403, 407; 50: 407, 408, 409, etc.; 51: 413, 414, 415, etc.;
     52: 420, 422, 423, etc.; 53: 427, 428, 430, etc.; 54: 434, 435, 436, etc.; 55:
     441, 442, 443, etc.; 56: 449; 57: 449, 450, 451, etc.; 58: 453, 454, 455, etc.;
     59: 459, 461, 462, etc.; 60: 465
     Lan1• 1: 3, 5, 6, etc.; 8: 56, 57, 59, etc.; 10: 94. 95, 96, etc.; 11: 104, 108; 14:
     129, 153; 19: 236; 20: 236, 238, 239, etc.; 21: 247, 258, 259, etc.; 22: 260,
     262, 265, etc.; 23: 298, 299, 300, etc.; 24: 321, 331; 25: 333, 334, 336, etc.;
     26: 340, 341, 342; 27: 347; 28: 351; 29: 356, 359, 360, etc.; 31: 371, 373; 32:
     374, 379; 33: 381, 382; 34: 387, 388, 392, etc.; 35: 394; 37: 402; 39: 407, 411;
     40: 413; 41: 423, 424; 42: 428; 43: 430, 431, 434; 44: 434; 45: 438, 439; 46:
     440; 47: 442, 448, 449; 48: 453, 454, 457
     Lan2• 49: 1, 2, 8, etc.; 50: 35; 51: 35; 52: 40, 50, 54, etc.; 53: 132; 54: 132; 56:
     158; 58: 202; 60: 231, 234; 61: 274, 279, 280, etc.; 62: 323; 63: 327, 338; 66:
     407; 67: 413; 68: 415; 70: 430, 431, 432, etc.; 71: 456, 459, 461, etc.
     Lan3• 72: 1; 73: 3, 8, 9, etc.; 74: 18, 19, 22; 75: 36, 37, 38, etc.; 76: 75, 78,
     85; 77: 92, 93, 94, etc.; 78: 111, 112, 115, etc.; 79: 127; 80: 153, 157,158, etc.;
     83: 189; 84: 201; 85: 208, 213; 95: 300; 97: 330; 98: 335; 99: 344, 346, 347;
     100: 350
     Lan4• 107: 2, 4, 6; 108: 26; 111: 85, 89, 92, etc.; 112: 102; 113:107; 114: 111,
     112,113, etc.; 121: 236, 255; 123: 267; 124: 267, 268, 277; 131: 319; 136:

357; 137: 388 Lan5• 142: 62; 143: 66, 70; 145: 125; 150: 223; 151: 248, 252; 154: 287, 335, 340; 155: 355, 357, 361; 156: 4, 7, 36; 157: 50, 53

Lan6• 159: 63; 164: 145; 165: 152,153, 161, etc.; 166: 188; 167: 223; 169: 264; 170: 294; 171: 3, 15, 16, etc.; 172: 50, 60, 61, etc.; 175: 97, 110, 123, etc.; 176: 153, 154,155, etc.; 177: 183; 179: 243, 244

Quest• 1: 3; 3: 7; 4: 8; 5: 13,16; 6: 18; 7: 23; 16: 63; 17: 66; 20: 72, 74; 23: 80; 25: 87; 26: 87; 29: 99; 31: 108; 34: 117; 47: 153; 49: 158; 61: 190; 73: 229, 230, 231; 79: 261, 262; 83: 273; 85: 279

Death• 1: 1, 3, 5, etc.; 2: 28, 30; 3: 34, 39; 4: 43, 55; 5: 55, 56, 57, etc.; 6: 75; 7: 78, 81; 8: 81, 83, 84, etc.; 9: 95; 11: 114,115,118; 12: 120, 121, 122, etc.; 13: 127, 128, 133, etc.; 14: 137, 138, 139, etc.; 15: 153,154, 155; 16: 164,165,167, etc.; 17: 171, 172,173, etc.; 18: 181, 182, 183, etc.; 19: 195, 204; 20: 206, 207, 208, etc.; 21: 210, 211, 212, etc.; 22: 219, 221, 222, etc.; 23: 225, 226, 227, etc.; 24: 246, 250, 251, etc.; 25: 252, 258, 259

Post1• 1: 147, 148; 3: 165, 166, 168, etc.; 4: 174, 176, 179, etc.; 5: 184, 189, 194, etc.; 6: 199, 202; 7: 207, 209, etc.; 8: 214, 222; 9: 226, 229, 230; 10: 235, 237, 239, etc.; 11: 243, 244, 248, etc.; 12: 249, 250, 251, etc.; 13: 254, 256, 257, etc.; 14: 262, 263, 265, etc.; 15: 268, 269, 273, etc.; 16: 277; 17: 1, 5; 19: 21; 20: 26, 29; 23: 59, 60; 24: 62, 63, 64, etc.; 25: 68, 71, 72, etc.; 26: 77, 78, 80; 27: 94, 97, 99; 28: 104, 106, 114; 29: 117, 118, 122, etc.; 30: 132, 135; 31: 141; 32: 151, 152, 153; 33: 158, 159; 34: 159, 160, 161, etc.; 35: 173; 36: 173, 174, 176, etc.; 37: 193, 199; 38: 199, 200, 201, etc.; 39: 215; 40: 216, 217, 219, etc.; 41: 228, 229, 242, etc.; 42: 249, 250, 251, etc.

Post2• 43: 25, 30; 44: 35; 46: 40; 48: 56, 57; 50: 63, 66; 51: 69, 75; 52: 80, 81; 53: 88, 91, 92; 54: 93, 95, 98; 56: 106, 107,115; 57:120; 58:124; 59: 131; 60:1, 2, 5, etc.; 61: 22; 63: 45; 64: 53; 66: 80; 67: 86, 89, 90, etc.; 68:106,113, 119; 69: 129; 70: 131, 133, 134, etc.; 74: 17; 75: 19, 25; 76: 31; 77: 37; 78: 41, 45, 47, etc.; 79: 57; 83: 95, 99; 84: 111, 113, 125; 85: 131; 87: 165, 167; 88: 173,175, 179; 94: 241; 96: 267; 98: 283; 101: 313; 103: 325; 105: 335; 107: 359; 108: 367, 369; 111: 385, 389, 391, etc.; 114: 19; 120: 498; 121: 77, 79; 122: 81, 87; 123: 87, 89, 91, etc.; 126:119; 130: 151; 131:173; 132:179; 133: 187; 134: 201, 207; 135: 207, 209, etc.; 136: 223; 137: 233, 235, 239, etc.; 138: 251; 139: 262, 268, 269, etc.; 140: 279, 280, 498; 141: 292; 142: 301, 303, 304; 143: 311, 313, 316; 145: 355; 149: 394; 151: 407, 409; 152: 415, 417; 153: 424, 429, 430; 154: 435, 436, 443; 155: 447, 449, 451; 156: 453, 454, 455, etc.; 157: 461, 465; 158: 465, 467, 469, etc.; 159: 472, 475; 160: 490, 491

Arthur² [the Less] [*Artus¹*]

Post2• 122: 87; 123: 91, 93, 95, etc.; 136: 217, 219, 221, etc.; 137: 233, 235, 237, etc.; 148: 375; 157: 461, 463, 465

Arun (river) [*Aisurne*] *see also* Arsonne

Merl• 26: 199

Arundel (city) [*Arondel*]

Merl• 18: 160, 161, 162, etc.; 19: 168; 20: 171; 24: 190; 25: 191; 26: 198,199, 200, etc.; 27: 202, 205; 32: 255

Asalim the Poor
    Post2• 78: 51
Ascension [Day/Sunday]
    Hist• 1: 38
    Merl• 14: 142; 55: 441
    Lan1• 20: 236
    Lan3• 77: 109; 78: 116, 119
    Lan4• 107: 1, 2; 108: 21
    Post2• 52: 81; 60: 21
Asgares the Sad
    Post2• 84: 113; 85: 137,139
Assen (King) [*Assen*]
    Post1• 37: 192
Assumption (Feast of the)
    Lan1• 1:9
Atamas *see also* Knight of the Spring
    Post2• 146: 364, 365
Ataz
    Post2• 78: 51
Athean (castle) [*Athean*]
    Death• 3: 39
Athens (city) [*Athenes*]
    Hist• 27: 91
    Post2• 109: 371; 119: 49
Aube (river) [*Aube*]
    Merl• 53: 431; 57: 449
Audolus [*Audolus*]
    Merl• 29: 218
Augustine *see* Saint Augustine
Augustus Caesar [*Auguste, Cesar*]
    Hist• 4: 135; 8: 210, 211; 26: 30, 33
Augut (castle) [*Augut*]
    Post2• 70: 131
Aula (forest)
    Post2• 134: 205
Aupatris (giant) [*Aupatris*]
    Post2• 57: 123
Ausile [*Abilas*] *see also* Abilas
    Lan5• 143: 104
Ausurne (river) [*Assume*]
    Lan2• 53: 129; 63: 332; 67: 409; 69: 418
    Lan3• 73: 8, 9
Autragais [*Autragais*]
    Lan1• 23: 305
Autun (city) [*0(s)tun*]
    Merl• 52: 427; 54: 437, 438

Banin [of Trebe] [*Banin*]
     Merl• 5: 98; 6: 109; 33: 258; 34: 272; 46: 376; 60: 465, 466
     Lan1• 2: 13, 14, 15, etc.; 20: 238, 239, 240, etc.
     Lan4• 121: 239, 240
     Lan5• 152: 278
     Lan6• 162: 96, 112; 173: 78, 79; 174: 86
     Post2• 78: 49
Baradam
     Post2• 130: 151, 153
Baradan the Young
     Post2• 78: 51
Baram
     Post2• 123: 99
Baramal (King) [*Baramaus*]
     Merl• 20: 172
Barbary (land) [*Barbaric*]
     Merl• 56: 449
     Post2• 128: 133
Barren Wasteland [*Deserte*]
     Lan6• 172: 56
Baruch (castle) [*Barut(h)*]
     Hist• 27: 98
Bast *see* Urien[2]
Bastard (horse)
     Post2• 85: 135
Baudon [*Baudon*]
     Post2• 54: 98; 56: 107, 108, 109, etc.
Baufumes (King) [*Baitramés, Baufumes*]
     Merl• 30: 232, 234, 235
Beast *see* Bizarre Beast
Beaumont *see* Aces
Beautiful Retreat (castle)
     Post2• 71: 147
Bed of Wonder [*Lit*[1] *des Mervelles*] *see also* Adventurous Bed
     Lan6• 169: 259
Bedivere [the Constable] [*Bedoi(i)er*]
     Merl• 53: 428, 429, 431; 54: 435, 436, 438, etc.
     Lan1• 10: 97, 99; 22: 261
     Lan4• 111: 90, 91; 112: 97
Bedoin (Count)
     Post2• 142: 305, 307
Belande (city) [*Belande*]
     Merl• 11: 131
Belcis (King) [*Belcis*]
     Merl• 54: 437

Benoic³ (meadow) [*Benoïc(h)*]
    Lan1• 2: 21
Benoic⁴ (queen) [*Benoïc(h)*] *see also* Elaine [of Benoic]
    Merl• 50: 408
    Lan1• 5: 37; 10: 86, 88, 94; 16: 197; 19: 232, 236
    Lan5• 154: 301
    Lan6• 175: 120
    Post2• 99: 293
Bernant of North Wales (King) [*Belinant¹*] *see also* Belinant
    Lan2• 61: 277
Berry [*Berri*]
    Merl• 5: 98
    Lan1• 1: 1; 8: 57
    Lan6• 165: 152
Bertelay/Bretelai [the Old/the Red] [*Bert(h)olai)*
    Merl• 29: 219; 37: 310, 311, 312; 38: 312, 313; 46: 375
    Lan3• 74: 23, 29; 77: 96, 98; 78: 121; 79: 125, 127,132; 80:153, 154, 161, etc.
Bestoc (castle) [*Bestoc*]
    Lan6• 176: 158, 159
Bethany (land) [*Betanie*]
    Hist• 4: 123, 124
Bethlehem (city/land) [*Bethleem*]
    Hist• 4: 138; 13: 304
Betinia *see* Aroans
Beyond [the Borders] *see* Land Beyond [the Borders]
[Bizarre] Beast [*Beste² Glatissant*] *see also* Questing Beast
    Post1• 1: 150; 2: 153, 158, 160; 13: 258, 259, 260
    Post2• 83: 111; 85: 125, 129, etc.; 91: 197; 97: 275-7; 145: 343
Black¹ Chapel [*Noire Chapele*]
    Death• 24: 246, 251,252
Black² Cross [*Crois⁵ Noire*]
    Merl• 10: 129
    Lan4• 131: 320, 324
Black³ Isle [*Isle²¹ Noire*] *see also* Mador the Black
    Lan1• 10: 99
Black⁴ Knight *see also* Lancelot²
    Lan2• 52: 87, 93, 95, etc.
Blaharis [*Blaaris²*]
    Merl• 39: 324
Blair [*Blaires*]
    Merl• 14: 142
Blaise [*Blaise*]
    Merl• 1: 18, 19; 2: 26, 27, 35; 3: 35, 36, 41, etc.; 4: 70, 74, 80; 5: 97; 6: 106, 108; 7: 121; 22: 179, 180; 23:180; 28: 206, 207; 29: 222; 32: 256; 36: 292, 293; 37: 300; 38: 314, 315; 46: 375, 376; 49: 406; 52: 421, 422; 57:

Brodan
    Post2• 78: 51
Broken Sword [*Espee³ Brisiee*]
    Quest 81: 266
Bron [*Bron*]
    Hist• 30: 131; 34: 199, 202, 203, etc.; 35: 223, 232; 39: 282
    Merl• 29: 221
Brumand [the Proud] [*Brumant*]
    Lan6• 171: 21, 25, 26, etc.; 174: 86
Brun [the Merciless/the Ruthless] [*Brehu*]
    Merl• 21: 177; 24: 188; 36: 294, 297
    Lan1• 35: 396; 37: 398, 399, 400, etc.; 39: 405, 406, 408, etc.; 41: 422, 423
Brut (castle)
    Post2• 86: 141
Brutus (King)
    Post2• 86: 141, 143
Burgundy [*Bo(u)rgoigne*]
    Merl• 28: 209; 52: 427; 53: 431
    Death• 20: 206, 207
Byanne [*Byanne*]
    Merl• 58: 455
Bylas [*Bylas*]
    Merl• 24: 191

Cabarentin [of Cornwall] (King) [*Cabarentins*] *see also* Esbarantin
    Lan4• 124: 267
    Lan6• 171: 36; 172: 64; 175: 88, 123
    Death• 23: 230, 238
Cabrion (lady) [*Briestoc*]
    Lan3• 87: 218, 221
Cadant [*Chadians*]
    Lan6• 174: 86
Cador [*Cador*]
    Merl• 52: 425; 54: 435, 436
Cadwain of Carmurain [*Karadoains*]
    Lan1• 27: 347
    Lan2• 51:39;54: 142
Caelenc (King) [*Caelenc*]
    Merl• 15: 146, 147
Caerleon *see* Carlion
Caesar *see* Julius Caesar
Caiam (city)
    Post2• 156: 453
Caiaphas [*Caÿphas*]
    Hist• 2: 69, 70; 3: 78, 112, 115, etc.
    Post2• 132: 177

Lan2• 60: 233; 61: 246, 256; 63: 326, 327, 330, etc.; 64: 365, 373, 379; 66: 407

Camelot[1] (city) [*Camaalot*[1]] *see also* Alma, Limangin, Lucas, Luzes, Tanadal

Hist• 34: 195, 199; 41: 302

Merl• 22: 179, 180; 23: 180, 183, 184, etc.; 24: 186, 191; 49: 401, 402; 50: 407, 410, 411; 51: 414, 419

Lan1• 21: 260; 22: 260, 264, 271; 33: 383; 44: 434, 435; 45: 438, 439; 47: 441, 442, 450, etc.

Lan2• 49: 1; 52: 105, 108; 54: 133

Lan3• 74: 18; 77: 89; 80: 154, 159; 84: 197

Lan4• 107: 1, 2; 111: 84, 85; 121: 233, 254; 128: 310; 130: 314; 131: 319, 321

Lan5• 144: 110, 113, 118; 146: 131, 133; 147: 148; 149: 203, 209; 150: 221; 151: 241; 152: 284; 153: 284, 285; 154: 294, 295, 338, etc.; 155; 346, 356, 357, etc.; 156: 2, 8; 157: 52

Lan6• 159: 62; 164: 139, 145, 146, etc.; 165: 151, 167; 167: 216, 221, 226; 169: 247, 274; 171: 3, 4, 6, 14, etc.; 172: 61; 176: 153, 155, 171, etc.; 177: 179; 178: 207; 179: 244

Quest• 1: 1, 2, 3; 5: 13, 14; 8: 25; 45: 147; 47: 152; 49: 159; 85: 279

Death• 1: 1, 4, 6, etc.; 2: 22, 29; 3: 30; 4: 48, 49, 50; 5: 55, 58, 60, etc.; 6: 68, 72, 73, 75; 7: 75, 78, 81; 8: 81, 83, 87, 90, 92, etc.; 9: 93, 95, 97; 10: 98, 101; 11: 119; 12: 122; 13: 127, 132, 136; 14: 137, 139, 141; 15: 161, 162; 22: 220, 222, 224; 23: 225, 237

Post1• 6: 200; 8: 213; 9: 232, 233; 14: 262, 264; 19: 20; 23: 60, 65; 25: 69, 72, 73; 26: 76; 27: 81, 82, 96; 28: 104, 106, 108, etc.; 29: 121, 122, 123; 31: 139, 142; 34: 159, 168; 36: 174, 177, 178, etc.; 38: 210, 211, 212; 39: 215, 216; 40: 217, 219, 223; 41: 229, 232

Post2• 48: 56; 52: 81, 84; 53: 89, 90; 54: 94; 58: 124; 59: 131; 60: 1, 5, 21; 61: 23; 63: 36; 65: 65; 67: 86; 73: 3; 74: 9; 75: 27; 78: 41; 79: 53; 85: 131; 92: 221, 225; 105: 335; 121: 77, 79, 81; 123: 97; 134: 201; 135: 209, 211, 213; 136: 219, 223, 227, 231; 137: 233, 235, 237, etc.; 138: 251, 253; 139: 262, 268, 269, 277; 140: 277, 287, 499; 141: 292, 293; 142: 303; 144: 331; 145: 355, 357; 147: 367; 148: 373, 382; 150: 401; 152: 415; 153: 421, 427; 155: 443, 448; 160: 490

Camelot[2] (forest) [*Camaalot*[1]]

Lan4• 124: 267; 131: 320

Lan6• 171: 16; 177: 178; 179: 242

Death• 6: 73; 7: 78; 11: 113; 13: 127

Post1• 41: 232

Post2• 52: 81, 84; 54: 99; 61: 23; 73: 3; 78: 47

Camengues/Camugnes (castellan) [*Camugnes*]

Merl• 20: 173; 21: 177

Camille [*Camille*[1]]

Hist• 37: 267, 268

Camugnes *see* Camengues

Cart[2,3] (knight) *see* Knight of the Cart
Cart[4] (story) [*Contes*[1] *de la C(h)arete*] *see also* Charrette
  Lan3• 76: 83
Case (castle) [*C(h)astel*[41] *de la Casse*]
  Lan5• 149: 207, 208; 150: 213
  Lan6• 164: 140
Casibilant [*Cassibilans*]
  Lan5• 143: 101
Castle of ... *see* following noun
Castle Passing [*Chastel*[32] *du Trespas*]
  Lan5• 151: 262, 263; 156: 13, 38
  Lan6• 158: 56, 57, 58, etc.; 159: 70; 162: 106; 172: 54
Cat *see* Hill of the Cat
Catanance
  Post2• 100: 305
Catelina
  Post2• 119: 49
Catenois [*Catenois*]
  Merl• 54: 435, 436
Caulas[1] [the Chieftain] [*Caulas*[1]]
  Merl• 31: 236, 241, 242
Caulas[2] the Red [*Caulas*[2]]
  Merl• 57: 453
Celeca (lake)
  Post2• 94: 247
Celibe (forest) [*Celibe*]
  Quest• 63: 198
Celice (river) [*Celice*]
  Hist• 35: 218
Celidoine [*Celidoine*]
  Hist•18: 406, 414; 19: 427; 20: 435; 22: 496; 23: 496, 497, 498, etc.; 24: 533,
  534, 535, etc.; 27: 95, 100, 102; 28: 103, 104, 115, etc.; 29: 125; 31: 134,
  143,144, etc.; 32: 146, 149; 33: 169, 171, 180, etc.; 34: 207; 40: 296; 41: 296,
  297, 298, etc.
  Merl• 29: 221
  Quest• 41: 135, 136
Celinant [*Belinan*[1]]
  Lan6• 178: 210, 211, 215, etc.
Celinas [*Celynas*]
  Merl• 30: 224
Celis (castle) [*Celys*]
  Post2• 114: 17
Celise[1] (=Saraide) [*Saraide*]
  Lan2• 64: 361
Celise[2] (river) [*Celice*]
  Post2• 114: 17

Dark² (river) [*Tembre*]
     Lan3• 76: 83
Darnantes (forest) [*Darnantes*]
     Hist• 35: 218, 223, 224, etc.
     Merl• 28: 208
     Lan1• 6: 43
David (King) [*David*]
     Hist• 6: 164; 7: 180; 17: 371, 373; 21: 464, 465, 469, etc.
     Lan1• 3: 23; 15: 192; 21: 256
     Lan2• 49: 14
     Lan5• 142: 27
     Lan6• 162: 97
     Quest• 3: 7; 21: 74; 25: 86; 36: 125; 68: 218; 69: 220; 70: 223
     Death• 6: 70
     Post2•75: 19; 81: 79
Dawn (forest) [*Aube¹*]
     Quest• 76: 246
Day¹ of Branches *see also* Palm Sunday
     Post2• 92: 219
Day² of Judgment *see also* Judgment [Day]
     Quest• 77: 252
     Post2• 96: 273
Day³ of the Purification *see* Purification
Dead¹ (Tower of the) *see* Tower of the Dead
Dead² (Valley of the) *see* Valley of the Dead
Death of King Arthur (story)
     Death• 1: 1
Deep Valley [*Val¹² Parfont*]
     Merl• 36: 297
Delimaz the Poor
     Post2• 78: 51
Demophon [*Demophon*]
     Post1• 32: 147
Denmark¹ (king) [*Danemarc(h)e*]
     Merl• 21: 174
     Quest• 11: 40
     Post1• 34: 159
Denmark² (land) [*Danemarc(h)e*]
     Merl• 16: 155; 17: 158; 21: 174
     Quest• 81: 267
Desert (land/title) [*Deserte*] *see also* Taulat, Blioberis
     Post2• 130: 151, 153
Deserted Forest
     Post2• 147: 369
Desired Knight (Galahad) [*Bon Chevalier¹*]
     Quest• 3: 7

Donadix
    Post2• 123: 97; 126: 111
Doon [of Carduel] [*Do*] *see also* Girflet
    Merl• 13: 138, 140; 27: 205, 206; 32: 254, 255; 57: 453
    Quest• 14: 55
Dorilas [*Dorilas*[1]]
    Merl• 16: 151; 19: 169, 170; 31: 236, 242; 36: 294; 47: 390, 391
Dorin [*Dorin*]
    Lan1• 8: 53, 57, 69; 11: 103; 12: 118; 14: 124, 125; 15: 186; 17: 215
    Lan6•175: 114,116
Douglas [*Doulais*]
    Merl• 39: 327
Dover (port) [*Do(u)vre*]
    Merl• 18: 160; 22: 179; 32: 255, 256; 33: 356; 57: 450
    Death• 22: 219; 23: 225, 227
Dragan
    Post2• 74: 15
Driadam [*Driadam*]
    Post2• 64: 51
Drian[1] [*Drian(t)*[2]]
    Post2• 60: 1; 66: 74, 76, 77, 78; 69: 121, 127
Drian[2] [the Gay/the Merry/of the Wild Forest] [*Drian(t)* [3]]
    Merl• 6: 103; 7: 112; 15: 148; 20: 173; 57: 453
    Lan3• 84: 195, 196, 197, etc.
Druas the Cruel [*Druas*]
    Lan5•141: 1,3. 4, etc.
Drulios of the Hamlet [*Drulios*]
    Merl• 6: 103
Dry[1] Island [*Ille*[10] *Seche*]
    Lan4• 125: 292
Dry[2] Island with the Green Pine [*Isle*[28] *Seche du Pin Vert*]
    Post2• 65: 70
Duiche (castle)
    Lan3• 100: 355
Dun [-Issout] (castle/lord) [*Dun*]
    Lan1• 8: 58; 14: 165, 166, 168
Dyabiaus [*Dyabiaus*]
    Quest• 23: 81
Dyoglis [*Dyoglis*]
    Merl• 47: 391
Dyonas/Dionas [*Dyonas*]
    Merl• 28: 208, 209, 211; 35: 280; 46: 376, 377; 47: 390; 48: 396
Dyonis [*Dyonis*[1]]
    Lan5• 143: 101

East [*Orient*[1]]
    Hist• 4: 137
Easter
    Hist• 1: 36, 39; 29: 125; 41: 304
    Merl• 5: 85; 9: 128; 12: 133; 14: 141
    Lan1• 20: 236, 237, 238
    Lan2• 63: 329
    Lan3• 77: 108; 78: 111, 115; 80: 171, 172
    Lan5• 157: 54
    Lan6• 159: 60, 61, 66; 164: 125, 139, 140, etc.; 165: 165; 171: 25; 176: 170;
    177: 205; 178: 220; 179: 244
    Quest• 77: 251; 82: 270
    Death• 16: 165,166
    Post2• 52: 81; 113: 14
Ebron (valley) [*Ebron*[1]]
    Hist• 17: 388
Ector *see* Antor
Eden *see* Paradise of Delight
Eglantine [*Eglente*]
    Merl• 20: 171
Egypt [*Egypte*]
    Hist• 4: 131, 138; 7: 183; 8: 218; 25: 11, 14, 20; 29: 125
    Post1• 33: 155
Egyptian (s)
    Hist• 4: 131, 132; 5: 155; 8: 200; 9: 234; 10: 263; 23: 522
Einaguis
    Post2• 153: 425
Eladinan
    Post2• 78: 51
Elaine[1] *see also* Amite
    Post2• 73: 3
Elaine[2] [of Benoic] (Queen) [*Helaine*[1]] *see also* Queen of Great Sorrows
    Merl• 5: 99; 33: 259; 34: 277; 60: 465
    Lan1• 3: 24, 31; 5: 37; 10: 86; 19: 232, 233
    Lan6• 162: 114
    Post1• 31: 143
    Post2•99:293,295;141:289
Elaine[3] the Peerless [*Heliene*]
    Lan1• 8: 59
    Lan2• 65: 400, 406
Elcan
    Hist• 2: 47
Elians
    Post2• 155: 445
Eliant [*Elianz*]
    Death• 14: 138

Epiphany
  Lan1• 10:93
 Eric [*Erec*]
    Post2• 61: 22, 23, 24; 62: 25, 26, 27, etc.; 63: 46; 64: 47, 48, 49, etc.; 67: 89,
    100; 68: 101, 102, 103, etc.; 69: 121, 130; 70: 131, 132, 133, etc.; 74: 15, 17;
    75: 17; 77: 37; 79: 55; 113: 8, 9, 11; 114: 14, 15, 17, etc.; 115: 25, 26, 27, etc.;
    116: 32, 33, 35, etc.; 117: 38, 39, 41; 118: 41, 43, 44, etc.; 119: 45, 47, 57, etc.;
    120: 59, 61, 63, 497, etc.; 121: 69, 71, 73, etc.; 122: 83, 85; 139: 274, 275;
    144: 328, 331; 152:415,417
Ernol, Count [*Herno(u)l*]
    Quest• 73: 232, 233
Errant's Hermitage
    Lan5• 151: 248
Esbarantin of Cornwall (King) [*Cabarentins*] *see also* Cabarentin
    Lan5• 155: 356
Escalon the Dark (castle) [*Escalon*]
    Lan3• 87: 235; 92: 266; 95: 284; 96: 310; 101: 360
Escalone (kingdom)
    Lan3• 80: 169
Escalot[1] (castle) [*Escalot*]
    Death• 1: 14, 15; 2: 22; 3: 35, 36, 38, etc.; 4: 50; 6: 66, 67
Escalot[2] (maiden) [*Escalot*]
    Death• 8: 89, 91, 92; 11: 107
Escan(t) of Cambenic (Duke) [*Escan(t)*]
    Merl• 7: 110, 116, 118; 21: 177; 23: 186; 24: 188, 189; 36: 293, 294; 45: 365,
    367, 369, etc.; 47: 383, 391; 48: 395, 396, 400; 53: 427; 54: 437
    Lan2• 60: 217; 61: 278
Escavalon (location of battle/residence) [*Escavalon(s)*]
    Lan3• 82: 182
    Lan4• 113: 105
Esclabor [the Unknown] [*Escaliborc[1]/Esclabor(t)*]
    Post2• 87: 165, 167; 93: 225; 136: 217, 227; 137: 233, 241, 249; 145:
    345, 353; 149: 393, 394
Esclamor[1] [*Esclamor[1]*]
    Lan6• 174: 86; 175: 98, 99, 100, etc.; 176: 168
Esclamor[2] of the Red City [*Esclamor•*]
    Lan6• 162: 93
Escorant/Escorante (King) [*Escorant*]
    Quest• 84: 276; 85: 277
    Post2• 151:411; 152:411
Escose (city) [*Escolte*]
    Hist• 32: 163
Esterbury (place) [*Estreberes*]
    Lan2• 64: 376
Estorel [the Poor] [*Estorel*]
    Lan2• 52: 48, 49

Estral (castle) [*Estraus*] *see also* Kay of Estral
    Lan3• 96: 313
Estrangorre (land) [*Estrangort*] *see also* Caradoc[2]
    Merl• 7: 110; 11: 131; 20: 171, 173; 26: 198; 47: 384; 48:
    400; 58: 455, 456
Estrangort (city) [*Estrangort*] *see also* Gaswain
    Merl• 11: 132; 20: 171, 173; 26: 199; 32: 252
    Lan1• 33: 383
    Lan4• 129: 311; 136: 354
Eteocles of Thebes (King) [*Ethioclés*]
    Merl• 30: 230
Euphrates (river) [*Eufrate(s)*]
    Hist• 3: 121; 4: 123; 20: 447; 30: 126
    Quest• 65: 202
Evadain (King) [*Evadain*]
    Merl• 48: 395, 400
Evadeam[1] (King) [*Evadeam*[1]]
    Merl• 58: 456
Evadeam[2] the Dwarf [*Evadeam*[1]]
    Merl• 58: 457; 59: 464
Evaine [of Gaunes] (Queen) [*Evain(n)e*] *see also* Gaunes[5]
    Lan1• 4: 32, 36; 19: 234
    Quest• 50: 165
Evalach [the Unknown] (=Mordrain) [*Evalac(h)*]
    Hist• 4: 131, 132, 133, etc.; 5: 155, 159, 161; 6: 162, 165, 166; 7: 196; 8: 197,
    200, 202, etc.; 9: 222, 223, 228, etc.; 10: 248, 250, 252, etc.; 11: 264, 265; 12:
    284, 286, 288, etc.; 17: 360, 361, 362, etc.; 23: 500
    Quest• 10: 32, 33, 34; 25: 84; 41: 134, 135
    Post2• 80: 69, 71
Evalachin (castle) [*Valacin*]
    Hist• 8: 208, 209, 216, etc.; 9: 222, 224
Evander (King) [*Evander*]
    Merl• 54: 435, 436
Evangelist
    Hist• 35: 224
    Post2• 93: 231
Eve [*Eve*]
    Hist• 21: 453, 455, 456, etc.; 32: 153
    Merl• 1: 3
    Quest• 33: 113; 67: 210, 211, 212, etc.; 69: 219; 77: 251
    Post1• 9: 231
Evieran of Ganaor
    Post2• 78: 51
Excalibur (sword) [*Escalibor*]
    Merl• 5: 94, 95; 15: 146, 147; 16: 153; 30: 230, 235; 31: 240; 37: 306; 39: 317,
    328; 41: 340, 342; 43: 354, 355, 356; 44: 358, 362; 45: 367, 368; 48: 394

Fury/Wrathful (sword) [*Courec(h)ouse*]
    Merl• 15: 146, 147; 30: 234, 235

Gadran
    Post2• 78: 49
Gadras the Black
    Lan3• 85: 204
Gadrasolain [*Gadrasalain*]
    Lan2• 71: 477, 479, 481
Gaheriet [*Gaheriet*[1]]
    Hist• 37: 270
    Merl• 4: 73; 5: 96; 10: 128; 12: 134, 136, 137; 13: 139; 18: 160; 23: 183, 184, 185, etc.; 25: 192, 195; 26: 195, 196, 197; 27: 204; 32: 252; 33: 262, 266; 34: 275; 37: 302, 305; 41: 343, 344, 345; 43: 350, 351, 352, etc.; 44: 357, 358, 359, etc.; 45: 366, 367, 368, etc.; 47: 385, 388, 389; 48: 400; 51: 415; 55: 442, 443; 57: 453
    Lan1• 41: 420, 421, 422, etc.
    Lan2• 51: 39; 52: 62
    Lan4• 112: 97; 131: 319; 140: 408, 410, 416
    Lan5• 142: 62; 143: 62, 63, 65, etc.; 147: 159, 160, 161, etc.; 155: 386, 387, 393, etc.; 156: 1, 8, 10, etc. Lan6• 167: 232; 168: 234, 236; 170: 285; 171: 5, 8; 172: 50, 56, 57, etc.; 175: 88, 95, 107, etc.; 177: 182
    Quest• 13: 51; 14: 52, 53
    Death• 1: 13, 17, 18, etc.; 2: 19, 20, 22, etc.; 8: 85, 90; 9: 94; 11: 108, 109, 110, etc.; 12: 122, 123, 124, etc.; 13: 129, 130, 131, etc.; 14: 138, 147; 15: 158, 159; 18: 191; 22: 220, 222, 224
    Post1• 1: 147; 15: 273; 23: 59; 25: 75, 76; 26: 80; 27: 81, 85, 86, etc.; 41: 240; 42: 249
    Post2• 48: 55; 53: 88, 89, 90, etc.; 54: 93, 94, 97, etc.; 55 101, 102, 103, etc.; 56: 106, 107, 108, etc.; 57: 116,117, 118, etc.; 58: 123, 124,125, etc.; 59: 129, 130,131, etc.; 60: 2, 3, 4, etc.; 61: 22; 66: 77; 67: 96, 97, 98, etc.; 68: 111; 69: 121; 70: 135, 136, 137, etc.; 71: 141; 77: 37; 78: 47, 49; 91: 203, 205; 92: 209; 97: 275; 98: 281, 283; 111: 387, 389, 391, etc.; 121: 75, 77; 122: 83; 124: 101; 126: 109, 111; 139: 269; 143: 315, 316; 144: 328, 329, 331, etc.; 145: 333, 334, 335, etc.; 146: 359, 365; 153: 418, 419, 421, etc.; 154: 430, 431, 433, etc.; 155: 445
Gaheris [the White/of Carahan/of Carahew/of North Wales] [*Gaheris*]
    Lan1• 27: 347
    Lan2• 52: 51
    Lan3• 94: 283; 97: 331
    Death• 7: 76, 78; 8: 81, 84
    Post2• 155: 445
Gaidou (King) [*Gaidou*]
    Merl• 30: 233
Gaius [*Gains*]
    Hist• 2: 73

etc.; 135: 353, 354; 136: 354, 355, 356, etc.; 137: 371, 372, 373, etc.; 138: 389; 139: 408; 140: 408, 409, 410, etc.

Lan5• 141: 6, 11; 142: 13, 17, 35, etc.; 143: 62, 66, 67, etc.; 144: 110, 114; 147: 147, 163, 164; 149: 190, 192, 202, etc.; 150: 222; 151: 244; 152: 284; 153: 284, 285; 155: 348, 350, 357, etc.; 156: 1, 2, 8, etc.; 157: 54

Lan6• 158: 54, 55, 56, etc.; 159: 68, 70, 71; 162: 96, 101, 109, etc.; 164: 139, 140, 141, etc.; 166: 174, 179, 180, etc.; 167: 218, 224, 225, etc.; 168: 235, 236, 237, etc.; 169: 257, 263, 271; 170: 285, 289, 290, etc.; 171: 1, 2, 3, etc.; 172: 52, 53, 54, etc.; 173: 69, 70, 71, etc.; 174: 83, 87; 175: 87, 88, 94, etc.; 176: 168, 170; 177: 182, 198

Quest• 1: 4; 2: 6; 4: 11; 5: 14,16; 6: 16, 17, 18, etc.; 7: 21, 22, 23; 8: 25; 13: 51; 14: 51, 52, 53, etc.; 44: 146; 45: 147, 148; 46: 149, 150, 151; 47: 151, 152, 153, etc.; 48: 154,155; 49:155,157,160, etc.; 63:196,197; 78: 260; 79: 261, 262

Death• 1: 2, 3,13, etc.; 2: 19, 20, 22, etc.; 3: 30, 31, 32, etc.; 4: 40, 46, 47, etc.; 6: 66, 69, 72, etc.; 7: 75, 76; 8: 82, 83, 85, etc.; 9: 94; 10: 98, 100, 101, etc.; 11: 107, 108, 109, etc.; 12: 121, 125; 13: 129. 130, 131, etc.; 14: 137, 138, 141, etc.; 15: 158, 159, 160; 16: 164, 165, 166, etc.; 17: 172, 180; 18: 181, 182, 183, etc.; 19: 195, 196, 197, etc.; 20: 204, 205, 206, etc.; 21: 210, 211, 212, etc.; 22: 220. 221, 222, etc.; 23: 225, 226, 237, etc.

Post1• 1: 147; 13: 261; 14: 262, 263; 15: 273, 274; 17: 11, 12; 23: 58, 59; 25: 68, 69, 70, etc.; 26: 77, 79, 80, etc.; 27: 81, 82, 84, etc.; 28: 113; 34: 161, 162,164; 40: 222, 228; 41: 230, 231, 232, etc.; 42: 249 Post2• 43: 19, 20, 21, etc.; 44: 34, 35; 45: 35, 36, 38, etc.; 46: 40, 41, 42, etc.; 47: 43; 48: 53, 54, 55, etc.; 49: 59, 60, 61; 50: 61, 62, 63, etc.; 51: 68, 71, 72, etc.; 52: 77, 78, 79, etc.; 53: 85, 88, 89, etc.; 54: 98, 99; 55: 105; 56: 115; 57: 122; 58: 125, 126, 128, etc.; 59: 129, 130, 131, etc.; 60: 1, 2, 5, etc.; 61: 22, 23; 64: 47, 48, 49, etc.; 65: 71; 66: 72, 73, 74, etc.; 67: 89, 95, 96, etc.; 68:108, 111; 69: 122, 123, 124, etc.; 73: 3; 74:15; 75: 23; 76: 31, 33; 77: 35, 37, 39; 78: 39, 45, 47, etc.; 79: 55, 57; 84: 109, 111, 115, etc.; 86: 139; 88: 171,173,175, etc.; 89: 179, 181,183, etc.; 90: 185,187, 189, etc.; 91: 197. 201, 203, etc.; 92: 209, 211, 213, etc.; 97: 275; 101: 313; 106: 337; 107: 349, 351, 353, etc.; 108: 361, 363, 365, etc.; 110: 377, 379, 381; 111: 381, 383, 385, etc.; 112: 397, 399, 401; 113: 3, 5, 7, etc.; 114: 14; 118: 41, 43, 44, etc.; 119: 45; 120: 63, 65, 67, etc.; 121: 69, 71, 73, etc.; 123: 97, 99; 124: 99; 126: 115; 136: 225; 139: 262, 269, 271, etc.; 144: 328, 329, 331, etc.; 145: 333, 335, 337, etc.; 146: 365; 148: 382; 149: 387, 388, 389, etc.; 152: 415, 417; 153: 418, 419, 421, etc.; 154: 433, 436, 437, etc.; 155: 443, 447, 449, etc.; 156: 453, 454

Gay¹ (castle) [*Gais Chasteaus*]
   Lan3• 84: 195; 89: 249
Gay² Gallant [*Gais Galantis*]
   Lan1• 25: 336 Lan2•51:39
Gazel (castellan) [*Gazel*]
   Merl• 36: 294
Gazevilte (castle) [*Gazevilte*]
   Merl• 17: 159 Lan1• 8: 59 Lan2• 65: 399; 67: 414

Herlen, King [*Herlen*]
    Quest• 44: 143
Herlion the King [*Helyois*]
    Lan4• 112: 97
Herman [*Hermans*]
    Merl• 54: 440
Hermit Segre *see also* Segre
    Lan4• 137: 386
Hermitage[1] of the Cross [*Crois[1]*]
    Lan2• 63: 326
Hermitage[2] of the Crossing [*Quarefor*]
    Lan2• 63: 326
Hermitage[3] of the Hedge [*Ermitage[1] de la Haie*]
    Lan4• 133: 344, 345
Hermitage[4] of the Mount [*Ermitage[2] del Mont*]
    Lan4• 139: 407
Hermit's Spring [*Fontaine[2] a l'Ermite*]
    Lan2• 61: 317, 318
Hermoine [the Hermit] [*Hermoine*]
    Hist• 11: 282; 13: 304; 27: 100
Hernil de Rivel *see* Hervi of Rivel
Herod[1] [*Herode[1]*]
    Hist• 3: 122
Herod[2] [Tetrarch] [*Herode[2]*]
    Hist• 4: 125, 137, 138
Hervi/Hervieu/Hernil [of Rinel/Rivel] [*Hervi[2]*]
    Merl• 14: 143; 16: 152, 153; 17: 157; 30: 223, 224, 228, etc.; 31: 238, 241; 33:
    259; 34: 275; 37: 305; 38: 313; 39: 331, 332, 334; 48: 398; 50: 411; 51: 417
    Lan1• 10: 98, 99
    Lan2• 51: 39; 52: 65, 66, 67
    Post1• 12: 254; 34: 170
Hidden Island *see* Montenant
High[1] Rock (castle)
    Post2• 68: 106
High[2] Walls (castle) [*Haul Mur*]
    Merl• 6: 109; 46: 376
    Lan1• 14: 162, 163, 169; 16: 199
High[3] Wild Forest *see* Pellinor
Hill[1] (castle) [*C(h)astel[66] del Tertre*]
    Lan5•151:253,256
Hill[2] of the Cat (=Hill[3] of the Lake) [*Mons[5] du Chat*]
    Merl• 55: 444
Hill[3] of the Lake (=Hill[2]) [*Mons[6]du Lac*]
    Merl• 55: 444
Hill[4] of the Spring (location of prison)
    Lan5• 148: 172

Merl• 17: 159

Lan1• 8: 59

Lan3• 75: 54

Lan6• 169: 273

Quest• 5: 16; 23: 79; 66: 204, 209; 73: 233; 75: 241, 244; 80: 265; 82: 271; 83: 273

Post2• 72: 153; 139: 268; 146: 359, 364; 148: 376

Maine[1] (King) [*Moine*]

Merl•2:20, 21,22, etc.

Maine[2] (river)

Lan1• 32: 374

Maissent *see* Saint Maissent Makabrez (King) [*Macabres*]

Lan6• 160: 86

Malaguin [*Malaguin*] *see also* King of the Hundred Knights

Lan1• 34: 388

Lan2• 52: 56; 61: 278

Malaguine (fortress) [*Malaguine*]

Lan2• 70: 451

Malakin the Castellan [*Malakins*]

Merl• 48: 395, 396

Malaquin[1] of Scotland (King) [*Malaquin[1]*]

Lan4• 124: 267

Malaquin[2] the Welshman [*Malaquin[2]*]

Lan4•119: 191

Maldalet (King) [*Maudalet*]

Merl• 12: 135

Malduit [the Giant] [*Malduit[1]*]

Lan5•151: 251, 252, 259, etc.

Lan6•159: 71; 172: 51

Malec [*Malec*]

Merl• 16: 151

Malehaut[1] [Bluff] (city) [*Malehaut*]

Merl• 11: 131; 18: 163; 44: 364

Lan1• 48: 456

Lan2•49:2, 6, 9; 50: 31; 52: 53

Malehaut[2] [Bluff] (lady) [*Malehaut*]

Lan2• 49: 31; 51: 39; 52: 42, 54, 55, etc.; 54: 132, 134; 58: 203, 204, 211, etc.; 59: 215; 62: 323; 66: 407; 70: 436, 441, 444, etc.; 71: 453, 454, 455, etc.

Lan3• 74: 18; 77: 89, 104; 80: 153, 167, 173. 89: 247; 97: 315; 100: 354; 102: 367, 369

Lan4• 107: 2; 112: 99

Lan5• 149: 209

Malés the Dark [*Males*]

Merl• 14: 143; 48: 398; 50: 411

Mallias of the Thorn [*Melior[1]*]

Lan4•119: 190

Malore [*Maloré*]
    Merl• 16: 153, 155
Malruc of the Rock (Duke) [*Mauruc*]
    Merl• 6: 103; 7: 112, 117; 15: 148
Malta (city)
    Hist• 40: 284
Manassel [*Manasses*[1]]
    Lan2•63:351,352
Manasses [of Gaul] [*Manasses*[2]]
    Post1• 40: 226; 42: 249, 250
Manathes [*Manaches*[1]]
    Hist• 12: 295
Manatur [*Mana(r)tur*]
    Hist• 10: 246, 247, 248
Manuel [*Manaal*]
    Hist• 40: 293
Many Years (maiden) *see* Maiden of Many Years
Marabon (Master)
    Lan3• 75: 56
Marabron [*Marabron*]
    Lan6• 159: 74, 75, 76, etc.
Marador [*Marados*]
    Lan4• 116: 164; 117: 167
Maragond/Margondes[2] (King) [*Margondre*]
    Merl• 19: 168, 169, 170; 21: 176; 48: 400
Marahant [*Marehan(t)*]
    Hist• 37: 252, 253, 254, etc.
Maran (castle) [*Maran*]
    Lan6• 177: 181
Maranz [*Maranz*]
    Lan6• 169: 244, 245
Marat of the Tower
    Post2• 78: 51
Marcel [*Marchel*]
    Merl• 53: 433
March (castle) [*Marche*[1]]
    Post2• 142: 298
Marche (Queen)
    Lan6• 164: 122
Marches of Scotland [*Escoc(h)e*]
    Lan6• 167: 212
Marcoisa/Marcoise (river) [*Marcoise*]
    Quest• 31: 106; 44: 145; 77: 246
    Post2• 104: 327
Marec [*Marec*]
    Lan2• 63: 328, 336

Mares [*Marés*[2]] *see also* Roestoc[2]
    Merl• 21: 177
Margalant [*Murgalant*•]
    Merl• 25: 192; 26: 195, 196
Margan [*Margan*]
    Lan2• 64: 377
Marganant [*Marganant*]
    Merl• 16: 151
Marganor [*Marganor*[x]]
    Merl• 7: 116,120,121; 18:162
    Lan2• 61: 278, 282, 284, etc.; 65: 393, 396, 397, etc.
Margarit (King) [*Morgans*]
    Merl• 7: 113
Margon the Wine Steward [*Margon*]
    Merl• 48: 393, 394, 395, etc.
Margondes[1] [*Margondes*[1]]
    Merl• 47: 385; 48: 400
Margondes[2] *see* Maragond
Margondre [of the Black Castle] [*Margondes*[1]]
    Lan4• 114: 115, 123, 131; 115: 131, 132
Margoras (King) [*Margoras*]
    Merl• 30: 234
Margot[1] [*Margot*]
    Merl• 30: 233
Margot[2] Rock (place) [*Roche*[26] *(Margot)*]
    Merl• 21: 177; 23: 186; 24: 188
Mariale [*Marial(l)e*]
    Lan5• 152: 268, 269
Mariel Bridge [*Pont*[8] *Maruel*]
    Lan6• 171: 10, 11
Marien [*Marien*]
    Lan6• 174: 86; 175: 90, 91, 92
Marigart the Red [*Marigart*]
    Lan4• 138: 397, 398
Marins
    Post2• 54: 94
Mark [of Cornwall] (King) [*Marc*]
    Death• 6: 71
    Post1• 9: 230, 232; 10: 233, 242; 16: 280; 41: 240
    Post2• 76: 27; 84:113; 93: 239; 108: 367; 113:11,13,14; 122: 83; 123:97; 134: 207; 135: 207, 209, 211, etc.; 136: 223; 137: 233,235,237, etc.; 138:251,253,255, etc.; 139: 261, 268, 269, etc.; 141: 292, 293; 159:489; 160: 489, 490,491, etc.
Marlagan
    Lan4• 125: 285

etc.; 47: 385, 386, 387, etc.; 48: 395, 396, 397, etc.; 49: 401, 402, 403, etc.; 50: 407; 51: 413, 414, 415, etc.; 52: 420, 421, 422, etc.; 53: 427, 428, 431, etc.; 54: 436; 55: 441, 442, 443, etc.; 56: 445, 448; 57: 450, 451, 452, etc.; 58: 457, 458; 59: 458, 460, 461, etc.; 60: 466

Lan1• 6: 38, 39, 41, etc.

Lan2• 53: 130; 54: 143

Lan3• 75: 46, 52, 54, etc.; 95: 300, 301

Lan4• 108: 32

Lan6• 171: 21

Quest• 21: 76; 22: 77, 78; 34: 116

Death• 23: 228, 229

Post1• 2: 153, 154, 155, etc.; 3: 164, 165, 168, etc.; 4: 174,175, 176, etc.; 5: 185, 186, 187, etc.; 6: 196, 197, 198, etc.; 7: 203, 207, 211, etc.; 8: 224, 225; 9: 231, 232, 233; 10: 233, 235, 236, etc.; 11: 242, 243, 244, etc.; 12: 249; 13: 254, 255, 256, etc.; 14: 264, 265, 266; 15: 266. 270, 271, etc.; 16: 279, 280; 17: 7, 8, 12; 19: 22; 20: 27, 28, 29, etc.; 22: 47; 23: 57, 58, 59; 24: 60, 61, 62, etc.; 25: 72, 73, 74, etc.; 26: 76, 78, 79, etc.; 27: 97, 98, 99, etc.; 28: 114, 115; 29: 124, 128, 129, etc.; 30: 131, 132, 133, etc.; 31: 139,140,141, etc.; 32: 145, 148, 149, etc.; 33: 154, 155, 156, etc.; 34: 159; 36: 191; 37: 191, 192, 193, etc.; 38: 206; 39: 214; 40: 228; 42: 254

Post2• 49: 59; 50: 62; 52: 78, 83; 53: 86, 88, 89, etc.; 59: 130; 64: 60; 67: 85; 74: 13; 75: 21; 113: 14; 144: 321; 150: 399

Merlin's[1] Bed [*Lit*[1] *Merlin*]

    Lan6• 172: 55

Merlin's[2] Castle

    Lan6• 170: 289

Merlin's[3] Island/Isle [*Isle*[20] *Merlin*] *see also* Island of Marvels

    Post1• 23: 60

    Post2• 48: 55

Merlin's[4] Rock [*Perron*[5] *Merlin*]

    Lan2• 54: 143

Merlin's[5] Tower [*Tor*[9] *Merlin*]

    Lan4• 121: 237

Michael's Day *see* Saint Michael's Day

Mid-Lent

    Merl• 8: 124; 12: 135

    Lan6• 165: 163, 164

Midians (king of the)

    Hist• 19: 418

Migloras [*Migloras*]

    Merl• 37: 305

Mill (Castle of the) [*Castel*[12] *del Molin*]

    Lan4• 136: 356

Minadap (King) [*Minadap*]

    Merl• 30: 232, 234, 235

Hist• 12: 293; 13: 302, 321; 15: 338; 16: 338; 17: 353, 401; 27: 95, 97, 98, etc.; 29: 125; 31: 137, 139; 33: 171, 173, 179, etc.; 39: 279, 280, 281; 41: 296, 297

Quest• 10: 33; 25: 84, 85, 86; 28: 93; 41: 135, 136, 138; 66: 206, 207, 208; 80: 262, 263

Post2• 80: 67; 103: 323; 140: 279; 150: 401

Mordred [*Mordret*]

Hist• 32: 161; 35: 224; 37: 271; 38: 275

Merl• 4: 73; 5: 96; 10: 128, 129; 27: 204, 205; 33: 265; 37: 300; 56: 449

Lan2• 60: 230, 231

Lan4• 131: 319; 139: 408; 140: 408, 411, 412, etc.

Lan5• 149: 190, 192, 193, etc.; 155: 397; 156: 10, 11

Lan6• 158: 59, 60; 159: 71; 166:174,175,176, etc.; 167: 204, 205, 206, etc.; 168: 235, 236, 237, etc.; 170: 285, 289; 171: 5, 15, 20, etc.; 172: 50, 54, 55, etc.; 177:182,193,197, etc.

Death• 2: 22, 23; 11: 109; 12: 125; 13: 127, 135; 16: 166, 171; 17: 171, 172, 173, etc.; 20: 209; 21: 210, 211, 212, etc.; 22: 219, 220; 23: 225, 226, 227, etc.; 25: 252, 253, 255, etc.

Post1• 1: 147; 7: 203, 206; 13: 255; 15: 274

Post2• 58: 124; 60: 5, 6, 9, etc.; 61: 22, 23; 64: 50, 51; 66: 76, 77, 78; 67: 93; 78: 49; 79: 55; 111: 387, 389, 393; 112: 393, 395, 397, etc.; 123: 97; 139: 262, 263, 265, etc.; 153: 419, 424, 427, etc.; 154: 433, 435, 442; 156: 453, 454, 455, etc.; 157: 461; 158: 472; 159: 472, 473, 475, etc.

Moret of the Way [*Moret*]

Merl• 7: 112

Morgan [the Fay] (Queen) [*Morgain*]

Merl• 4: 73; 29: 215; 32: 253, 254; 40: 338

Lan3• 93: 275, 276, 277, 278; 95: 296, 297, 298, etc.; 96: 304, 306, 309, etc.; 97: 313, 316, 317, etc.; 99: 346, 347; 100: 348, 349, 352, etc.; 101: 357, 358; 102: 367, 368, 369, etc.; 104: 381

Lan4• 108:21; 110:74

Lan5• 149: 173, 174, 175, etc.; 154: 335, 338; 155: 346; 156: 4; 157: 47, 48, 49, etc.

Lan6• 158: 57, 60; 159: 60, 61, 62-3, 70; 162: 98; 171: 28; 172: 51

Death• 5: 55, 56, 57, etc.; 7: 75; 11: 114; 24: 250

Post1• 2: 163; 3: 164, 166; 6: 199, 201; 14: 262, 266; 15: 266, 268, 269, etc.; 32: 152; 34: 168; 36: 174, 178, 179, etc.; 37: 199; 38: 199; 39: 212, 213, 214; 40: 217, 218, 219, etc.; 41: 228, 229, 230; 42: 250, 251

Post2• 52: 83, 84; 77: 37; 99: 291, 293; 111: 389, 391, 393; 123: 91, 93; 153: 424; 158: 469

Morgan's Chapel

Lan3• 92: 271, 273

Morholt [of Ireland] [*Morholt*]

Post1• 41: 233, 234, 235, etc.

Post2• 46: 43; 47: 43, 44, 45, etc.; 48: 46, 47, 48, etc.; 49: 59, 60; 50: 61, 62, 63, etc.; 51: 67, 68, 71, etc.; 52: 77, 78, 79, etc.; 53: 85; 56: 115; 58: 125, 126,

128, etc.; 59: 129, 130, 131, etc.
Moses[1] [*Moÿses*]
    Hist• 6: 163; 20: 440
    Quest• 18: 69
Moses[2] [*Maÿs*]
    Hist• 34: 200, 201, 202; 35: 223, 227, 228, etc.; 36: 241
    Lan4• 108: 32
    Post2• 136: 227, 229; 147: 367
Mount (hermitage) *see* Hermitage of the Mount
Moydas (King) [*Moydas*]
    Merl• 45: 367, 368
Murgalant of Trebeham [*Murgalant*[1]]
    Merl• 48: 400
Mute Maiden
    Post2• 67: 91
Mysenes (King) [*Micenes*]
    Merl• 21: 176

Nabin[1] [*Nabins*[1]]
    Lan6• 174: 86; 175: 89, 90
Nabin[2] [*Nabins*[2]]
    Merl• 24: 189
Nabor[1] [*Nabor*[1]]
    Hist• 28: 105, 106, 107, etc.; 29: 124; 33: 184
Nabor[1] [*see* Nascor[2] and Aglinde]
    Post2• 119:50,55
Naborn *see* Mabon[1]
Nabunal [the Seneschal/of Tharmandaise] [*Nabunat*]
    Merl• 46: 377, 378; 48: 395, 400; 53: 427
Nabur[1] [*Nabur*[1]]
    Hist• 8: 222; 10: 260, 263
Nabur[2] [the Unruly] (Duke) [*Nabur*[2]]
    Post1• 7: 206
Nadien
    Lan6• 174: 86
Nadres (city) [*Nadres*]
    Merl• 56: 449
Nantes[1] (city) [*Natanc*]
    Merl• 9: 126, 127
Nantes[2] (city) [*Nantes*[1]] *see also* Hoel[3]
    Merl• 60: 465
Napins [*Napins*]
    Merl• 48: 400
Narbaduc (King)
    Lan4• 121: 253

Saint[19] Stephen (church) [*Estevene, Saint*]
    Hist• 34: 199
    Merl• 37: 302, 308; 39: 329, 330; 50: 408; 51: 414
    Lan3• 74: 22
    Lan6• 167: 221; 171: 6, 20
    Death• 7: 78; 11: 107; 13: 132; 15: 161
    Post1• 14: 262; 25: 69; 40: 217
    Post2• 54: 94; 78: 41; 105: 335; 121: 81; 154: 441
Salamander (city/district) [*Salemandre*]
    Hist• 4: 128; 31: 135
Salebrun (King) [*Salebrun*]
    Merl• 19: 164; 41: 339; 48: 395, 396
Salergne *see* Falerne
Salerno *see* Falerne
Salisbury[1] (city) [*Sale(s)bieres*]
    Merl• 3: 49, 51
    Quest• 85: 280
    Death• 1: 1
    Post2• 157: 461; 159: 487
Salisbury[2] Plain [*Sale(s)bieres*]
    Hist• 38: 275
    Merl• 3: 50, 52, 53; 45: 373, 374; 46: 376, 377, 382, etc.; 47: 383, 384, 386,
    etc.; 49: 407
    Lan6• 172: 61
    Death• 16: 167; 23: 228, 231, 232; 25: 258
    Post1• 15: 274
    Post2• 156: 454, 457, 459; 159: 472
Salust [*Saluste(s), (Saint)*]
    Hist• 11: 267, 279; 13: 303, 304; 17: 401
Samaliel [*Samaliel*]
    Post2• 142: 299; 143: 307, 309, 310, etc.
Samson [the Strong] [*Sanson (Fortin)*]
    Hist• 26: 41, 61
    Quest• 36: 125
    Death• 6: 70
Samuel [*Samuel*[1]]
    Hist• 2: 48
Sanades
    Post2• 136: 233
Sanasesio
    Post2• 78: 51
Sanebron [*Senebruns*] *see also* Falerne
    Merl• 21: 177
Sansedoine [*Sansadonies*] *see also* Nohaut[1]
    Merl• 21: 177

Sapharin[1] (King) [*Sapharin[2]*]
> Merl• 15: 145, 147; 16: 149, 150, 151, etc.

Sapharin[2] (King) [*Sapharin[1]*]
> Merl• 21: 176

Sapient of Baghdad [*Sapiens*]
> Lan2• 71: 488

Sapinoie (forest) [*Sapinoie*]
> Merl• 38: 314, 315; 39: 315
> Lan4• 114: 112

Saracen (s)
> Hist• 4: 128, 129, 130, etc.; 7: 183; 19: 427; 25: 11; 28: 105, 106; 30: 132, 133; 31: 143; 32: 149, 169; 34: 195; 35: 209, 210, 211, etc.; 37: 267; 40: 285, 293
> Merl• 54: 441
> Lan1• 14: 130
> Lan2• 63: 329
> Lan4• 121: 253; 131: 321; 132: 335
> Lan6• 164: 123
> Quest• 73: 231, 232
> Death• 6: 70

Sarah [*Sarra*]
> Hist• 4: 128

Saraide (=Celise) [*Saraide*]
> Lan1• 11: 102

Sarduc the Blond [*Sarduc*]
> Lan4•119: 190

Sardup [*Sardup*]
> Merl• 16: 151

Saret
> Post2• 78: 51

Sarmedon[1] [*Sarmedon[1]*]
> Merl• 15: 147

Sarmedon[2] (King) [*Sarmedon[2]*]
> Merl• 50: 409

Sarpenic (forest) [*Sarpenic*]
> Lan4• 114: 130; 119: 208; 120: 208

Sarras[1] [of Logres] [*Sarras[1]*]
> Lan6• 164: 139, 141, 142, etc.; 165: 169; 166: 169

Sarras[2] (city) [*Sarras[1]*]
> Hist• 4: 128, 129; 8: 208, 209; 9: 224, 226; 10: 264; 11: 284; 12: 286, 294, 296; 13: 302, 303, 304, etc.; 14: 322, 331; 17: 382, 401, 403; 19: 426, 427; 25: 11; 27: 102; 28: 114, 115; 29: 125; 30: 126; 31: 137, 138; 33: 171, 172, 173, etc.
> Merl• 39: 334
> Quest• 10: 32, 33; 25: 84; 41: 134; 75: 241; 81: 268; 82: 271; 84: 275; 85: 279

Sorestan[2] (king) [*Sorestan*]
    Lan5• 149: 180
Sorestan[3] (queen) [*Sorestan*]
    Lan5• 149: 173, 180; 154: 332
Sorhalt (King) [*Sorhaus*]
    Merl• 14: 142
Sorhaut (city) [*Sorhaut*[2]]
    Merl• 9: 124, 128; 10: 128, 131; 11: 131,132; 18: 164; 19: 166, 167; 20: 171;
        21: 174; 24: 190; 25: 191
    Lan2• 69: 418, 419
    Lan3• 73: 14, 17; 75: 68; 76: 88; 80: 164
Soriondes (King) [*Sorionde*]
    Merl• 21: 175; 24: 190, 191; 25: 192, 193, 195; 26: 195, 196,197
Sornegrieu [of the Land of the Irish] (King) [*Sornegrieu*]
    Merl• 14: 142; 15: 145, 147; 16: 149, 150, 151, etc.; 21: 176
Sorneham [of Newcastle] [*Sornehan(t)*]
    Lan5• 141: 1, 7, 9, etc.; 142: 59, 60; 143: 86, 87, 88, etc.
Sorrowful Queen [*Roine*[6] *Dolerouse*] *see also* Elaine [of Benoic], Queen of Great
    Sorrows
    Lan4• 136: 370
    Lan5• 155: 397; 156: 2
Sortibran[1] [*Sortibran*[1]]
    Merl• 16: 153, 155
Sortibran[2] [*Sortibran*[2]]
    Merl• 44: 361
South Wales (king/kingdom) [*Sorgales*], [*Sugales*] *see also* Belinant
    Merl• 20: 171; 48: 395
    Lan2• 71: 468
Spain [*Espai(n)gne*]
    Hist• 16: 339
    Merl• 53: 428; 54: 439; 56: 448, 449
Spiritual Palace [*Palais*[2]*Esperitel*]
    Hist• 7: 169
    Post2• 134: 201; 151: 409; 152: 412, 413
Spring[1] (hill) *see* Hill of the Spring
Spring[2] (knight) *see* Atamas, Knight of the Spring
Spring[3] of Adventure *see* Spring of Healing
Spring[4] of Adventures *see* Adventures (Spring of)
Spring[5] of Healing (=Spring of Adventure)
    Post2• 146: 359, 364; 150: 395, 401, 403
Spring[6] of Marvels [*Fontaine*[22] *des Merveilles*]
    Post2• 62: 26; 64: 49
Spring[7] of the Pine [*Fontaine*[18] *del Pyn*]
    Lan2• 55: 147; 56: 161; 64: 373, 374; 70: 435
Spring[8] of the [Two] Sycamores [*Fontaine*[20] *des Deux Sicamours*]
    Lan6• 164: 140, 142, 146, 148; 166: 184

Ugly Hero/Worthy [*Lait Hardi*] *see also* Acanor
 Merl• 15: 148; 31: 237, 239
 Lan2•51:39
 Lan4• 119: 192; 131: 319
 Lan6• 162: 96; 173: 78
 Post2• 68: 102, 103, 104, etc.; 70: 134; 72: 151,152
Ulfin[1] [*Ulfin*[1]]
 Quest• 63: 198
Ulfin[2]/Urfin [*Urfin*]
 Merl• 3: 44; 4: 59, 60, 61, etc.; 5: 89, 90, 92, etc.; 6: 102, 106, 107; 7: 111,
 112, 115, etc.; 8: 123; 15: 146, 148; 16: 151, 154,155; 30: 228; 32: 247; 33:
 258, 262; 37: 308, 309, 311; 38: 312; 46: 375
 Post2• 3: 164, 165, 166, etc.
Unbridled Heart (=Lionel)
 Lan1• 11: 108
 Lan3• 86: 215
Underwater Bridge [*Pont*[12] *sous Aigue*]
 Lan3• 76: 86
 Lan4• 107: 19; 110: 70; 111:82
Urfin *see* Ulfin[2]
Urglay (abbey)
 Hist• 39: 282
Urien[1] of Bast (King)
 Lan5• 156: 6
 Post2• 92: 213
Urien[2] [of Garlot] (King) [*Urien*[1]]
 Hist• 38: 275
 Merl• 5: 88, 96; 7: 110, 115, 117, etc.; 9: 124, 125; 19: 165, 166, 167, etc.; 20:
 173; 22: 178; 24: 190, 191; 25: 191, 194, 195; 26: 197, 200; 32: 252, 253, 255;
 33: 262; 34: 273; 36: 293, 294, 295, etc.; 37: 300; 39: 320; 45: 372, 373; 47:
 385, 386; 48: 400; 50: 408; 51: 414, 416; 53: 427; 54: 437, 438
 Lan1• 10: 99; 22: 261; 23: 309; 47: 444
 Lan2• 51: 38; 52: 56; 53: 132
 Lan3• 76: 83, 84; 77: 102; 79: 125; 81: 176; 88: 239; 91: 256; 96: 305
 Lan4• 139: 402
 Lan5•151:244, 248, 256, 263
 Lan6• 175: 136
 Quest• 47: 153
 Death• 9: 94
 Post1• 6: 201, 202; 14: 262; 15: 273, 274; 34: 168,170; 35: 172; 36: 174, 175,
 177, etc.; 38: 212; 39: 212; 40: 227; 41: 229; 42: 248
 Post2• 48: 56; 51: 68, 74, 75; 52: 79, 82, 84; 53: 88; 78: 51; 89: 179; 143:
 309; 156: 454
Uther[1] *see* Uther Pendragon
Uther[2] Pendragon [of Britain] (King) (=Uther) [*Uterpandragon*]
 Hist• 7: 184, 185

Merl• 2: 20, 21; 3: 35, 36, 37, etc.; 4: 58, 64, 77; 5: 89, 90, 92, etc.; 6: 102, 106,107; 9: 127; 10: 128, 129; 20: 172; 27: 206; 29: 217, 221; 30: 231; 31: 238; 32: 247

Lan1• 1:2, 3, 6; 6: 41; 10: 98

Lan2• 71: 468

Lan3• 76: 83, 84, 85; 95: 300

Lan5• 150: 223; 151: 248, 250, 251

Lan6• 176: 157

Death• 23: 228

Post1• 1: 147; 2: 155, 156, 162, etc.; 3: 164, 165, 168, etc.; 24: 61, 62

Post2• 53: 91; 96: 261, 267; 119: 47; 139: 261; 140: 279; 144: 321

Uther[5] Pendragon Abbey (=Galahad's Marvel)

Post2• 139: 261

Utrenal

Post2• 78: 51

Vadaans the Black

Post2• 155: 445

Vadalon (King) [*Vadalon*]

Lan4• 118: 172, 173, 174, 175

Vadoan (king) [*Vadoan*]

Lan2• 52: 56, 67

Vagan [*Vagan*]

Quest• 8: 25

Post2• 79: 53

Vagan's Castle

Quest• 8: 25

Vagor [of Strange Island] (King) [Vagor[1]]

Lan6• 159: 64, 76; 160: 82; 172: 51

Valdon (count) [*Valdon*]

Lan5• 142: 29

Valigues (count) [*Valingues*]

Lan5• 143: 63

Valley[1] (count/king of the) [*del Val*[1]]

Quest• 35: 120

Post1• 34: 159

Valley[2] of the Dead [*Val*[9] *des Mors*]

Hist• 1: 25

Valley[3] of False Lovers [*Val*[3] *as Fans Amans*] *see* Valley of No Return

Valley[4] of No Return [*Val*[13] *sans Reto(u)r*]

Lan3• 92: 272; 93: 275; 95: 285; 96: 305, 307, 308, etc.; 97: 314, 321, 329, 331; 99: 345; 100: 349; 102: 370

Valleys of Galorre [*Vals*[3] *de Galor(r)e*] *see* Gravadain[2]

Vambieres (castle/city) [*Vandeberes*]

Merl• 9: 124, 125; 11: 132; 13: 140; 18: 162; 19: 164; 21: 175, 176; 22: 178; 26: 197; 46: 383